The Golden Age of
EUROPEAN RAILWAYS

PEN & SWORD
TRANSPORT

This edition published in 2013 by Pen & Sword Transport
an imprint of Pen & Sword Books Ltd, 47 Church Street, Barnsley, South Yorkshire S70 2AS

Text copyright © 2013 Christian Wolmar (Introduction, Great Western Railway, West Coast Main Line, Leeds–Carlisle, London Termini, Moscow–St Petersburg, Trans-Siberian Railway);
Brian Solomon (rest of text). The right of the authors to be identified as the authors of this work has been asserted by them in accordance with the Copyright, Designs and Patents Act 1988.
Concept, design, and layout copyright © 2013 Bookcraft Ltd   www.bookcraft.co.uk   Project manager John Button
A Bookcraft/Worth Press co-production

The endpaper maps are reproduced from *Il Strade Ferrate dell' Europa Centrale*, an 18-segment map published in 1857 by Vittorio Angeli, Turin.

Set in Stone Serif (text), Orbit and Orbit Antique (display), and designed by Bookcraft Ltd, Stroud, Gloucestershire, United Kingdom

All images included in this volume are in the public domain, with the exception of those credited in individual captions.
Most of the images come from books, brochures, maps, and postcards forming part of Bookcraft Ltd's 'Times Past Archive' (see www.memoriesoftimespast.com).

ISBN 978 1 78346 284 1

Pen & Sword Books Ltd incorporates the Imprints of Pen & Sword Aviation, Pen & Sword Family History, Pen & Sword Maritime, Pen & Sword Military, Pen & Sword Discovery,
Wharncliffe Local History, Wharncliffe True Crime, Wharncliffe Transport, Pen & Sword Select, Pen & Sword Military Classics, Leo Cooper, The Praetorian Press, Remember When,
Seaforth Publishing and Frontline Publishing.

For a complete list of Pen & Sword titles please contact
PEN & SWORD BOOKS LIMITED, 47 Church Street, Barnsley, South Yorkshire, S70 2AS, England
E-mail: enquiries@pen-and-sword.co.uk   Website: www.pen-and-sword.co.uk

1 3 5 7 9 10 8 6 4 2

Printed in Malaysia

The Golden Age of
EUROPEAN RAILWAYS

Consultant Editor: Christian Wolmar
Lead Author: Brian Solomon

The Elbe bridge at Dresden on the Saxony–Bohemian Railway, 1848 (above).

Gare St Lazare, Paris, painted by Paul César Helleu, 1879 (previous page).

CONTENTS

Göschenen station on the Gotthardbahn, Switzerland, 1910 (right).

A Dutch poster for the Amsterdam–Marseilles Riviera Express, 1901 (opposite).

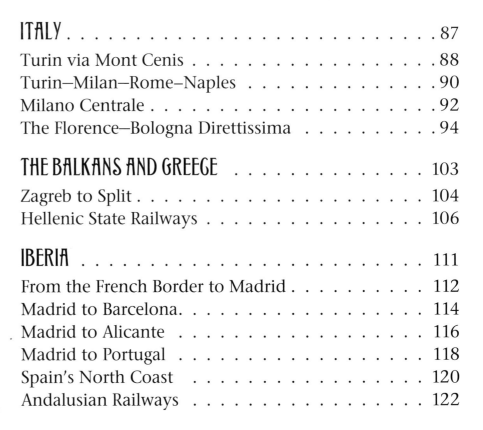

INTRODUCTION

Christian Wolmar

La Flèche d'Or–Golden Arrow, a poster designed by William Spencer Bagdatopoulos for Chemins de Fer du Nord Wagons-Lits in 1926.

The concept of a Golden Age of the railway in Europe appeals to everyone. The images in those familiar railway posters of the time, portraying the exotic appeal of the *Orient Express* or even the more prosaic, and indeed proletarian, attractions of seaside excursions offered by England's Southern Railway, are etched in the mind. They were produced by the best artists of the day in an era when the railway was king and was, for most people and for most journeys, the only way to travel substantial distances.

Golden Age posters celebrated an established and mature industry that was at the core of the society it was serving and was doing a fantastic job. However, it is not quite as simple as that. Golden ages are elusive affairs whose very existence is hard to pin down. The posters, like all advertising, rarely reflected the reality and the railways did not always live up to expectations. For many people living in the last decade of the nineteenth century, before the internal combustion engine had made any serious inroads into the railway's market, trains seemed nothing like an invention that was enjoying its heyday. Slow trains, dirty trains, infrequent trains, unsafe trains, old trains, expensive trains, uncomfortable trains – those were the complaints that could be heard across Europe from both rich and poor. The railways were a monopoly, and were the biggest and most powerful businesses in the world. It was not a recipe for good service.

There is a delicate balance between nostalgia for an age which may never have been, and celebrating an invention that not only changed the way people lived but also, at its best, represented the apogee of humankind's efforts to harness the natural world to good effect. The truth is that it took an awfully long time for the railways to overcome their utilitarian origins. Certainly, for the passenger there was little to celebrate about the early days of the railway. It is perhaps difficult to envisage just how crude were the initial efforts to provide train services for passengers when railways were in their earliest stage of development.

Beginnings

The railway age is widely recognised as beginning in September 1830 when the Liverpool and Manchester line in northern England first opened for service amid huge celebrations and a recognition that this was a truly epoch-making event. The Liverpool and Manchester was the culmination of centuries of efforts to improve and reduce the cost of transport with devices that used tracks and trucks to carry minerals, especially coal. Indeed, over the previous centuries, there had been numerous transport undertakings that were variously called tramways or railways. The existence of very basic 'tramways' where rails were laid at the mouth of mines to help transfer the ore to the nearest waterway can be traced back to the fourteenth century in Germany and quite sophisticated networks of such lines could be found as early as the mid-seventeenth century in the northeast of England. The Stockton and Darlington, completed in 1825 and often presented as the first 'proper' railway, is best viewed as the most sophisticated of these tramways rather than as the first example of a modern railway. It was little more than a single-track line around 25 miles long (just over 40 km) connecting two small towns and mostly carrying minerals in wagons dragged along the track by horses. It was used by only a few passengers who travelled in remodelled stagecoaches and while George Stephenson (1781–1848), the line's engineer and designer, provided some basic steam locomotives, their four-legged rivals were the main form of traction. Passengers

were an afterthought rather than the main customers of the railway, and were sometimes called upon to help heave their coaches up inclines.

The Liverpool and Manchester, also built by Stephenson and using his engines, was different in conception and scale from all its predecessors. The 31-mile line was far more advanced as it was double-tracked throughout, was powered entirely by steam engines, and connected two of the world's most important cities of the day. Crucially, it carried passengers and freight in both directions, taking untreated cotton to the Manchester mills and

'The Liverpool and Manchester Railway: The Viaduct across the Sankey Valley', a coloured engraving by T.T. Bury published in 1831.

returning cloth back to Liverpool for export. Passengers, too, travelled on the line extensively, and it was not long before Sunday School outings were lured onto its trains. It was not the comforts of the ride or the train that attracted them, for trains on the Liverpool and Manchester had just about every discomfort imaginable. The chain connections between carriages gave a jerky and disjointed ride made worse by the lack of brakes on the coaches and the bumpy track. There were no toilets and little protection from the elements, and stations consisted at best of a few boards laid onto the mud.

It was no better on the pioneering lines in other European countries. The first French line ran in the coal region between St Etienne and Lyon, and, for passengers, also used modified stagecoaches hauled by horses, which made for a bumpy and uncomfortable ride. They were, though, a modest improvement on the Liverpool and Manchester coaches, as their design was more elaborate and they had compartments separated out from one another, which made for more privacy and was a model that would be copied around the world. Moreover, some coaches were designed with two decks, with the lower ones provided with curtains which did offer some protection from the rain, although passengers on the upper floor still remained exposed.

In Austria, the notion that horses rather than steam locomotives were best equipped to haul trains survived well into the 1830s when a remarkable network of such lines, stretching more than 170 miles (273.5 km) in the valleys of Upper Austria and Bohemia, was built. These horse-powered trains offered no more comforts than the stagecoaches which they replaced. Soon, though, across Europe the advantages of steam locomotives proved all too obvious and the horses were put out to grass. In Germany, it was the bureaucracy that made life difficult for passengers. On the first major line, between Leipzig and Dresden, tickets were not obtainable in advance, and instead the office only opened 15 minutes before departure and passengers were forced to buy returns. Interestingly, such customer-unfriendly practices as only opening ticket offices briefly before the arrival of a train survived in many smaller European countries throughout the twentieth century.

Growth

All the difficulties of early train travel did not prevent the rapid spread of railway networks. Railways simply had too many advantages not to prove attractive to passengers, and indeed to freight. The immediate success of the Liverpool and Manchester and other pioneering lines, combined with improvements in locomotive technology, stimulated a period of rapid growth in railway construction during the middle years of the nineteenth century across the continent. Within a couple of decades of the opening of the Liverpool and Manchester, all major European countries had begun to establish rail networks, and while mostly this was undertaken with private money, in several countries governments influenced the location of lines and provided subsidies either directly by making capital available or indirectly through the provision of land or the passage of helpful legislation.

Belgium was an unlikely early innovator, stimulated by the desire of its government to use the railways as a way of establishing the country's separate identity from its neighbour, the Netherlands, from which it had just broken away. Work started on the first line in 1834 and remarkably, thanks to the very active involvement of government, by 1843 most of the network that forms the heart of the Belgian railway system had been completed.

The scale of ambition shown by Belgium was by no means unique, and spread to other nations who realised that railways had not only an unparalleled advantage in stimulating economic development, but also were an important tool of nation-building. There was a darker side, too. It was not long after the first tracks had been laid on the Liverpool and Manchester that troops were being sent to far-flung parts of the absolute monarchies of the day to quell rebellions, or wage war on neighbours. The importance of railways for various purposes, military as well as economic, was beginning

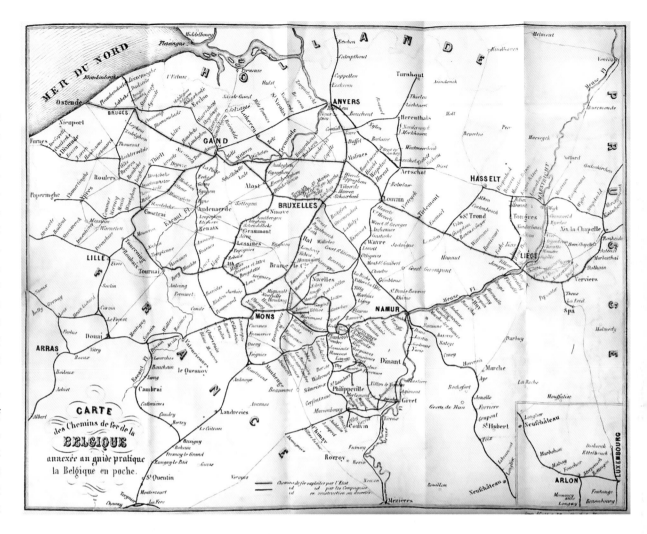

to be realised across Europe. Whereas the first lines in most countries were short, experimental affairs, perhaps linking a capital city with a port or as in Italy and Russia, connecting two royal palaces, soon more ambitious schemes through whole countries – and soon the entire continent – were being put forward. Building them, though, was another matter. There was no end of obstacles ranging from proprietors unwilling to yield a single inch of their land to the iron road and Luddite town authorities unconvinced that the railway would bring prosperity to perennial difficulties in finding investors and the sheer technical difficulties of what was still a very new invention.

Progress, therefore, was patchy and fastest where governments perceived the advantages in terms of both nation-building and military strategy. The contrast between France and Germany is interesting in this respect. Initially, Germany, which actually did not exist as a unified nation until 1870 but

The Belgian railway network in 1875 (above).

Rail-borne artillery being used during the Siege of Paris in 1870 (left).

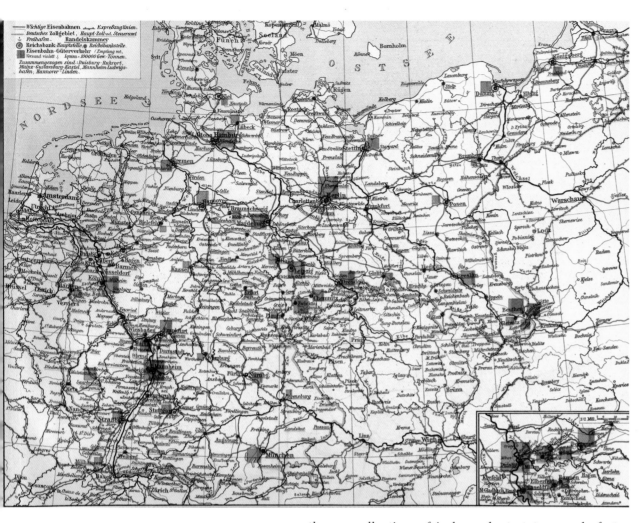

The German railway network in 1896, from *Steiler's Hand-Atlas*; express lines are shown with red dotted highlighting and goods volume by the coloured squares (above left).

Der Adler (*The Eagle*), built in 1835 by British railway pioneers George and Robert Stephenson, was the first locomotive to run successfully in Germany. It first ran between Nuremberg and Fürth on 7 December 1835 (above right).

was, rather, a collection of independent states, made faster progress than its neighbour. The Germans, like the Belgians, had quickly realised that the railways were the best mechanism for nation-building and built lines across their state borders, a scheme that helped to unify the nation. The French were hamstrung early on by philosophical discussions over the desirability of railways, but then, seeing the speed of progress by their neighbour, they also embarked on a massive railway-building programme. However, France, catching up quickly, later built a remarkable network of small lines, often narrow gauge, that connected every town and most villages, thanks to a law that gave local authorities access to central government funds to build railways. That became the pattern throughout Europe. Main lines were built, quickly followed by smaller branches with slow, infrequent trains which at least ensured that almost everyone was connected to the iron road. They would carry not only passengers but freight too – agricultural

produce on the way to market in one direction, manufactured goods bought by mail order or being delivered to local shops, in the other.

The railways became the only way to travel quickly and relatively comfortably, since for long distances they were far superior to their predecessors – stagecoaches on bumpy roads or, for freight, canals which were slow and froze over in winter. Consequently, the railways spread inexorably across Europe. Their advantages ensured that they were effectively a monopoly able to dictate terms and conditions to their customers, so the attitude of the early railways was that there was no need to spend money on creating expensive facilities when passengers were flocking to them anyway.

Therefore any reality of a Golden Age was a long time coming. Before the European railways could boast of anything like a Golden Age, they needed to have coherent networks with fewer changes of train, on-board facilities which meant corridor rather than compartment coaches and, possibly most important, a change in ethos by the train companies. They needed to become faster, more comfortable, offer decent facilities and, in modern parlance, become customer-focused.

Progress

Progress on all these fronts was relatively slow until the last quarter of the nineteenth century when rapid changes began to be made, and consequently it was not until the turn of the century that the very notion of a Golden Age can perhaps be entertained. Safety, for example, was barely considered in the early days as the very slowness of the trains and their

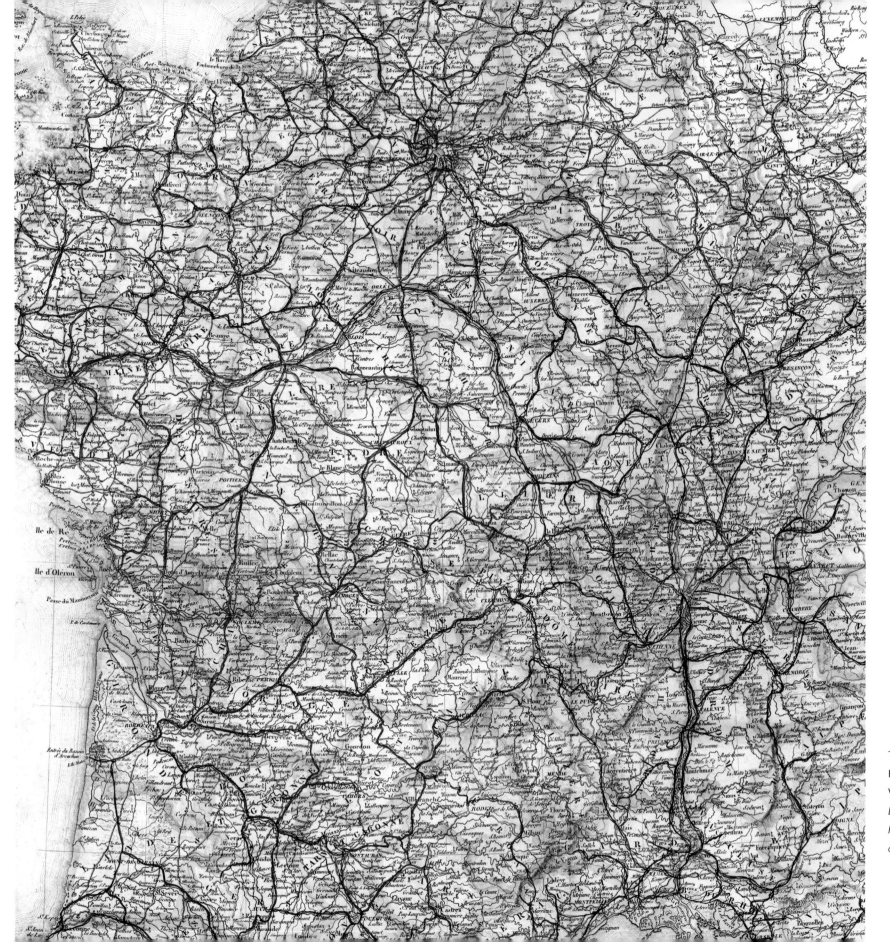

The railway network in France in 1875, from Le Vasseur's *Grand atlas Départemental de la France, de l'Algérie et des colonies.*

infrequency limited the potential for disasters. There were a few early mishaps, such as the 1842 Versailles accident in France, in which 55 people died in the resulting fire, but by and large accidents were few and far between. However, while by the 1850s accidents were becoming more severe and more frequent, it was not until later when there were several major disasters that the resulting public outcry forced governments and railway companies into action. In Britain, for example, the catalyst for legislation was a particularly cruel and unnecessary disaster, the Armagh accident of 1889 in Northern Ireland, in which 78 people, mostly schoolchildren, died. The accident occurred when a train carrying people on a Sunday outing proved too heavy to reach the top of an incline and, when some carriages were de-coupled, they rolled down the slope crashing into a train behind. The accident was eminently preventable had proper braking systems been fitted or, indeed, had the children not been locked into their compartments, and within weeks legislation requiring improved brakes and more sophisticated signalling systems was passed by the British Parliament.

Fares, too, were coming down as competition on parallel lines became more commonplace and as companies no longer needed to spend so much on expanding their networks. For example, in 1889, the first and third class fares on the Great Western between London and Penzance in Cornwall, a distance of 326 miles (nearly 526 km), were respectively three pounds, three shillings and six pence (£3.18 in decimal notation) and one pound, five shillings and eleven pence (£5.30) but by 1900 they had been reduced to two pounds, twelve shillings and ten pence (£2.64) and one pound, three shillings and five pence (£1.17). Similarly, the price for the 540-mile journey between Paris and Marseille was four pounds and five shillings (£4.25), reduced to three pounds, seventeen shillings and four pence (£4.87) in first class and from two pounds, six shillings and nine pence (£2.34), to one pound and fourteen shillings (£1.70) in third class. Note how the republican French seemed to favour third class in their reductions, used by the vast majority of travellers, while the British

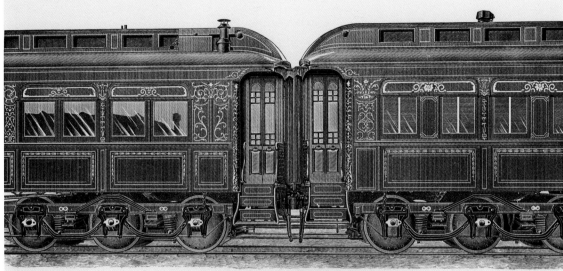

focused on alleviating the burden for their more affluent patrons! Fare cuts, though, were a continent-wide phenomenon. In Austria (which was still the core of the Habsburg Empire and consequently far bigger than today) the introduction of a zonal tariff system, a very advanced concept for the age, led to sweeping reductions in long-distance fares for all classes. Prussia, though, was an exception because its railways made an additional charge in respect of an improvement in the type of accommodation offered to passengers. These were the so-called 'concertina trains' which became the norm on its express services and had corridors that allowed passengers to circulate through the whole train rather than individual compartments with doors on both sides. The porter's area served as a buffet from which hot and cold dishes as well as drinks were served to passengers in their compartments, a huge improvement in service.

Corridors were an important innovation. Until the 1860s, virtually all European trains were of a compartment design and the change, oddly, was prompted by two murders. In December 1860, the body of the French Chief Justice, M. Poinsot, was found at the Gare de l'Est in Paris in the compartment of a train from Mulhouse in eastern France, and his fellow passenger in first class, clearly the murderer, was never found. The similar murder of Thomas Briggs on a suburban line in London four years later, for which a German national was eventually hanged, sent something of a shudder around Europe about the safety of train travel. Initially, peepholes allowing people to see into adjoining compartments were introduced

on some lines but while assuaging the fear of violence this did little, in practice, to prevent it. Doors that ran between each compartment were also installed on some railways, but again this was unsatisfactory as the occupants' privacy and comfort were disturbed by the passage of people through the doors. The Nord railway in France tried external corridors but these were perilous in the extreme. The solution, first put forward by a German engineer, Heusinger von Waldegg (1817–86), was to move the corridor to one side, and introduce sliding doors in each of the compartments rather than, as in America, have fully open-plan-style carriages.

In the last quarter of the century, corridor trains became standard throughout Europe. More important than preventing murder, they allowed the introduction of various passenger comforts. Toilets on trains began to appear in the 1870s, and not only did corridors allow passengers to relieve themselves, but also to purchase refreshments and food in dining cars. Initially providing fairly basic food, on longer-distance trains dining cars became a source of pride for the train companies and began to offer generous menus.

At first the connections between carriages were primitive, exposing passengers to the wind and rain, as well as the risk of finding themselves on the tracks, and at times they proved an insurmountable obstacle for women dressed in the wide-rimmed dresses and copious petticoats of the day. Later, however, corridor connections with leather, accordion-style covers provided adequate if not entirely watertight passage from coach to coach.

Wagons-Lits dining car in 1868 (above left).

Pullman vestibuled cars, c.1890 (above right).

Wagons-Lits day lounge and cabinet de toilette, 1868 (below).

WAGON-LIT, LE JOUR.

CABINET DE TOILETTE.

Good lighting was another relatively late addition to railway travel. As far back as 1863, English trains had pioneered gas lighting and oil lamps and, in Russia, candle lamps became commonplace. The first electrically lit coach was introduced on the London to Brighton line in 1881 but the batteries proved too heavy, and it was not until right at the end of the nineteenth century that the technology for electric lighting was perfected, with the Great Northern Railway of Ireland being an unlikely pioneer.

Because train travel was so patently superior to any other form of transport and had no rival until the arrival of the car and the lorry in the early twentieth century, the railways had been rather dilatory about reducing journey times. However, the trains began to speed up in tandem with the fall in fares, helped by technological developments as locomotives became faster and the tracks became smoother. With corridor trains, there was no longer the need to have 'comfort breaks' or stops for meals, an advance which also speeded up services. Lines built by penurious companies struggling to complete projects half a century before could now be improved with slow curves being replaced by faster sections of straighter track. Many single track lines were now doubled, cutting the time that trains waited at crossovers, which was always a source of great frustration for passengers. The major lines were expanded to four tracks, allowing passenger expresses to overtake stopping and freight trains that meandered along on the slower lines. Locomotives, too, were improving. The use of compound steam engines – in which both fuel economy and power is enhanced because the steam goes through two stages of pressurisation – became widespread.

Railway companies, too, began to be more conscious of the fact that their passengers would favour shorter journeys and realised that they would get more use out of their rolling stock by improving the timetable. All this investment paid off in terms of cutting journey times. For example, while in 1889 it took more than 14 hours to travel between Paris and Marseille on the fastest train (an average of just 37 miles per hour), a decade later it was just 13 hours, an average of more than 40 mph. The service between Vienna and Trieste, 372 miles apart (599 km), improved by two hours in that period to just 12 hours, an average of 31 mph, which was not bad given that the route crossed the Semmering mountain range, the first route to pierce the barrier of the Alps. In the more remote parts of Europe, however, train travel could still be remarkably slow. In Russia, for example, the mail trains, which were the fastest, ran at an average of just 20 mph while even on the prestigious Moscow–St Petersburg route, the ordinary passenger train speed was a ponderous 15 mph and even the fastest, the courier train, averaged just 28 mph.

Gauge standardisation was another important development. Although most companies in Europe – with the exception of Russia and the Iberian countries – used the standard four foot, eight inches gauge, some railways had been built to different gauges and this was a source of delay at connecting stations. The Great Western Railway in Britain, for example, had been built to 7 foot, ¼ inch, and in one momentous summer's day in 1892 all its remaining broad gauge track, more than 200 miles (about 322 km), was converted to standard.

The Trans-Siberian

This was a period, too, of great expansion where mountains, rivers or sheer distance were no obstacle. The most notable construction was the Trans-Siberian in Russia, the world's longest and most impressive railway. In 1888, the first section of what would become the 5,777-mile Trans-Siberian between Moscow and Vladivostok on the Pacific Coast was opened between two obscure stations, Samara and Ufa. The building of the complete line was authorised in 1891 by a decree from the Czar who wanted to cement the hold of the Russian state over the vast, sparsely populated territories of Siberia. Built as a state enterprise, the Trans-Siberian was largely completed by 1904 with a section, the China Eastern Railway, that ran through Manchuria and prompted the Russo-Japanese War which broke out as soon as the line was completed. While it was a marvellous and unparalleled engineering achievement, the railway was remarkably primitive and early travellers on the line complained of lengthy, unexplained stops, and of long periods travelling through the endless birch forests at a mere 12 mph. The whole journey at best would take two weeks, but passengers were advised to allow at least three weeks given the unreliability of the service. Accidents, mostly caused by derailments due to the terrible state of the track,

were frequent with almost 100 deaths in numerous crashes during 1901, before the line was fully open. The tight security was another irritating feature for the many international passengers, who used the line because it was a far quicker way of reaching China from Europe than the ships, although they were banned from taking photographs or even getting off the train to stretch their legs at many stations. The staff were famously obstreperous and uncommunicative, and spoke only Russian. Passengers suffered from other oddities, such as meals being served according to St Petersburg time even in the far east of Russia, seven time zones away.

No other railway could match the ambitious scale of the Trans-Siberian, but the last quarter of the nineteenth century saw unprecedented growth and, for the most part, the effective completion of railway networks. The main lines were, by and large, finished by the 1880s with the completion of several cross-border connections. The earliest international line had been built in 1844, when a French railway extended a mile or so over the frontier from Alsace to Basel in Switzerland, and the Alps had been breached with the 1857 completion of the Semmering

Japanese propaganda from the Russo-Japanese War of 1904 – 'The Russian Railway Carriage Falling to the Bottom of the Frozen Lake', an illustration by Utagawa Kakunimasa (above).

Building the Trans-Siberian Railway, a tinted photograph from 1902 (below).

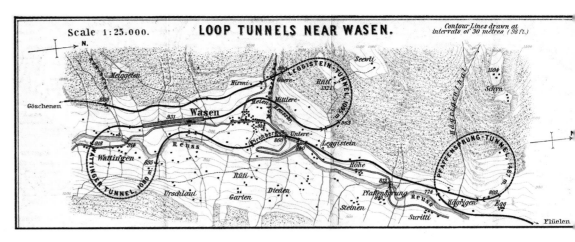

Loops in the St Gotthard railway at Biaschina seen in an 1899 photochrome (above left).

The loops in the St Gotthard line at Wassen (Wasen), a map from a 1905 guidebook (above right).

The opening of the Mont Cenis Tunnel on 10 September 1871, an engraving from the *Illustrated London News* (left centre).

Building workers during construction of the Mont Cenis Tunnel, a photograph from early 1871 (left bottom).

line between Vienna and Trieste, both at the time part of the Austro-Hungarian Empire. Spurred by the success of the Semmering, which quickly became a vital route for both passengers and freight, several other trans-alpine projects were promoted. A second line, the Brenner, which opened in 1867, was far easier from an engineering point of view as it required no major tunnelling. Switzerland, which joined the railway age surprisingly late in the late 1840s, was now key to this process. A much more impressive achievement was the Mont Cenis line between France and Italy. Work on the eight-mile tunnel through the Alps started at both ends as far back as 1857 and was expected to take 25 years, showing a breadth of ambition by the promoters. However, improvements in tunnelling techniques, notably with the use of a pneumatic drill to speed up the drilling of holes in which to place explosive charges, greatly accelerated progress. The French and Italian teams met on Boxing Day 1870, barely half-a-metre out of alignment. The railway, completed the following year, provided a route from Milan and Turin through to Lyon and eventually Paris, and soon there was an express service which left Paris at 8 a.m. and arrived in Rome at 6 a.m. the following day, a 22-hour journey at an average speed of 40 mph.

An even more impressive line, the St Gotthard which linked Germany and Italy through Switzerland was completed in 1882. It was the engineering miracle of the day. At nine miles (14.5 km), the St Gotthard had the longest tunnel in the world at that time, but it was the method used to bring the line up to that height which was innovative. The engineer, Louis Favre (1826–79), decided to cut enormous circular tunnels deep into the mountainside with a gentle and consistent gradient, raising the railway above itself. This inevitably added considerably to the length of the line. The railway between Lucerne and Chiasso on the Italian border is 141 miles long (227 km), a fifth of which consists of these loops, but gives passengers a spectacular ride. For example, at Wassen, passengers heading south emerge from one such loop above a church spire which they have just seen from below a few minutes before.

Railway Stations

Stations, initially dull minimalist depots thrown up as cheaply as possible became great palaces of the modern age, with companies competing to show off their munificence. Even in modest towns and small villages, the stations became the hub of a vast range of activity. At stations people mingled in unprecedented numbers, bringing or collecting their packages, meeting and greeting relatives and lovers, or seeing off sons to war or daughters to work as maids in the big cities. In Europe's

major cities the railway companies, which were by far the biggest businesses of their day, began to show off with splendid creations. Starting with the Gare de l'Est in Paris, built in 1852, the railway station changed and there was a rush to host the grandest of these modern cathedrals. The allusion to temples of worship is apt as the styles were, with the odd exception such as King's Cross in London, unashamedly retrograde, harking back to a past long before the railway age. They were built in a remarkably eclectic range of revival styles: Gothic, classic, Renaissance, Romanesque, even Baroque, possibly, as Jeffrey Richards and John M. Mackenzie say in their 1988 book *The Railway Station: A Social History*, 'to comfort and reassure those concerned about the newness of it all'.

It is difficult to choose the grandest European station: just to name a few is to leave out countless others, but competitors for the prize would include the massive Hauptbahnhof in Frankfurt in Germany, Paris's Quai d'Orsay which is now an art museum, the Gothic splendour of St Pancras in London or the Stazione Centrale in Rome, inspired by the Gare de l'Est. The railways began to improve stations in rural areas, too, realising that they were centrepieces of their localities. Many in Europe were built to a classic rustic style in keeping with the local vernacular and which, again, reflected the past rather than celebrated the modernity of the invention they served. It was only at the turn of the century that more modern styles began to be used for some of the larger stations. Notably the Art Nouveau movement reflecting the influence of nature and, later, modernism and Art Deco, in a belated attempt to reflect the role of the railway in the twentieth century.

Sleeper cars were another relatively late innovation. In America, where the long distances made them a necessity, they had been introduced early in the railway's history and Pullman cars soon became ubiquitous. In Europe, a few basic facilities were offered to overnight travellers, but sleeping cars were not introduced until the 1870s when an enterprising Belgian, Georges Nagelmackers, who had seen Pullman cars in America, introduced them on an express train service between Berlin and Paris.

The Orient Express

More notably, Nagelmackers was responsible for creating the *Orient Express* which perhaps can be perceived as the emblem of the Golden Age of European railways. Inaugurated in 1883, it crossed seven borders as it operated from Paris to Constantinople (Istanbul), a 1,800-mile journey made legendary by the reports of intrigue, illicit sex and, of course, thanks to Agatha Christie, murder. It took a few years before the full route could be established by direct train but Nagelmackers performed miracles in overcoming the bureaucratic problems of crossing European borders.

The story of the *Orient Express* neatly encapsulates the contradictions of what we want to believe was the Golden Age of railways. We are all familiar with the Agatha Christie version of the train with its cast of exotic characters and tales of diplomatic intrigue. The comfortable couchettes were, indeed, occupied by the elite of the day, the forebears of those prepared to pay £5,000 for the pleasure of travelling across

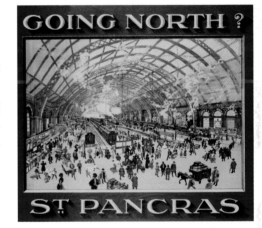

Paris's Gare d l'Est in 1870, the busiest of the city's stations at the end of the nineteenth century (top left).

Frankfurt Hauptbahnhof (main station) seen in a 1905 postcard (top right).

'Going North? St Pancras'; a famous London and North Eastern Railway poster from 1910 (above).

Georges Nagelmackers, creator of the luxury Wagons-Lits, photographed in Brussels on 4 January 1898 (above).

Mann Boudoir Car No. 15 was constructed in 1873; in this photograph Colonel William d'Alton Mann and Georges Nagelmackers are seen posing beside its running board (above centre).

A Simplon-Orient-Express poster designed by Jean de la Nézière in 1926 (above right).

the Atlantic in a Virgin Upper Class bed rather than strapped into an uncomfortable, economy class seat. However, while initially the *Orient Express* only had a few luxury carriages, it soon acquired basic ones for third class passengers who quickly became far more numerous than Hercule Poirot and his gang of suspects. They did not travel the whole route, but rather they were often emigrants travelling from one impoverished East European country to another, or maybe simply using the train for local purposes of business or pleasure. Their accommodation in cramped carriages with wooden seats and little ventilation was far removed from the more common, luxurious images of this great train.

Indeed, it was not only the poor and the thrifty who would have cause to question the notion of a Golden Age. Certainly the modern notion of customer service remained absent from the majority of rail services. Travelling down to the Côte d'Azur from London as late as in 1886, the Baroness de Stoeckl, a regular traveller on the route, found the experience distressing to say the least. She was relatively content until she reached Calais where, as she later described 'there was a wild rush for the buffet as in those days there were no restaurant cars on the trains'. Even though everyone ordered the same meal – *potage, demi-poulet, pommes purées, un demi de vin rouge* (soup, chicken, mashed potatoes, red wine) – within minutes the train officials were hustling them out with cries of '*cinq minutes*' (five minutes) long before the *poulet* and *pommes* could be enjoyed. After settling their bills and grabbing their coats, she describes how the passengers ran 'like maniacs along the platform, maids with anxious faces pointing to the various compartments, the porters shouting "*prenez vos places*" (take your places)'. There were

no lavatories or corridors and the Baroness reported mysteriously that 'most people took with them a most useful domestic utensil, the emptying of which necessitated the frequent lowering of the window'. As this was first class, one can only guess at the depredations in second. In fairness, though, perhaps the Baroness was travelling just as the train companies were improving their services. A few years later, Queen Victoria, a reluctant and at times frightened train traveller, was a regular passenger on the same train down to the French Riviera where she preferred Nice to Cannes, the choice of her son, the future British king Edward VII.

The big companies were at pains to show their prowess on their prestigious routes. In 1888, a speed contest erupted on the London and Aberdeen route between the London and North Western, using the west coast route, and the Great

Northern on the east coast. The prize was the lucrative hunting and shooting brigade who travelled from the English capital to Scotland for the annual grouse shoot, but company pride was at stake, too. Over the course of the race, where both companies employed dubious practices such as omitting the usual intermediate stops and carrying fewer coaches than normal, the time for the 500-mile run was cut from nine and ten hours respectively to around seven hours. Eventually, conscious of the dangers highlighted by an increasingly hostile press coverage, the companies compromised by adding some slack into the timetables but nevertheless the trains on both lines were still more than an hour faster than previously.

A Golden Age?

In the final years of the nineteenth century, the European railway networks were virtually complete and at their height. Hardly a town of any substance was without its train station, and few villages were more than a few miles from one. The service they offered was now universal and since most companies were monopolies, they generally made good profits. No longer needing to invest in expanding their networks, they could turn their attention to improving services and undoubtedly they did improve. If there was a Golden Age in Europe, this was it. But services were still patchy. Whereas the main line trains did offer considerable amenities and good frequencies, many regional services were inadequate at best,

with slow and infrequent trains, and branch lines that could never be profitable were neglected and offered a sparse service.

By the turn of the century, the major European powers – France, Germany and Great Britain, all had similar size networks in relation to their population, as they all averaged about two-thirds of a mile (one kilometre) for every 1,000 people. Spain and the Austro-Hungarian Empire lagged behind with networks that had around three-quarters as many railways in relation to the population, but this still gave them extensive networks with, for example, the Austro-Hungarian Empire boasting more than 18,000 miles (29,000 km) of line. These countries had, effectively, all the railways they needed, but they still built a few lines in the first decade of the twentieth century either to thwart competitors or to fill a gap in their network.

Nord Express poster by A.M. Cassandre, 1927 (left).

London-Vichy Pullman, a 1927 poster by Jean-Raoul Naurac (right).

The *Fliegender Hamburger* in 1933, in a press photograph (left) and an advertising leaflet (right).

While the two or three decades leading up to the First World War were a time of profitability for many railway companies, they were always under pressure to invest to improve the service offered to passengers with more frequent trains or more comfortable accommodation. Just as they were able to slow their expansion, the threat of competition from car and lorry emerged, wrecking any hopes they had of a period of consolidation. Then came the First World War when the railways of all the key players came under state control and were used extensively as part of the war machine. They emerged from the war battered – often quite literally – suffering from years of underinvestment and facing pressure from motorised transport, especially the lorry which soon began to take lucrative freight transport off the rails.

After the war there was a last-ditch attempt to maintain the pre-eminence of the railways in the face of this competition. It is, again, the posters and advertising that we often remember from this period and there are indeed numerous examples of great art being harnessed in the interests of the railway. Thanks to this publicity, the 1920s and 1930s are sometimes seen, too, as a Golden Age of the railway. Certainly the posters from that period are suggestive of a railway that would be the envy of rail passengers today and to be fair, they were not all misleading. The railway was improved by competition as rail managers realised that they had to respond to the

motor car, which was seen as a superior form of travel as it allowed far more freedom to the individual.

Electric and diesel trains, which were an improvement on steam locomotives, were seen as a way of modernising the railways and were introduced by various railways across Europe. Electric power in particular had a number of advantages, being cleaner, more efficient and ultimately cheaper, but the technology took time to develop. The first electric trains had been introduced in the 1880s, and by the early years of the twentieth century were being enthusiastically adopted in countries such as Switzerland and Germany thanks to their superiority on mountain routes. In the interwar period France and Italy, too, embarked on substantial electrification programmes, as did the UK on its suburban network south of the River Thames.

Diesels were another innovation that improved both efficiency and the service. Diesel engines were also nineteenth century invention, but it was not until the 1920s that the technical difficulties were overcome and they could become anything but a technical curiosity. The Germans were the first to fully exploit the concept. In 1933, the Reichsbahn launched a new, high-speed diesel service, the *Fliegende Hamburger* (Flying Hamburger) between Berlin and Hamburg which covered the 178-mile route at an average of 75 mph, requiring long periods of running at 100 mph. The train, which looked rather like a Zeppelin on rails, was

Terence Cuneo's famous painting of British Railways No. 60022 (formerly London North-Eastern Region 4468) *Mallard*, the Gresley-designed Pacific locomotive which established the world steam locomotive speed record of 184 km/h on 28 June 1937 (left).

Sir Nigel Gresley (1876–1941) (below).

Sir William Stanier (1876–1965) (bottom).

a revolutionary concept and could have been the spur to a Golden Age had not the service been brought to a close by the Second World War.

Steam engines, though, still had a last gasp at trying to prove their superiority, and again it was on the route between London and Scotland, where two rail companies, the London, Midland and Scottish and the London and North Eastern Railway, battled to provide the fastest service in the 1930s. They employed two illustrious locomotive engineers, William Stanier (1876–1965) and Nigel Gresley (1876–1941) respectively, who attempted to outdo each other in designing the most advanced steam locomotive and consequently allow the fastest services. Ultimately it was Gresley who prevailed with the famous run by *Mallard*

which achieved the remarkable speed of 126 miles per hour on a test run in July 1938. The companies also vied to provide customer services, with DJs, piped music, cinema coaches and even on-board typists and carriages with leather armchairs and hand-painted décor to attract passengers. It was the last vestiges of grandeur on the railways. Ultimately, there was no way that the railways could compete once the Second World War took its toll on them. The war laid asunder thousands of miles of Europe's railways, requiring them to invest massively in the aftermath, and together with the rapid rise of mass car ownership, this put paid to any chance of reviving the railways. It was now that the motor car would enjoy its own Golden Age, snuffed out only by its very success. But that's another story!

GREAT BRITAIN

The railway was one of the most significant products of the industrial revolution, successfully blending a fixed guided tramway with steam power, while borrowing transport models from established systems including stagecoaches, canals, and toll roads.

Britain was the first country in the world to develop the railway as a steam-hauled carrier of goods and passengers (a 'common carrier'), establishing a unified rail transport system in which the same organisation built and maintained purpose-made private infrastructure, procured equipment, and fully controlled operations.

George Stephenson was among the early railway engineering pioneers. His Stockton and Darlington Railway, opened in 1825, is considered to be the first steam-hauled common carrier railway, while his Liverpool and Manchester Railway, which opened in 1830, was the true beginning of the railway era, a prototype emulated around the nation and across the globe.

In its desire to procure more effective steam power, the Liverpool and Manchester held its famous Rainhill Locomotive Trials in 1829, aimed at encouraging competition between builders. The winner was none other than Stephenson's talented son, Robert, with his exceptional machine named *Rocket*, which blended all the successful

principles of locomotive design and influenced more than a century of locomotive building around the world.

The success of these early railways led Britain's first wave of railway fever, with lines proposed across the nation. While many adhered to the principles established by George Stephenson, including the width of the track (typically described as the 'track gauge') which he set at 4 feet $8^{1}/_{2}$ inches (1.44 m) between rail heads. There was one significant exception, Isambard K. Brunel, an eccentric visionary engineer who deemed Stephenson's gauge too restrictive for high speed operation; he built his Great Western Railway to the exceptional 7 foot $^{1}/_{4}$ inch track gauge, the widest ever adopted by a common carrier.

British railways began as relatively focused, privately financed lines and soon grew into regional competing networks. Railways penetrated almost every corner of the British Isles, with many towns served by two or more routes. Grouping in 1923 produced four large regional systems – the Great Western Railway (by then re-gauged to the Stephenson standard), the London, Midland and Scottish; the London and North Eastern; and the Southern Railway. All were blended together as the nationalised British Railways after the Second World War, but later re-privatised in the 1990s using a modern system of franchises which also separated infrastructure from both ownership of equipment and from train operations.

The railway across Chat Moss, on the Liverpool and Manchester Railway, 1831 (above).

The original 'Rocket' of 1829 (left).

Great Northern Railway Stirling 8-foot with a Scotland-bound express (below).

The opening of the Stockton and Darlington Railway in 1825 (opposite).

THE GREAT WESTERN RAILWAY

Isambard Kingdom Brunel's Masterpiece

It is not for nothing that the Great Western Railway's nickname was God's Wonderful Railway. Built by Isambard Kingdom Brunel, it has all the characteristics for which that great engineer is famous. It was built to the highest standards, using the best techniques of the day, and the fact that the route has barely changed to this day is testimony to Brunel's achievements.

But he so very nearly did not get the job. The group of Bristol businessmen promoting the scheme had chosen another route entirely until Brunel came down from the north and persuaded them to appoint him as the engineer for the line. It proved an excellent decision as otherwise the line might have been a windy slow route. Instead, he managed to convince them that they should not build a standard line on the cheap, but rather the best railway the world had ever seen.

After a lengthy Parliamentary process, the scheme was given the go ahead in 1835 and work started early the following year. Brunel insisted that there should be few curves and only gentle gradients. Moreover, to demonstrate the grandeur of the scheme, he embellished bridges and tunnels with all kinds of mock cases, using an eclectic range of classical, Tudor and Jacobean styles.

It was perhaps in trying to show off that Brunel made his most expensive mistake. The line was built to a gauge of just over 7ft (2.2 m), 50 per cent wider than the gauge used by Stephenson and that became adopted as

standard throughout Europe and much of the world. His idea was that this would enable people to travel in more comfort but actually his carriages were, oddly, not that much wider than those used elsewhere, and just half a century after the line was completed, it was converted to standard gauge.

When the line opened to Bristol in 1838, it was a veritable speedway, which, thanks to Brunel's engineering requirements, allowed trains to travel faster than on other contemporary lines. The performance of the railway was boosted, too, by the work of Daniel Gooch, the excellent locomotive engineer whom Brunel hired. He developed several innovative types of engine that enhanced the company's reputation for reliability and speed.

There was, though, an oddity which slowed down the trains. In order to help pay for the line, which was over budget

Isambard Kingdom Brunel in the famous 1857 photograph by Robert Howlett (above).

'Rain, Steam and Speed', J.M.W. Turner's painting of a GWR express crossing Brunel's Maidenhead Bridge in 1844 (right).

The locomotive shop, GWR Swindon Works, 1881 (far left).

The last broad gauge train to the West – the GWR 'Cornishman' photographed on 20 May 1892 (left).

because of the high engineering standards, Brunel came to an agreement with a pair of brothers, the Rigbys, to build a station and housing at Swindon. In return, every train had to stop there for long enough for people to buy refreshments from the Rigby's buffet. It was not until 1895 that the GWR bought itself out of that onerous contract.

The line had two of the most difficult structures built during that period, the Maidenhead Bridge, immortalised in the Turner painting, *Rain, Steam and Speed – The Great Western Railway* and at the time the widest in the world, and

the 2.8 km Box Tunnel near Bath. As the railway expanded westwards, there were other great structures, notably the unique 140 m Royal Albert Bridge connecting Devon and Cornwall which was completed just before Brunel's death in 1859.

No. 1 Tunnel, from an 1846 book of engravings of the Great Western Railway by John Cook Bourne (right).

GWR West of England Express, 4-cylinder 4–6–0 No. 4099 'Kilgerran Castle', July 1927 (below).

THE WEST COAST MAIN LINE

From London to Birmingham and the North

George Stephenson portrayed at the height of his career in an angraving of 1830 (above).

Grand Junction Railway locomotive No. 1868 *Columbine*, built in 1845, in the London Science Museum (right).

The opening of the Liverpool and Manchester Railway in 1830 created an immediate boom in railway building. It was obvious that London would have to be connected with the burgeoning industrial north, 200 miles away, but it was no easy task.

The route was, in fact, initially built as two separate railways, both terminating in Birmingham. As with so many early railway projects both in Britain and in Europe, the Stephensons, George and his son Robert, were strongly involved. The southern section was the London and Birmingham, a 180 km railway from Euston through Watford, Rugby and Coventry through to Birmingham, where it would meet the 125 km Grand Junction, which ran through Staffordshire to join the Liverpool and Manchester. George was the chief engineer for both projects, but in practice Joseph Locke was responsible for the Grand Junction while Robert Stephenson laid out the London and Birmingham.

These were the first two long-distance railways in Britain, and the task of convincing local landholders to allow them to be built was not easy. There was also much opposition from canal owners, and the first attempt to push through a bill for the Grand Junction failed. Oddly, a key objector was James Watt, the son of the great steam engine pioneer, who not only owned shares in canal companies but also an estate, Aston Hall, which was on the path of the railway near the centre of Birmingham. He refused to cede any of his land to the railway company, forcing the promoters to reroute the line in a way that initially made it impossible for the two lines to connect, although both terminated at Curzon Street where through passengers had to change trains.

Further south, too, there was no shortage of opponents. One of the most truculent was an old doctor, Sir Astley Cooper, who owned an estate in Berkhamsted, and told Robert Stephenson that the idea of a railway was 'preposterous in the extreme' and suggested that if 'this sort of thing be permitted to go on, you will in a very few years destroy the noblesse'.

But go on it did. Eventually these landowners were bought off at a price – some £700,000 was spent on buying the narrow slivers of land required for the two projects, about a fifth of the combined cost of the schemes. After permission was obtained

Entrance to London Euston Station on the London and Birmingham railway, 1838 (far left).

The Camden Town stationary steam engine chimneys and locomotive workshops in 1838 (left).

The Avon Viaduct, 1838 (below).

in 1833, work progressed relatively fast and part of the line was opened by 1838. The Grand Junction was the harder of the two to build, requiring four major viaducts and a 3 km cutting at Preston Brook which involved constructing an aqueduct to carry a canal over the railway. Although operated for a few years as separate railways, they soon merged, along with a few smaller companies, to create the London and North Western, a 400 km line which ran from London to Warrington, where it joined the Liverpool and Manchester, and through services were eventually made possible by the opening of the present station in Birmingham, New Street, in 1854.

Initially it took six hours to travel between London and Birmingham at a fare of £1 10 shillings (around £100 in today's money), and for many years the first part of the journey from Euston involved being hauled up the incline with the aid of a rope and stationary engine. Soon, however, services improved and speeded up, and connections with other Midlands and Northern cities could be made easily. The line was, and remains, the spine of the British rail network, connecting most of its major towns and cities.

LEEDS TO CARLISLE – THE SETTLE ROUTE

The Moorland Route of Tunnels and Viaducts

Aisgill and Deepgill Viaducts under construction, 1873 (insets opposite).

Old meets new – the newly-built steam locomotive *Tornado* on the Ribblehead Viaduct, October 2009 (opposite)

The Settle line on a map of 1910 (below).

The Leeds–Carlisle line was the last main line to be built in Britain. Constructed almost entirely by hand, it was intended to be an alternative route to Scotland for the Midland Railway. It was a brave enterprise, a line that went through virtually uninhabited countryside principally to serve long-distance passengers, but it also gave England one of its most scenic rail routes, the section through the moors between Settle and Carlisle.

The line was born of the fierce rivalry between the big late-nineteenth century railway companies as they forged main line routes to Scotland. There were already two main lines linking the two countries, but both were controlled by the Midland's rivals – the London and North Western on the west coast, and the Great Northern on the east coast. The Midland ran trains to Scotland from its new massive station at St Pancras, but was hamstrung by having to combine carriages with those of the London and North Western, which made life uncomfortable for Midland passengers by making them transfer at a chilly North Yorkshire station called Ingleton.

The Midland, therefore, embarked on the potentially foolhardy task of building a line across the North Yorkshire moors to give it a route of its own to Scotland. Work started in 1869, long after most other main lines had been completed, and was a tough, even heroic, enterprise. A young Tasmanian, Charles Sharland, surveyed a route, spending days tramping across the barren moors to try to work out a route with gradients that were not too high, managing to keep to just 1 in 100. Poor Sharland perished at the age of 26, soon after completing his task, his health broken by his efforts. His route, however, was used as the basis for the new line.

It took the labour of more than 6,000 men to complete the line, costing some £3.5m (around £300m in today's money). There was a human cost, too. Hundreds of these navvies, and some of their families, perished in a smallpox epidemic, and there were numerous fatal accidents, the Ribblehead Viaduct alone resulting in an average of one death a week during its five years of construction.

The line eventually opened in 1876, and became a successful addition to Britain's main line network, despite the difficult conditions encountered in winter. Overall, there are seventeen viaducts and fourteen tunnels along the 72 miles of the line between Settle and Carlisle, and among the stations, Dent, on a remote hillside some distance from the village of that name, is the highest station in England, some 350 m above sea level.

From Settle, the railway climbs over 200 m over twelve miles, then reaches the Blea Moor tunnel, nearly 2 km long and, according to the historian of the Midland Railway, Hamilton Ellis, 'a damp, terrible tunnel. It drove men mad so that they could go underground no more.' More appealingly, there is the elegant Ribblehead Viaduct, one of the grandest on the British rail network, which stretches more than 400 m on its twenty-four arches. It almost spelt the end of the line when British Rail, in the 1970s, argued it was too expensive to repair, but fortunately the line was reprieved after a strong campaign from local people and other users. Today it flourishes, and although no longer used for express trains it still carries significant amounts of freight, and is a honeypot for tourists and rail enthusiasts alike.

LONDON'S RAILWAY TERMINI

A Ring of Famous Stations

St Pancras Station under construction, 1868 (below).

The skyline of St Pancras Hotel (below right).

As railways spread around Britain, London found itself bestowed with a series of wonderful termini – and a few that were less pleasing on the eye. When an idea for a central station for the whole of London near present-day Faringdon was rejected by the city fathers, every railway company sought to have a terminus in London, and tried to outdo each other in terms of scale and grandeur. Londoners have been the beneficiary of this competition.

A ring of stations was built in the mid and late nineteenth century, linked by what became the Circle Line of London's Underground. London's first major terminus was Euston, which also boasted the country's first two railway hotels. It was not a particularly sensible place for a station, as in those days the locomotives were not powerful enough to haul trains up the incline to Camden. The opening in October 1837 had to be delayed because the cable which hauled the trains up the incline was not ready. The initial station was a modest affair with just two platforms, but in order to demonstrate its ambitious intentions the London and Birmingham Railway built a huge 72 ft/22 m high portico in classical style complete with Doric columns. Just over a decade later Euston gained a 'second splendour' in the words of historian Alan A. Jackson – the Great Hall, built in the Renaissance style with a double curved staircase

and a deeply coffered ceiling with plaster bas-reliefs in every corner. It outshone the interior of all subsequent London stations, but was sadly demolished in 1962.

Paddington was the other early station, and as it was built to a design by Isambard Brunel it could not be anything but grand. The main building, the Great Western Hotel, was not particularly exciting, but the train shed, with three graceful spans (later a fourth was built), gave the station a light and airy feel which it retains today.

Less than a mile away from Euston, two more magnificent and contrasting stations were erected over the next two decades. First was the simple, and consequently often underestimated, modern-looking King's Cross, two huge sweeping brown brick arches topped by an Italianate turret with a clock tower. Then next door, the Midland Railway, not to be outdone, built a Gothic temple backed by what was at the time the largest single-arch train shed in the world, designed by William Barlow. The station also housed the enormous Midland Hotel, designed by George Gilbert Scott, adorned with all kinds of ornate accessories including numerous dormer windows, a veritable spaghetti of chimneys, and a clock facing towards King's Cross, on a far higher tower and always showing a slightly different time as a statement of contempt for its rival. In the 1960s St Pancras nearly suffered the same

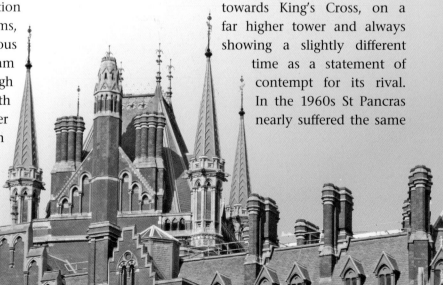

fate as Euston, but was saved by a public campaign led by the poet John Betjeman. Instead, St Pancras was refurbished in the first decade of the twenty-first century to accommodate the international Eurostar trains, with all its main original features being retained.

No other railway company was able to follow these examples, and other London terminuses were inevitably not as grand. The frontage of Charing Cross, for example, is typical – it is a hotel in a vaguely Renaissance style but with a rather cramped feel, the result of its central location on the Strand next to Trafalgar Square and its proximity to the river. Liverpool Street was a banal building interspersed with roadways, and also fronted by a hotel, the unremarkable Great Eastern. London Bridge and Waterloo, shared by various railways, were cobbled together over the Victorian era, though the latter, which boasts more platforms than any other in the UK, was eventually rebuilt in Imperial Baroque style dominated by a Victory Arch over a twenty-year period in the early twentieth century. Victoria, too, suffered from being shared by two railways with an impenetrable dividing wall, although eventually in the early twentieth century it gained a reasonably elegant frontage.

Modest Marylebone, the last new station, built as the terminus of the Grand Central, is a pleasing and rather comely redbrick terminus that was once, rather accurately, described by the architectural historian Nikolaus Pevsner as resembling a 'public library in a large provincial town', but lacking the monumental confidence of its predecessors.

'The Railway Station' (Paddington, 1886), an engraving by William Powell Frith (1819–1909) (above).

The Paddington train shed today (left).

THE WEST HIGHLAND RAILWAY

Across Scotland's Moors and Mountains

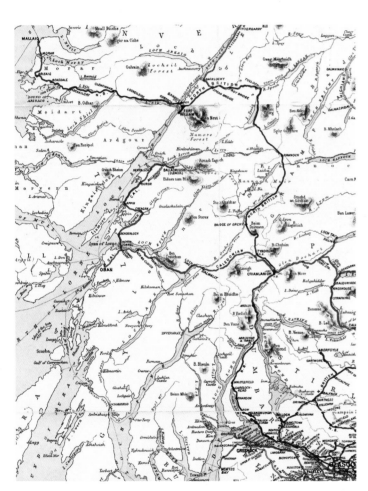

The West Highland Line on a map of 1910 (above).

A poster describing the line, 1906 (right).

The Glenfinnan Viaduct (opposite).

Building and maintaining the line, photographs from the early 1900s (insets opposite)

In 1894 the West Highland Railway opened to the popular Scottish Highland tourist destination of Fort William. Seven years later, operations commenced on a 64 km extension to the fishing port at Mallaig, which also served as a gateway to the Isle of Skye. D.T. Timins, writing in *Railway Magazine* in 1901, described this extension as 'one of those very rare cases in which the electric spark of a common interest flashes between the positive element of commercial advantage and the negative element of philanthropic undertaking.' Considering the sparse population of the Scottish Highlands, it is curious that such a difficult railway was built at all. Yet it was seen as a means of opening up the sublimely scenic region to tourism, while also benefiting the local population.

Leaving Glasgow, the West Highland climbs above the Clyde Estuary, offering magnificent views to the south. There are junctions at Craigendoran and Crianlarich, the latter picturesquely ringed by mountains and serving as a connection with the line west to Oban. Among the most difficult parts of the railway to build was the stretch across Rannoch Moor (the largest moor in Scotland), owing to the peculiar terrain, exceptionally remote land and a dearth of roads. After leaving the relative oasis of Rannoch Moor station, the line crosses a double-intersection

steel Warren truss and climbs sharply, cresting at Corrour Summit, 410.6 m above sea level. Descending toward Fort William, the line follows the crystalline waters of Loch Trieg, offering one of the most stunningly beautiful views afforded from a railway window.

Fort William has a small stub terminal station, and while some through carriages were operated to Mallaig, most passengers continuing to the line's terminus were compelled to make a cross platform change of trains.

The Mallaig extension is characterised by difficult engineering, including eleven tunnels and several significant viaducts, the most famous being the curved 21-arch concrete Glenfinnan Viaduct. Passengers departing from Fort William were awed by views of Ben Nevis, towering 1,342 m above sea level.

Orkney Is

Hoy
Burray
St. Margarets
S. Ronaldshay

Pentland Firth

C. Wrath
Dunnet H.ᵈ
Duncansby H.ᵈ
Scrabster
John o'Groats Ho.
Roan I.
Thurso
Durness
Nybster
Reay
Georgemas
Tongue
Halkirk
Bilbster
Scotscalder
Wick

Butt of Lewis

L. Roag

North Minch

Bernera I.
Stornoway
Eye Pen.

Lewis

Scourie
Forsinard
Altnabreac
Altnaharrow
Kinbrace
Lybster

Lochinver
Kildonan

L. Shin
Loth
Helmsdale
Elphin
Lairg
Rogart
Brora

Broom
Invershin
Mound
Golspie
Dornoch Firth
Ullapool

Little Minch
Aultbea
Dornoch
Poolewe
Bonar Br.
Edderton
Lochbroom
Tain
Moray Firth
Gairloch
Kildary
Fearn
Invergordon
Burghead
Hopeman
Lossiemouth
Cullen
Novar
Findhorn
Banff
Macduff
Linlochewe
Lochtuachart
Garve
Cromarty
Alves
Garmouth
Buckie
Portsoy
Dingwall
Bredie
Elgin
Auchnasheen
Strathpeffer
Forres
Fochabers
Tillynaught
King Edward
Conan
Nairn
Mulben
Keith
Glenbarry
Torridon
George
Dunphail
Rothes
Grange
Rothiemay
Turriff
Shieldaig
Culloden
Carton
Craigellachie
Beauly
Dufftown
Huntly
Fyvie
Strathcarron
Auchnoshellach
Clunes
Inverness
Dava
Rothie Norman
Garty
Portree
Raasay
Grantown
Ballindalloch
Insch
Inveramsay
Jeantown
Advie
Luonsden
Strome Ferry
Cromdale
Skye
Balmacarra
Grantown
Strathdon
Alford
Broadford
Carr Bri.
Bromhill
Monymusk
Glenelg
Boat of Garten
Nethybridge
Tillyfourie
L. Ness
Aviemore
Lumphanan
Torphins
Canna
Armadale
Kincraig
Aboyne
Drum
Rum
Ft. Augustus
Newtonmore
Kingussie
Crathie
Banchory
Eigg
Laggan
Braemar
Ballater
Muck
Unachan
New Mill
Drumlithie
Banavie
Dalwhinnie
Fourdoun
F. William
Dalnaspidal
Laurencekirk
Ardnamurchan pt.
Blair Athol
Marykirk

58°

A

RAILWAY MAP

OF THE

BRITISH ISLES

Scale

10   5   0   10   20   30   40   50   60   70

English   Miles

SCALE, 1:1,774,080, 28 ENGLISH MILES TO 1 INCH.

Railway Lines:- The frequency of communication is shown by engraving the railway lines in varying strength according to the number of daily trains running on each section, viz:-

Lines over which less than 10 trains run each way daily are shown thus .... ———

Lines over which between 10 and 20 trains run each way daily are shown thus .... ———

Lines over which more than 20 trains run each way daily are shown thus .... ———

Steamship route distances in Nautical Miles or Knots.

Towns generally are inserted according to their importance in the railway system - but no town is inserted that has not a railway station, or is not connected with a station by regular daily coach advertised in the Railway Companies tables, or is not a port with regular and frequent steam communication.

nnaird Hd.

Fraserburgh

Lonmay

ichen

clay

Longside   Peterhead

Cruden   Buchan Ness

on

Newburgh

ERDEEN

re

llethen

nhill

aven

Ardnamurchan Pt. · Struan · Kirkmichael · Brechin · Montr
Coll · Rannoch · Killiecrankie · Pitlochry · Kirriemuir · Forfar · Guthrie
S⁺ of Mull · Ballachulish · Kenmore · Aberfeldy · Ballinluig · Alyth · Glamis · Fricklein · Colliston · Monikie · Inverkeillor
Tobermory · Appin · Loch Tay · Guay · Blairgowrie · Alyth Jn. · Coupar · Angus · Broughty Ferry · East Haven · Carnoustie
Ulva · Lochaline · Killin · Dunkeld · Stanley · Strathord · Inchture · Tn · Jn · Newport · Firth of Tay
Mull · Connel Ferry · Tyndrum · Luib · Killin Jn. · Methven · Tn · Tayport · Bell R⁴
Salen · Craignure · Oban · Dalmally · Crianlarich · Comrie · Crieff · Perth · Forteviot · Errol · S⁺ Fort · Leuchars · S⁺ Andrews
Iona · Loch Awe · Lochearnhead · Muthill · Auchterarder · Newburgh · Cupar · Boarhills · Fife Ness
Portsonachan · Ardlui · Strathyre · Crieff Jn. · Greenloaning · Ladybank · Largo · Crail
Scarba · Portinsherrich · Inversnaid · Callander · Dunblane · Kinross · Milnathort · Leslie · Anstruther
Ford · Inveraray · Tarbert · Trossachs · Aberfoyle · Alva · Dollar · Lochgelly · Thornton · Elie · May I.
Colonsay · Lochgoilhead · Buchlyvie · Stirling · Larbert · Denny · Cowdenbeath · Kirkcaldy · Firth of Forth
Jura · Ardentinny · L. Lomond · Balfron · Killearn · Grangemouth · Bo'ness · Burntisland · N. Berwick
Lochgilphead · Ormidale · Helensburgh · Drymen · Buckhaven · Queensferry · Drem · Dunbar
Islay · Tighnabruaich · Dumbarton · Kilsyth · Falkirk · Linlithgow · Granton · Leith · Portobello · E. Linton · Inner
Dunoon · Milngavie · Kirkintilloch · EDINBURGH · Musselburgh · Haddington · Grant's Ho.
Tarbert · Bute · Greenock · Renfrew · Glasgow · Bathgate · Dalkeith · R⁴
Rothesay · Wemyss Bay · Paisley · Airdrie · Coatbridge · Crofthead · Midcalder · Penicuik · Gorebridge
Largs · Johnstone · Rutherglen · Motherwell · Wilsontown · Auchengray · Leadburn · Tynehead · Dunse
Beith · Barrhead · Kilbride · Hamilton · Law Jn. · Carstairs · Broomlee · Fountain Hall · Lauder · Green
Millport · Kilbirnie · Lugton · Stonehouse · Ayr Rd · Dolphinton · Eddleston · Stow · Gordon
Dalry · Stewarton · Strathaven · Lanark · Newbigging · Lyne · Peebles · Galashiels
W. Kilbride · Kilwinning · Kilmarnock · Lesmahagow · Douglas · Symington · Innerleithen · St Boswells · Melrose
Ardrossan · Irvine · Glenbuck · Biggar · Lamington · Selkirk · Maxton · Roxb
Port Ellen · Brodick · Barassie · Hurlford · Newmilns · Inches · Broughton · Hassendean · Jedburgh
Arran · Troon · Mauchline · Muirkirk · Abington · Elvanfoot · Hawick
Lamlash · Annbank · Auchinleck · Cumnock · Leadhills · Stobs · Shankend
Campbeltown · Ayr · Rankinston · New Cumnock · Sanquhar · Moffat · Riccarton · Deadwater
Carradale · Dalrymple · Patna · Kirkconnel · Beattock · Steele Rd · Kielder · Plashetts
Sanda · Maybole · Carronbridge · Thornhill · Wamphray · New Castleton · Belling
North Channel · Ailsa Craig · Kilkerran · Dalmellington · Penpont · Closeburn · Langholm
Rathlin I. · Girvan · Carsphairn · Moniaive · Auldgirth · Lochmaben · Lockerbie · Kershope · Penton
Giants Causeway · Pinmore · Dalry · Amisfield · Canobie · Riddings
Portrush · Bushmills · Ballycastle · Knocknacarry · Pinwherry · Ballantrae · Barrhill · New Galloway Sta · Parton · DUMFRIES · Ecclefechan · Gretna · Haltw
Coleraine · Portstewart · Dervock · Armoy · Glenwhilly · Cas. Douglas · Annan · Longtown
Macfin · Ballymoney · Parkmore · Glenarm · Newton Stewart · Dromore · Tarff · Dalbeattie · Port Carlisle · Carlisle
Garvagh · Knockanally · Carnlough · New Luce · Kirkcowan · Gatehouse · Br of Dee · Kirkcudbright · Siloth · Wigton · Wreay
Kilrea · Rasharkin · Cushendall · Stranraer · Glenluce · Wigtown · Kirkcudbright · Broomfield · Brayton · Lyneside · Brampton
Upperlands · Cullybackey · Ballymena · Dunragit · Whauphill · Whithorn · Port Carlisle · Abbey · Cotehill · Armathwaite
Garryford · Portglenone · Kells · Portpatrick · Port William · Solway Firth · Maryport · Bull Gill · Calthwaite · Lazonby
Kilrea · Carrickfergus · Belfast L. · Donaghadee · Mull of Galloway · Workington · Harrington · Siddick · Cockermouth · Plumpton · Penrith
Antrim · Bangor · Newtownards · Whitehaven · Keswick · Troutbeck · Shap
Belfast · Holywood · Greyabbey · Lisburn · L. Neagh

56°

Eyemauth
Burnmouth
Berwick
Tweedmouth
Scremerston
Holy
Beal
I.
oldstream
Belford
Wooler
Lucker
Chathill
Ckriston Bank
Eglingham
Little Mill
Long Houghton
Alnwick
Bilton
Warkworth
Rothbury
Amble
Brinkburn
Chevington
Ewesley
Wildrington
Longhirst
Woodburn
Morpeth
Newbiggin
Scots Gap
Meldon
Blyth
Reedsmouth
Plessey
Hartley
Chollerton
Monkseaton
Wall
Killingworth
Tynemouth
NEWCASTLE
S. Shields
Hexham
Wylam
Cleadon Lane
Langley
Gateshead
Pelaw
Allendale
Sunderland
Lintz Gr.
Penshaw
Ryhope
Consett
Chester
Murton
Seaham
Rowley
Leamside
Durham
Shincliffe
iheads
Waterhouses
Castle Eden
Wolsingham
Byers for.
Coxhoe
E.
Hartlepool
Wear Valley
Ferryhill
W.
Bp. Auckland
Sedgefield
Redcar
Saltburn
ddleton
Cockfield
Stokesley
Staithes
y Barnard Castle
Middlesbro'
Kettleness
Stockton
op
Darlington
Eaglecliffe
Guisboro'
Whitby
Barras
Bowes
Picton
Castleton
Hawsker
Robin Hood

415 miles

425 miles

N O R T H

S E A

IRISH SEA

I. of Man

Douglas
Ramsey
Peel
Castletown
Port Erin
Port Soderick
Calf of Man

Lurgan
Portadown
Armagh
Banbridge
Newry
Warrenpoint
Dundalk
Drogheda
Navan
Balbriggan
Skerries
Malahide
Howth
DUBLIN
Kingstown
Bray
Wicklow
Wicklow Hd.
Arklow
Gorey
Enniscorthy
Wexford
Rosslare Hr.

Downpatrick
Ardglass
Newcastle
Kilkeel
Greenore
Greencastle

Holyhead
Holy I.
Anglesea
Amlwch
Cemaes
Rhosgoch
Valley
Beaumaris
Conway
Bangor
Carnarvon
Llanberis
Bettws
Festiniog
Criccieth
Pwllheli
Braich-y-Pwll
Bardsey I.
Harlech
Barmouth
Towyn
Aberdovey
Borth
Aberystwyth

Llandudno
Colwyn
Rhyl
Abergele
Holywell
Flint
Denbigh
Mold
Ruthin
Wrexham
Corwen
Bala
Llangollen
Ruabon
Oswestry
Dolgelly
Machynlleth
Welshpool
Montgomery
Newtown
Llanidloes
Rhayader

Chester
Crewe
Nantwich
Whitchurch
Shrewsbury
Much Wenlock
Ch. Stretton
Bishops Castle
Knighton
Ludlow

Moor Row
Cleator Moor
Egremont
Ambleside
Kendal
Coniston
Windermere
Ravensglass
Sellafield
Barrow
Morecambe
Lancaster
Fleetwood
Blackpool
Southport
Preston
Chorley
Ormskirk
Wigan
LIVERPOOL
Birkenhead
Manchester
St. Helens

St. George's Channel

Barras · Picton · Robin Hood Bay · Grosmont · Scarborough

kby Stephen · Dalton · Cowton · Battersby · Goathland · Peak · Hayburn Wyke

Richmond · Catterick Br. · Welbury · Levisham · Forge Valley · Scalby

Tn · Askrigg · Leyburn · Northallerton · Pickering · Seamer · Filey

awes · Finghall Lo. · Bedale · Otterington · Helmsley · Slingsby · Weaverthorpe · Speeton · Flamborough

Buckden · Melmerby · Thirsk · Gilling · Rillington · Bridlington · Flamborough Hd.

head · Grassington · Pateley Br. · Boroughbridge · Cas. Howard · N. Grimston · Wetwang · Tarnaby · Lowthorpe

orton · RIPON · Copgrove · Alne · Easingwold · Kirkham Abbey · Nafferton · Driffield

Settle · Darley · Knaresborough · Strensall · Warthill · Lockington · Hornsea

Hellifield · Bolton Abbey · Ripley · Stamford Br. · Sigglethorne · Whitedale

HARROGATE · Wetherby · YORK · Pocklington · Arram · Beverley

arby · Otley · Tadcaster · Mkt. Weighton · Burton · Cottingham · Hornsea

Skipton · Arthington · Escrick · North Cave · Whitedale

Keighley · Ilkley · Shipley · Ch. Fenton · Bubwith · HULL · Withernsea

BRADFORD · LEEDS · Selby · Howden · Holland · Patrington

Burnley · Laister Dyke · Castleford · GOOLE · Brough · Barton · Ulceby

Halifax · Dewsbury · Normanton · Snaith · Hedon

Rochdale · Todmorden · Wakefield · Balne · Thorne · Brocklesby · Habrough · Spurn Pt.

Bury · Huddersfield · Brockholes · Elmsall · Barnetby · Gt. Grimsby · Cleethorpes · R. Humber

OLDHAM · Marsden · Shepley · Cudworth · Arksey · Scawby · Brigg · Holton · 360 miles · Hamburg

Staleybridge · BARNSLEY · DONCASTER · Finningley · Wirton · Moortown · N. Thoresby · 390 miles · Hamburg

Greenfield · Penistone · Wath · Mexbro' · Haxey · Northorpe · Holton · Mkt · Ludborough · 210 miles

ockport · Glossop · Wortley · Swinton · Bawtry · Gainsborough · Rasen · Grimoldby · Saltfleetby · Rotterdam

Woodley · Wadsley Br. · Rotherham · Donington · LOUTH · Mablethorpe

Marple · Hayfield · SHEFFIELD · Woodhouse · Stow Park · Wragby · Aby · Sutton

Chapel · Eckington · Worksop · Sutton · Langworth · Saxilby · Kingsthorpe · Alford · Willoughby

Buxton · Dronfield · RETFORD · Horncastle · Firsby · Burgh · Skegness

Millers Dale · Staveley · Tuxford · LINCOLN · Spilsby · Croftbank

MACCLESFIELD · CHESTERFIELD · Langwith · Bardney · Woodhall · Wainfleet

N. Rode · Bakewell · Clay Cross · Carlton · Swinderby · Kirkstead · Old Leake

Bakewell · Darley · MANSFIELD · Navenby · Tattershall · Sibsey · The Wash

Congleton · Rowsley · Stratton · Southwell · Digby · Longrick · BOSTON

Leek · Matlock · Pinxton · Newark · Claypole · Swineshead · Wells · Sheringham

Barslem · Wirksworth · Newstead · Sleaford · Cromer

HANLEY · Ambergate · Pye Br. · Hucknall · Barkstone · Aswarby · Donington Rd. · Hunstanton · Holt · Gunton

Stoke · Ashbourne · Kimberley · Rolleston · Daybrook · Elton · Billingbro · Surfleet · Holbeach · Heacham · Walsingham · Melton · N. Walsham

DERBY · Ilkeston · Spondon · NOTTINGHAM · GRANTHAM · Corby · Spalding · Sutton Br. · Wolferton · Fakenham · Corpusty · Aylsham

Uttoxeter · Eggington · Trent · Harby · Gt. Ponton · Bourne · Wisbech · Massingham · Reepham · Wroxham

Stone · Weston · Cas. Donnington · Melton Mowbray · Counter Drain · Postland · KING'S LYNN · County School · Dereham · Drayton

BURTON · Melbourne · Loughboro' · Ashwell · Peakirk · Magdalen Rd. · Holme · Yaxham · NORWICH · Helmby

Rugeley · Ashby · Coalville · Oakham · Essendine · Murrow · Glynhirne · Swaffham · Watton · Wymondham · Caister

Gnosall · Moira · Syston · Losely · STAMFORD · Littleham · Peterboro' · Middledrove · Downham · Stoke Ferry · Stow · Forncett · Gt. Yarmouth

Lichfield · Elford · Shackerstone · Seaton · Wansford · March · Hilgay Fen · Brandon · Wretham · Roydham · Lowestoft

Brownhills · Tamworth · LEICESTER · Wigston · Rockingham · Whittlesea · Manea · Littleport · Thetford · Tivetshall · Bungay · Beccles

WALSALL · Bosworth · Hinckley · Kibworth · Weldon · Oundle · Chatteris · Littleport · Barnham · Diss · Brampton

Sutton · Whitacre · Nuneaton · Mkt. Harbro' · Desborough · Holme · Ramsey · Sutton · Lakenheath · Eye · Southwold

Dudley · Ullesthorpe · Shilton · Welford · Thrapstone · Thorpe · Ely · Mildenhall · Mellis · Darsham

hampton · Wednesbury · BIRMINGHAM · COVENTRY · KETTERING · Cranford · Huntingdon · Earith Br. · Fordham · Ingham · Thurston · Haughley · Finningham · Framlingham

Kings Norton · Hampton · Finedon · Wellingboro' · Kimbolton · Buckden · St. Ives · Kennet · Bury St. Edmunds · Parham

aster · Barnt Gr. · Kenilworth · RUGBY · Brixworth · Welton · St. Neots · Newmarket · Stowmarket · Wickham · Aldeburgh

Bromsgrove · Redditch · Hatton · Marton · Daventry · NORTHAMPTON · Sharnbrook · Lg. Stanton · Woodbridge · Melton

Warwick · LEAMINGTON · Weedon · Blisworth · CAMBRIDGE · Shelford · Lavenham

Droitwich · Stratford · Southam · Billing · Old · Shelford

54

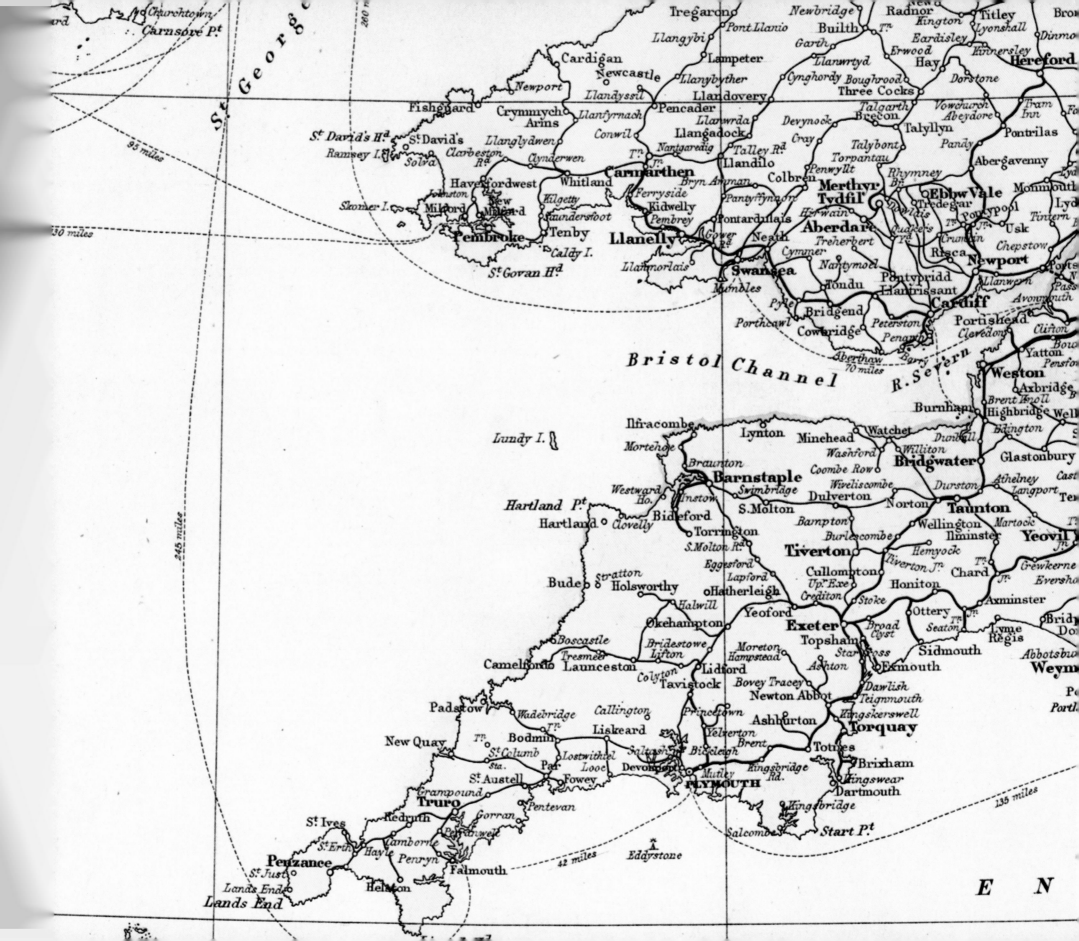

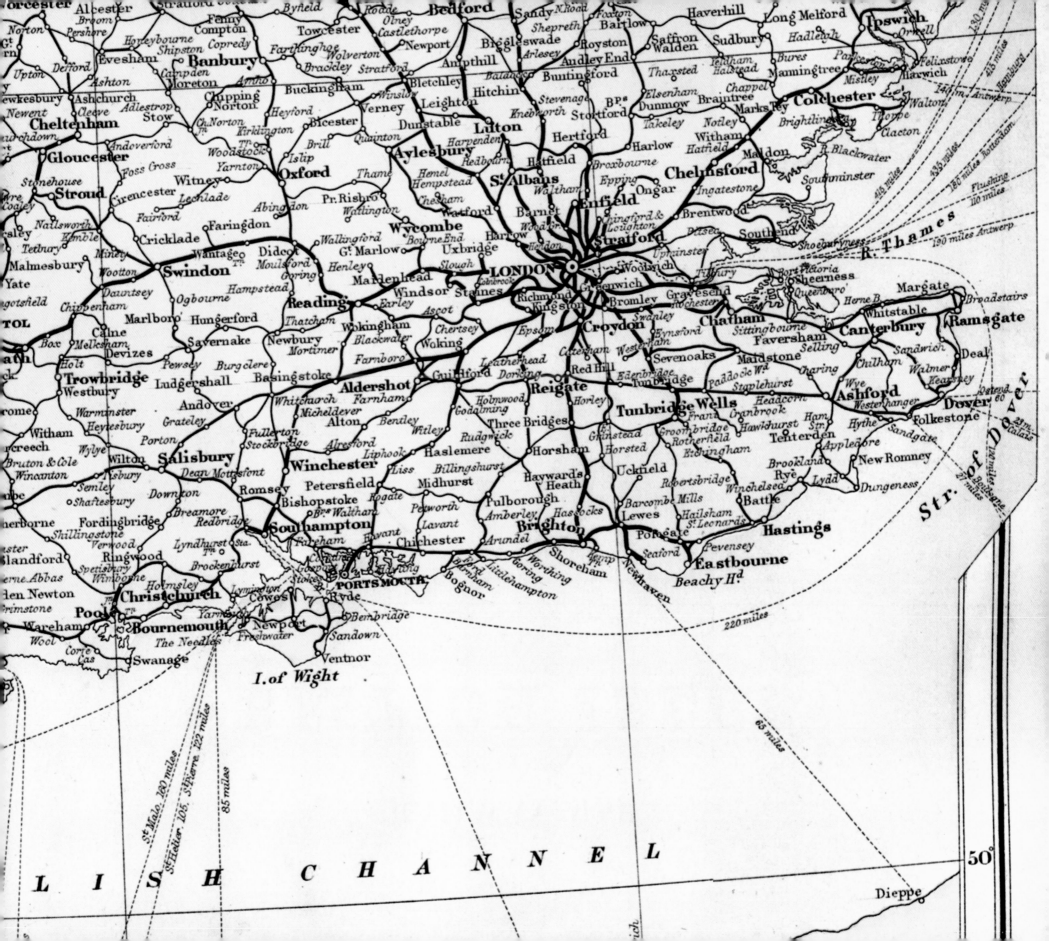

IRELAND

Ireland's integral relationship with Britain in the nineteenth century encouraged its early adoption of steam railways despite its largely agricultural economy and relatively impoverished population. Irish railways developed as regional networks, each accurately described by name, and largely remained in their respective territories. There were comparatively few instances of territorial incursion or construction of redundant infrastructure. Dublin and Kingstown Railway (D&KR) opened in 1834 between its namesake points and was the earliest line. More significant developments were the Great Southern and Western (GS&WR), Midland and Great Western Railway (M&GWR) systems. Dublin and South Eastern and Great Northern Railway networks were formed through consolidation of earlier lines. While the most significant railways centred on Dublin, there were several non-radial systems that did not serve Dublin, including the Waterford and Limerick Railway, the Cork, Bandon and South Coast, and lines centred on Belfast, as well as myriad narrow gauge lines in the country's western counties.

As Ireland's capital, largest population centre, and a primary port, Dublin was a natural focus for railway building. Over a 25-year period, from 1834, when D&KR opened its terminal at Westland Row on the south-eastern edge of the city centre, railways built independent Dublin terminals around the historic centre. It was only after the last of these stations was in place that efforts were made to make connections between railways serving Dublin. In 1864, the M&GWR extended a line to Dublin Port at North Wall, and this formed the pattern for links with other lines. GS&WR built a connection from Islandbridge (near its Kingsbridge terminus), which tunnelled beneath the Phoenix Park and reached the M&GWR extension near Glasnevin. Interchanges were built with the Great Northern route near its Amiens Street station. Ultimately the GS&WR extended its own line all the way to North Wall, parallel to M&GWR's, while in 1891 the loop line was built over the River Liffey, linking Westland Row and Amien Street terminals and providing a connection with the M&GWR route.

The establishment of the Irish Free State in 1922 and the partition of Ireland resulted in a violent civil war which saw great damage done to Irish railways. In 1924 the Irish government encouraged an amalgamation of lines in the south; the D&SE, the GS&WR and the M&GWR were grouped into the new Great Southern Railways. Cross-border lines between the new Republic of Ireland and Northern Ireland, including the Great Northern Railway and some narrow gauge lines, remained independent for the time being. The GSR network was effectively nationalised in the mid-1940s as part of a government-controlled semi-state company called Coras Iompair Éireann (Irish Transport Company), which also incorporated bus, lorry and canal services.

Lisburn station in about 1905 (above).

The original Boyne Viaduct at Drogheda, painted by Roger Curzon in 1878 (Drogheda Municipal Art Collection, Highlanes Gallery) (oppposite).

The Dublin and Drogheda Railway at Baldoyle Bridge, 1846 (left).

THE GREAT SOUTHERN AND WESTERN RAILWAY

The Main Line to Cork

The Great Southern and Western Railway (GS&WR) began construction near Dublin in 1845, and initiated services over 90 km of line between Carlow and its Dublin terminus at Kingsbridge in August 1846. Ultimately the GS&WR developed as the largest and most important railway in Ireland. Its trunk line was a double-track route via Portarlington, Thurles, and Mallow to Cork, where it reached a temporary terminal in 1849. From 1855, the GS&WR served Cork city more directly via a long tunnel to its Glanmire Road station. Affiliated lines connected Cork with Youghal with a branch to Cobh (Queenstown), an important deep-water port town. Secondary GS&WR routes connected Dublin with Waterford, Limerick, Killarney, Tralee and Athlone, with various branches reaching towns within its territory.

In 1901 the GS&WR acquired the Waterford, Limerick and Western (formerly the Waterford and Limerick), which connected the two towns of its name as well as reaching from Limerick via northern County Kerry to Tralee, and from Limerick northward toward Sligo. GS&WR's Dublin–Cork trunk line crossed the WL&W's line at Limerick Junction, a remote windswept station which existed mainly to allow passengers to change trains, and involved a unique track arrangement which required all trains to reverse into the station's platforms.

For many years the GS&WR's premier services were its Day Mails between Dublin and Cork. After 1876 these were extended to Cobh to facilitate connections with trans-Atlantic steam ships. Originally, Day Mails only carried first and second

Youghal station in the 1890s (below).

Kilcummer Viaduct on the GS&WR Fermoy Branch which opened in 1860, painted by Robert Stopford in 1862 (below right).

class passengers, but by the end of the nineteenth century third class passengers – previously confined to glacially-slow all-stops 'parliamentary' runs – were also accommodated. At that time, trains were working a 3-hour 55-minute express schedule. Other important runs included the *American Mail*, and from 1898 and 1914 the famed *Killarney Expresses* bringing wealthy tourists to the scenically-situated resort town, one of several resorts where the GS&WR operated premier hotels.

GS&WR's Cork–Rosslare Boat Express at Waterford, hauled by 4–4–0 No. 309 (painting by Jack Hill).

THE GREAT NORTHERN RAILWAY

From Dublin to Belfast and the North of Ireland

The aftermath of the Armagh collision of 12 June 1889, Ireland's worst railway disaster (right).

Express GNR locomotives, 1907: 4–4–0 No. 131 Uranus and 4–4–0 No. 174 Carrantuohill (below).

The Great Northern Railway (GNR) was created in 1875–76 from the unification of several older railways, principally the Ulster Railway company (established in 1836) and the Dublin and Drogheda Railway (established in 1844). The earliest Irish railways lacked common track gauge, and the Ulster Railway had been constructed to a very unusual broad gauge measuring 6 feet 2 inches (1.88 m) between the rails. This disparity of gauge in Ireland resulted in the Board of Trade mandating a standard in 1846. But, instead of adopting the 4 foot 8½ inch (1.44 m) standard used in Britain and by Ireland's pioneer Dublin and Kingstown Railway, it took an unusual approach by roughly averaging the gauges in use, deciding upon the broad 5 foot 3 inch (1.6 m) gauge as the Irish standard, which has remained in use to the present day. Existing lines were required to re-gauge to this standard.

GNR formed the second largest Irish network after GS&WR, and its most important route was between Dublin and Belfast – Ireland's largest and most prosperous cities. This had been completed in 1855, with the opening of the impressive 170 m long continuous-girder viaduct over the Boyne at Drogheda. GNR's network also reached Derry (Londonderry), Armagh, Clones, Cavan and Bundoran, along with numerous short branches.

Its line to Armagh gained notoriety because of the terrible collision between two trains that occurred on 12 June 1889, killing 78 passengers, 22 of them schoolchildren. Public outcry to the tragedy resulted in legislation affecting railways across the British Isles mandating implementation of fail-safe braking systems and improved signalling. Another of GNR's branches gained fame for its quaint operation – the short branch from Fintona Junction to Fintona survived with a horse-drawn tram until the mid-twentieth century, a century after most railways adopted mechanical propulsion.

The partition of Ireland in 1922 resulted in the GNR straddling the new demarcation between northern and southern counties, its lines crossing the border seventeen times. This complicated operations considerably, since customs inspection stops were established at key points. Even on the main Dublin–Belfast route all trains were forced to stop at Dundalk and Gorgahwood. After the Second World War, introduction of the through non-stop *Enterprise* services between Dublin and Belfast allowed for customs checks at terminal stations, thus speeding the service on the 181 km run. Similarly, the seasonal *Bundoran Express* (Dublin–Bundoran), carrying tourists to the popular seaside resort and pilgrims to the shrine at Lough Derg, avoided customs checks altogether by running non-stop through the northern counties, reversing direction at Dundalk.

GNR operations remained independent of consolidations in the southern counties longer than most other railways, but in the mid-1950s its operations were divided between northern and southern state-run railway operators.

The Fintona horse tram during its last days of operation in 1957 (above left).

No. 171 *Slieve Gullion* passing through Goraghwood with the down Dublin–Belfast Enterprise, 28 June 1952 (N. W. Sprinks) (above right).

The Great Northern station at Great Victoria Street, Belfast in 1890 (left).

THE MIDLAND AND GREAT WESTERN RAILWAY

Westward to Galway and Sligo

An MGWR poster from the early 1890s (below).

The Shannon Bridge at Athlone, still in use today (Niall McAuley) (below right).

MGWR Grendon 2–4–0 No. 2 at Broadstone Shed, Dublin, 1865 (painting by Norman Whitla) (opposite).

The original Broadstone Station in the 1850s (inset opposite).

The Midland and Great Western Railway was born from disagreement among board members at the GS&WR. Its charter, in 1845, authorised construction west from Dublin 80 km to Mullingar, and beyond to Longford, while requiring the railway to acquire and maintain the financially destitute Royal Canal. The railway established its Dublin terminal adjacent to the canal basin at Broadstone, located less than a kilometre from Dublin's General Post Office, and nearby Smithfield, famed for its livestock markets. Its Broadstone passenger station was executed in neo-Egyptian style, unusual for a railway terminal design, but the company never developed as did its counterparts in England or Europe. From its earliest days postal and livestock traffic were key to the M&GWR's prosperity. Early construction coincided with Ireland's Great Famine, which greatly affected the regions served by the railway; in many respects the M&GWR facilitated the depopulation of the very territory it served.

Train services commenced on 28 June 1847, with four round trips on the 42 km section between Broadstone and Enfield. Services were extended to Mullingar in October 1848, and west to Galway in July 1851. The M&GWR envisioned the development of Galway Bay as a premier trans-Atlantic port, while simultaneously vying for territory with its arch-rival, the GS&WR. Mullingar was developed as a junction between the routes toward Galway and Sligo, and served as a hub for livestock traffic. Building northwest, the M&GWR spanned the Shannon on a 244 m bridge near Drumsna, and reached Sligo in 1862. At Athlone it connected with the GS&WR's branch from Portarlington via Tullamore, and had a junction with

its own extensions to Counties Roscommon and Mayo; it reached Castlerea in 1860 and Ballina in 1862. The railway achieved its zenith in the 1890s with significant extensions from Galway to the Connemara port at Clifden, and from Westport to Achill Island, both lines proving popular with tourists.

Despite its relatively gentle grade profile, M&GWR's nineteenth century passenger trains travelled at leisurely speeds, its timekeeping a sore point with impatient travellers, but purchase of more powerful locomotives in 1902 improved matters. Among its most popular trains were the *Tourist Express* which ran to Galway and Clifden, with a section to Achill. Following the consolidation with GS&WR and other lines as Great Southern Railways, various M&GWR routes were scaled back; the Clifden and Achill branches were closed, and the Broadstone terminal was closed to passengers in 1936.

THE DUBLIN AND SOUTH EASTERN RAILWAY

Rails Round Bray Head

The Dublin and South Eastern name was adopted in 1907 to reflect the recent opening of the Dublin, Wicklow and Wexford's route via New Ross to Waterford. Although officially the name was short-lived (D&SE was among those lines consolidated in 1925 as Great Southern Railways), the route from Dublin south along the east coast toward Wexford continued to be known as the 'Southeastern'.

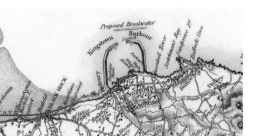

Significant among D&SE's historical components was the pioneering Dublin and Kingstown Railway (D&KR). Engineered by Wicklow-born William Dargan, a protégé of Britain's acclaimed engineer Thomas Telford, and built to British standard gauge on heavy stone sleepers, it linked the city-centre terminal at Westland Row (renamed Pearse Station in 1966) with the suburban port at Kingstown (Dún Laoghaire). The line was later re-gauged to the Irish standard of 5 foot 3 inches (1.6 m), and the original construction with rigid track replaced with a more forgiving structure. Yet portions of Dargan's original engineering have withstood the test of time; several of the line's original arch bridges remain in use to the present day. Dargan was later involved with many significant railway projects, and is often known as 'the father of Irish railways'.

On 17 December 1834, the locomotive *Hibernia* led the D&KR's first timetabled service, leaving Dublin to the cheers of the assembled crowd. Colourfully described as the world's first suburban railway, from its beginning it thrived on suburban passenger traffic and mail business, connecting with packet boats travelling between Holyhead and Kingstown. An 1840s-era extension of the line between Kingstown and Dalkey was initially operated as an atmospheric railway; the trains were propelled in the uphill direction by a vacuum cylinder, and by gravity on their downhill return. This novel form of propulsion was functional but unreliable, and after a few years the system was replaced with conventional steam power.

Dublin, Wicklow and Wexford built a line parallel to the D&KR's, taking an inland route from its Harcourt Street terminal near Dublin's St Stephen's Green, and running southward through Dublin's suburbs toward Bray. It continued beyond Bray via a coastal route to Wicklow, then inland via Rathdrum, Avoca and Enniscorthy, eventually reaching Wexford and Waterford. Among the most scenic sections was the precarious stretch around Bray Head, made famous by a horrific crash in 1867 when a train making its way north from Enniscorthy plunged through the bridge over Brandy Hole, killing two people and injuring more than twenty. Seaside erosion plagued the line, and several sections were eventually re-engineered, including Bray Head, where abandoned rock cuttings and tunnels survive to give passengers clues to the original alignment.

The route of the Dublin and Kingstown Railway, Ireland's first passenger railway, which opened in 1834 (above).

A contemporary engraving of the Brandy Hole accident, August 1867 (below right).

Dublin and Kingstown Railway at Blackrock, an 1840 engraving by Andrew Nicholl (National Library of Ireland) (opposite).

IRISH NARROW GAUGE WONDERS

At The Edge of Railway Engineering

The Tralee and Dingle Railway in its last year of operation (above).

Among Ireland's preserved railways is this vestige of the County Donegal Railways Joint Committee line at Lough Finn (upper right)

Moyasta Junction on today's preserved West Clare Railway (lower right).

The most interesting and by far the most scenic Irish railways were the various narrow gauge lines at the periphery of the network. Numerous slim gauge lines were built to serve towns beyond the reach of Ireland's broad gauge routes. Of these, the Tralee and Dingle achieved nearly mystical status, in part because of the sublimely beautiful territory it served, but also because of its infrequent and elusive operations in later years. This 50 km 3 foot (0.9 m) gauge route connected its namesake towns by crossing the spine of the Dingle Peninsula via a twisting steeply graded line over a 213 m pass. In addition, it served the village of Castlegregory via a short branch. Its locomotives were fitted with cow-catcher style pilots because the line was largely unfenced. Another peculiarity was the 13 km beyond Blennerville, where its tracks shared the road. In 1896, passenger trains required 2 hours and 40 minutes to make the journey, while cattle trains travelled at an even more leisurely pace.

Made famous in a popular song by Percy French, the 85 km West Clare Railway linked Ennis (on the Waterford and Limerick, later Great Southern and Western) with Kilkee and Kilrush; each was served by a separate branch which joined at rural Moyasta. The route developed in the 1880s, and though absorbed by Great Southern Railways in 1925, it survived until 1961, longer than most of the Irish narrow gauges.

County Donegal was served by two narrow gauge networks. The County Donegal Railways Joint Committee connected Derry (Londonderry) with Strabane, Letterkenny, Donegal town and Ballyshannon, with branches to Glenties and Killybegs, a network that in 1905 extended to 169 km. Northern Donegal was reached by the spectacularly remote Londonderry and Lough Swilly Railway.

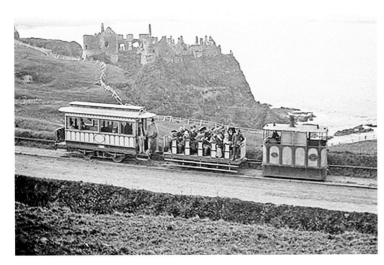

Among the most unusual Irish railways was the Listowel and Ballybunion, which was adapted from the French-designed Lartigue monorail system. This supported trains on a single elevated rail positioned 3 feet 6 inches (1 m) above the ground with non-load-bearing guide rails below. L&B's 14.8 km route opened to traffic in 1888 and closed as an effect of the Irish Civil War in the 1920s. In September 1896 the railway offered four daily round trips, which required a 40-minute journey.

County Antrim's Giant's Causeway Tramway allowed tourists to reach that natural wonder on one of the world's first public electric railways.

The Giant's Causeway Tramway at Dunluce Castle, 1906 (above left).

Changing points at Ballybunion on the Listowel and Ballybunion Railway, 1910 (above).

The opening of the Listowel and Ballybunion Railway in 1888 (left).

MAP

OF THE

RAILWAYS OF IRELAND,

1907.

Reproduced with necessary additions and alterations, by permission, from the Official
Railway Map of Ireland published at the Railway Clearing House, London, in 1906.

Scale:- Nine Statute Miles to One Inch

Miles 10 8 6 4 2 0   10   20   30   40 Miles

REFERENCE.

NOTE.—*Railways constructed under Tramways
and Light Railways (Ireland) Acts* } shown thus
Railways under construction
(*To be completed early in 1908.*)
Coach Routes
Joint Lines

GREENISLAND VIADUCTS
COUNTY ANTRIM, NORTHERN IRELAND
by NORMAN WILKINSON R.I.

LMS

The Greenisland Loop Line on the Northern Counties Committee opened in 1934 was constructed to obviate the necessity of trains to and from Belfast and Stations in the North running via Greenisland. The new line is approximately three miles in length and has a continuous gradient of 1 in 75. The Main Line Viaduct which is the largest reinforced concrete railway viaduct in the British Isles is 650 feet long and has a maximum height of 70 feet above the level of the stream. The Main Arches in the Main Line and Down Shore Line Viaducts have a span of 89 feet. Over 32,000 tons of concrete, reinforced with 700 tons of steel, were required for the construction of the two viaducts.

Valentia station in 1900 (National Archives of Ireland).

BENELUX

As a nation, Belgium was only five years old when it became the first country in continental Europe to operate a steam railway. There had been earlier railways, but they had begun commercial operations with horse-power rather than steam. Belgium's pioneering line connected Brussels and Malines, and inaugurated operations on 5 May 1835 with the spectacle of a triple-headed thirty-carriage train. The following year this line was extended to Antwerp, thus giving Belgium a direct interface between its railway and international sea trade. The port of Ostend was connected in 1843, and during the mid-nineteenth century Belgium engaged in a frenzy of railway building that extended lines to every major point in the small nation. By 1884, its network boasted 4,297 km. While its railways were centred on Brussels, urban-industrial conurbations such as Charleroi benefited from intensely developed networks which gave Belgium the densest railway system in Europe.

In the Netherlands, the necessity for improved transportation encouraged early railway development despite vested canal interests. There were two significant schemes underway by the late 1830s. Dutch railway promoters enamored by British railway technology made the unusual choice of adopting broad gauge, based on Brunel's Great Western Railway, despite the adoption of the Stephenson 4 feet 8$\frac{1}{2}$ inch (1.44 m) standard by neighbouring countries. The Holland Railway built in a south-westerly direction with the aim of connecting Amsterdam, The Hague and Rotterdam, and put the Netherlands on the European railway map when its British-built Patentee-type *De Arend* hauled its first train between Amsterdam and Haarlem in September 1839. The railway reached Rotterdam eight years later.

Meanwhile, jealous concerns of rapid railway development in Belgium, where proposed routes connecting the port of Antwerp with industrial areas of the Prussian Rhineland threatened to eclipse Dutch trade, propelled an ambitious Dutch engineering project known as Nederlandsche Rhijnspoorweg-Maatschappij (Netherlands Rhenish Railway) that built eastward from Amsterdam. Although progress was slow, it finally reached its Prussian connections in 1854, at which time the folly of the Dutch broad gauge experiment was boldly evident. Re-gauging was soon forthcoming, while the Holland Railway followed with re-gauging its lines a decade later.

During the mid-nineteenth century, numerous Dutch railway schemes connected cities across the Netherlands using a mix of public and private financing and operations. By the mid-1880s, the network reached more than 2,000 km. However, although by 1900 its route structure was largely complete, many lines were still limited to single track. By the early twentieth century railway construction and consolidation had produced two primary systems – Hollandsche IJzeren Spoorweg-Maatschappi (Dutch Railways) and Staatspoorwegen (Netherlands State Railway). The latter was in effect a private company providing services using state infrastructure. These lines were consolidated as a single state railway called Nederlandse Spoorwegen (NS) in 1938.

Among significant Dutch routes was the original route running 87 km from Amsterdam to Rotterdam via The Hague; an important 27 km passenger line from Hoek of Holland (Hook of Holland) to Rotterdam; and a 72 km line from Rotterdam east to Nijmegan. J.P. Pearson remarked on his travels on Dutch railways in 1904 that the State Railway's second class carriage in which he rode was 'quite of the German type, upholstered in yellow brown plush velvet, and fitted with lavatory accommodation, umbrella stand and hat peg.' What he found more unusual was the Netherlands Central Rotterdam–Utrecht express train led by a 'fine yellow 4–4–0 fitted with a brass dome.' The colour of the locomotive seemed peculiar to British eyes, yet today NS trains are predominantly painted yellow, which remains an unusual railway colour in Europe.

Belgian stations large and small – Mons in the late 1920s, and the nearby village of Flénu in 1898 (above).

A train crossing the Zijl Bridge on the Haarlemmermeer Railway between Haarlem and Amsterdam, Holland, 1910.

THE BELGIAN NORTH SEA CROSSINGS

The English and Merry Ostend

A typical cross-channel steamer of the 1900s, the *Nelson* plied between the southern English ports of Dover and Folkestone and the Belgian ports of Blankenberghe and Ostende (below).

The beach at Ostende, with the Kursaal (a large public hall) in the background (right).

Belgium's strategic location between northern France, the Netherlands and Germany, combined with the importance of its North Sea ports, meant that from an early date it had a considerable international traffic. While Belgian Railways initially imported British locomotives, they soon developed a domestic locomotive business that proved among the most innovative on the continent. Among Belgian contributions to locomotive design were the Walschaerts valve-gear and the Belpaire firebox, both of which were rapidly and widely adopted by railways around the world.

Bradshaw's Guide of 1884 offered travellers this portrait of the nation: 'The General Aspect of Belgium is level, indeed it contains no ridge that would be properly called a mountain', noting that southern Belgium was picturesque and romantic, while northern areas were typically flat plain. Unfortunately, *Bradshaw's* neglected to mention that the area around Liège in eastern Belgium was afflicted with exceptionally steep grades. Originally these were worked as inclined plains with stationary engines using cables to haul trains. By 1871, Belgian railways had developed some extraordinarily large locomotives to work this route as 'bankers' assisting trains up grades.

During the nineteenth century, railways led to the growth of considerable North Sea traffic between Great Britain and the continent. Among the most popular routes across the Channel between England and France were: Dover–Calais, Folkstone–Boulogne, New Have–Dieppe, Southampton–Harve, Southampton–Cherbourg. Ships also ferried passengers between England and Dutch ports with daily schedules between Harwich and the Hook of Holland, and Gravesend to Rotterdam. For passengers heading toward Germany and Central Europe, one of the most popular crossings was between Dover and Ostend, while there were also services from Harwich to Antwerp. Unlike other North Sea ports, noted for their dreary docks and bleak environs, in Victorian times the Belgian port of Ostend was in itself a popular seaside destination. *The Railway Magazine* profiled Ostend in 1898, gleefully announcing, 'there are few merrier places than Ostend during the season, which begins in July and closes in September.' Ironically, for many international travellers their only experience with Belgian railways would have been on an overnight sleeper from Ostend to the German frontier at Aachen.

BLANKENBERGHE. Le Bateau d'excursion Nelson.

Le Nelson entrant le port   Ostende

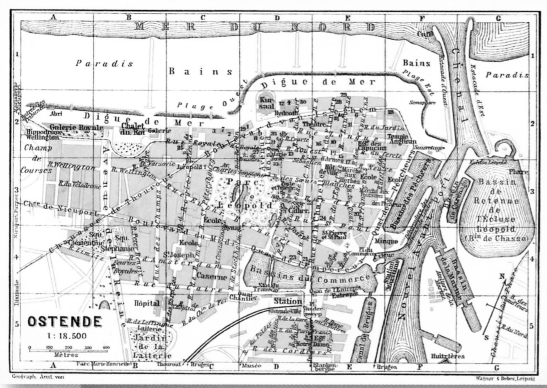

A plan of Ostend from the 1910 edition of Baedeker's *Belgium and Holland* (above left).

Two photographs of a busy Ostend station in the early 1940s (above and left).

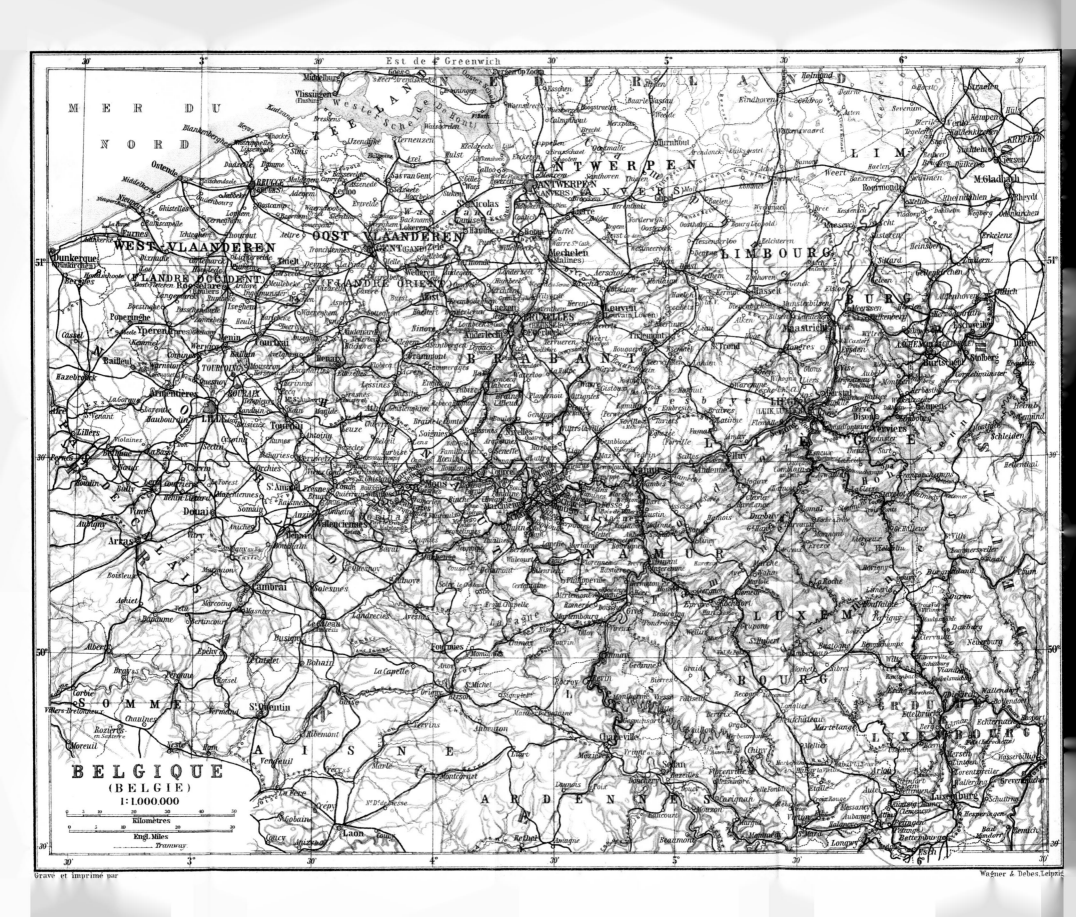

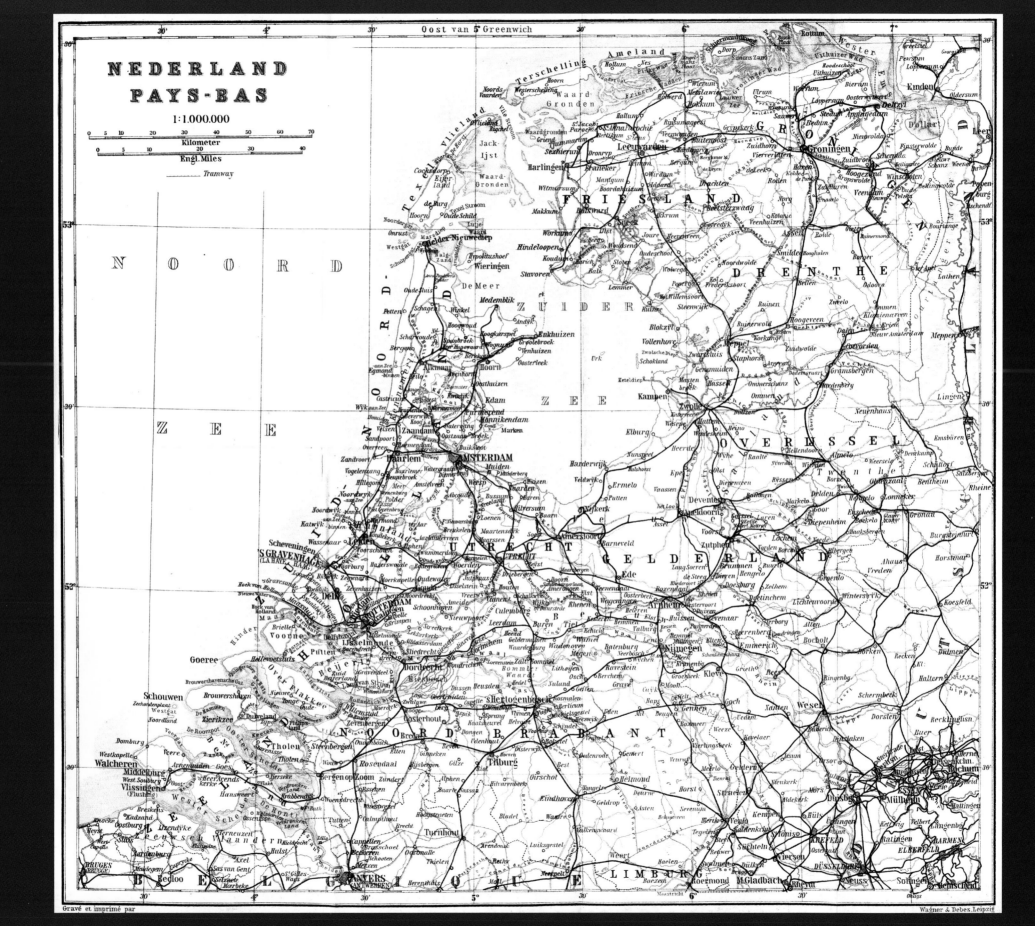

NEDERLAND
PAYS-BAS

1:1.000.000

Kilometer

Engl. Miles

Tramway

Gravé et imprimé par

Wagner & Debes, Leipzig

FRANCE

French railways are unquestionably some of the finest and most famous in the world, and rightfully the source of great national pride. In the late nineteenth century, Paris had developed as the premier hub for luxury passenger trains, services epitomised by the *Orient Express*. In the early twentieth century, French express trains vied with those in Britain, Germany and America as the fastest scheduled services in the world. After the Second World War, France led the way in railway development; its steam locomotives were among the finest ever conceived, while its push toward ever faster trains led to the development of a whole new high-speed railway system and the debut of the famed *train à grande vitesse* (TGV) in 1981. Continued improvements have allowed for sustained top speeds of 320 km/h, and in tests more than 560 km/h.

Yet compared with Britain, Belgium and Germany, in the early years France was relatively slow to adopt railways. While it considered steam railways as early as 1826, and a limited service railway opened between Lyon and St Etienne in 1832, France's first full-service railway (Paris–St Germain) did not begin service until August 1837, and a national railway movement did not gain momentum until the 1840s. Fears that the new mode of transport would destroy the French way of life fueled opposition by agricultural and canal interests which delayed railway schemes by decades. Under the rule of Napoleon III, French railway development finally took shape, and state planning focused major routes to suit national strategic interests.

Six regional companies were established, each named to describe their respective service territories. Five radiated from the Paris hub like spokes of a wheel – Réseau du Nord (Northern), Réseau de l'Est (Eastern), Réseau de Paris–Lyon–Méditerranée, Réseau de Paris á Orléans, and Réseau de l'Ouest (Western). The sixth network, Réseau de Midi, as its name implies, served the south. In the late 1870s a state-run railway, called Chemin de Fer de l'Etat, was also developed to serve Brittany and the north Channel ports.

By 1909 the French network had reached over 48,000 km and was deemed the fourth largest in the world, after the USA, Russia and Germany. After the First World War France reclaimed its lands in Alsace–Lorraine, lost to Germany after the Franco-Prussian War in 1871; the railways here which had been part of the Eastern network were then operated as the Alsace–Lorraine railways.

French railways suffered from growing highway competition during the 1930s, resulting in consolidation schemes that culminated in 1938 with the creation of the nationalised Société Nationale des Chemins de Fer Français (SNCF). SNCF preserved railways as a competitive mode, and was assigned the Herculean task of rebuilding French railways after the Second World War. However, nationalisation resulted in a dramatic trimming of the network. Routes totalling an estimated 11,000 km were abandoned, and many redundant facilities consolidated.

The locomotive *La Fontainebleau*, built for the Paris–Lyon Railway by Alexis Barrault in 1847 (opposite)

Exactitude, a stylish Etat poster by Pierre Fix-Masseau, 1932 (below)

PARIS—LYON—MEDITERRANÉE

The Route of the Côte d'Azur Rapide

The Paris—Lyon—Méditerranée route was the product of an 1850s union of earlier railway schemes, and effectively linked Paris with southeast France and the Côte d'Azur (the Mediterranean Riviera) via Dijon, Lyon and Marseilles. Operated as the Chemin de Fer de Paris à Lyon et à la Méditerranée, and known by its initials PLM, it developed as one of the most important national routes and a premier international line connecting France with western Switzerland, Italy and beyond. Famed for its express passenger trains from the late nineteenth century, in the twentieth century this was one of Europe's most important and busiest international routes.

By 1907 PLM operated more than 9,800 km of line, including lines in Algeria. It remained among the most important routes under SNCF, and in the 1950s author S. Kip Farrington estimated in his book *World Railways* that it was accommodating 120 trains daily. PLM's primary trunk line was the 1,100 km route from Paris to Mentone, near the Italian frontier. Both operationally and scenically this consisted of two distinct segments. The first was the south-easterly sprint from Paris via Lyon to Marseilles. This crested just one summit, located south of Laroche, 23 km north of Dijon, where the route crossed from the Seine to the Rhône watershed at an elevation of 405 m. Despite this height, the line featured very gentle main line grades. Avid railway traveller J.P. Pearson wrote of his journey toward Lyon, 'I found, looking out in the early morning light north of Dijon,

The famous French-manufactured 'Coupe-Vent' or 'C' locomotive (shown here around 1910), which pulled prestigious trains such as the PLM's *Côte d'Azur Rapide* at speeds of over 110m km/h.

that the views on the left were fine. Ascending along here and there were splendid viaducts in white stone and one very long deep cutting.' He further noted that 'beyond Sens, the canal aqueduct of the Vanne crosses above the railway.' Between the historic town of Arles and Lyon, the railway line followed the Rhône valley.

By contrast, the second segment, running from Marseilles south toward Italy, featured difficult engineering with numerous tunnels and trackwork perched precariously above the Mediterranean. While the run from Paris to Marseilles was famous for its speed, often listing among the fastest end-to-end express runs in Europe, the more sinuous nature of the line beyond Marseilles resulted in trains working at a more leisurely pace. Author Vivian Rowe described the line in his book *French Railways Today* as one of the most picturesque routes in Europe. Having nearly reached the Mediterranean at Marseilles, the line turns sharply inland and tunnels into the Sainte-Baume massif, emerging 2 km later high above the deep azure waters of the sea. The view is fleeting, as the line winds inland. From Fréjus to the Italian border it runs above the seashore on a rocky shelf providing the stunning Mediterranean views for which the Riviera is famous.

Among PLM's famous early twentieth century name trains was the de-luxe *Côte d'Azur Rapide* introduced in 1904. Aimed at wealthy travellers, this carried three luxurious carriages, a restaurant car, a Wagons-Lits saloon, and a special carriage designed for the needs of invalids. Significantly for the period, the train boasted electric lights and hot and cold running water.

Posters advertising the Paris–Riviera route: Côte d'Azur Pullman express,1929 (opposite); Services de la Mediterranée, 1893 (above left); Les Trains du Soleil, 1931 (above middle); La Côte d'Azur, à Une Nuit de Paris, 1926 (above right); Le Soleil Toute l'Année, 1928 (above, far right).

The Mistral Paris–Marseille express, hauled by a 221P steam locomotive, 1956 (below right).

Advertisement, with prices, for the trip to the Riviera from Paris, April 1914 (left).

Vincent Van Gogh, *Avenue of Plane Trees near Arles Station (The Blue Train)*, 1888 (below).

PARIS–ORLÉANS

Home of the Chapelon Pacifics

In the 1830s French railway visionaries anticipated a pan-European railway network radiating from Paris. The Réseau de Paris à Orléans network, or P-O (not to be confused with the shipping company Peninsula & Orient) was the first of the six primary French long-distance routes to connect its principal cities. Extending from Paris, and reaching Orléans in 1843 and Tours from 1846, it was finally completed to Bordeaux, 583 km from Paris, in 1853.

As a pioneer railway it faced considerable resistance in rural areas that feared change, along with well-established canal interests that despised competition. In particular, P-O experienced objections to direct routes serving historic city centres; as a result its early stations serving Tours and Orléans were built some distance from the centres of those cities. Branches were later constructed to serve the centres of both, but as a result these important centres of population were not directly on P-O's main line. *Bradshaw's Guide* advised travellers that 'The express trains do not always run into these towns.' Passengers for Orléans changed at Les Aubris junction; those for Tours changed at Saint-Pierre-des-Corps junction.

Paris-Orléans's designer André Chapelon.

P-O's expresses included *Le Drapeau* (*The Flag*), and the de-luxe *Côte d'Argent Express*, while the P-O route notably also hosted the first leg of Europe's famous Paris–Madrid–Lisbon *Sud Express*. In 1912 *Bradshaw's* listed running times for the *Côte d'Argent Express* included a 9 p.m. departure from Paris Quai d'Orsay, arriving at the Spanish frontier at 8.25 a.m. the following morning via the Midi system. Here passengers changed for the train's broad gauge equivalent for the Iberian portion of the journey.

P-O's locomotive chief André Chapelon refined compound locomotive design to a high art. Among his most famous machines were four-cylinder compound Pacifics for express passenger service, featuring external high-pressure cylinders feeding internal low-pressure cylinders. Chapelon's designs are regarded among the finest steam locomotives ever

P-O's *North Star*, typical of the early English engines whose advanced technology dominated French railways from 1830 until around 1845 (above).

Pacific 4546 of the P-O, saved by the SNCF and displayed at the Cité du train at Mulhouse (French National Railway Museum) (left).

Classic posters: an Etat poster for *Plages et Bains de Mer de l'Océan*, by René Pean, 1908 (above); a d'Orléans poster for *Chateau d'Amboise*, 1922 (right)

conceived, and he continued to build engines well into the SNCF era, including impressive three-cylinder compound 4–8–4s as well as highly-refined simple engine types. Although the travelling public may have been largely oblivious to the technical perfection of Chapelon's engines, they were undoubtedly pleased by their smooth running qualities at high speeds.

The P-O electrified some of its main routes in the 1930s, with wires reaching Saint-Pierre-des-Corps by 1935 and all of its main routes by 1939. Power was initially supplied by hydro-electric generation.

CHEMIN DE FER DU MIDI

And the Paris–Toulouse Route

2 - Les Locomotives (C⁰ du Midi)

Machine pour trains de voyageurs, à grande vitesse

Midi high-speed 2–4–0 type passenger locomotive No. 163, 1895 (above).

Period posters: L'Auvergne, Viaduc de Garabit, 1930 (right); Bordeaux, 1887 (opposite, left); Luchon, la Reine des Pyrénées, 1895 (opposite, top right); Biarritz, 1935 (opposite, bottom middle); Saint Jean de Luz, 1920 (opposite, bottom right).

France's southern regional railway, Chemin de Fer du Midi — commonly known as simply the 'Midi' — was entirely focused on the region it served. It was the only major network that did not serve Paris, and relied on its connections to run through expresses to and from the capital. Centred on Bordeaux, where Midi connected with the P-O system, its routes reached southward to the Pyrénées, the Mediterranean, and the Spanish frontier.

The Midi's principal line from Bordeaux to Irún hosted the famed *Sud Express*. This exclusive all-Pullman train, often described as Europe's most luxurious train, operated seasonally, in winter and spring, for the benefit of Europe's social classes wanting to migrate south in the cooler months. Wealthy travellers would frequent inland towns such as Pau and Cauterets, together with a string of favoured destinations along the southern Mediterranean and the Iberian peninsula.

In addition to seasonal holiday traffic, the Midi ran expresses on its southerly routes running via Toulouse and Narbonne toward the Spanish border at Port Bou. Departing from Paris, these sprinted along P-O's 716 km run to Toulouse, swinging from P-O's Bordeaux line near Orléans at Les Aubris, and benefiting from long stretches of straight track as far as Argenton. By comparison, Midi's route beyond Toulouse was characterised by a sinuous steeply-graded profile requiring much slower operations, but providing passengers with memorable views. Vivian Rowe, author of *French Railways of To-Day,* noted that beyond Toulouse lay the mountains of the Massif Central, while near Carcassonne were vast Languedoc

vineyards famed as the largest wine-producing region in France. After reaching Narbonne the route curved southward towards Perpignan, running toward the Mediterranean; between Argelès and Port Bou the line skirted the sea. Rowe also commented that the Paris–Port Bou run was among France's longest.

In its late steam era, the Midi's premier expresses were hauled by refined Pacific-type locomotives. To maximise efficiency and power, these were both superheated and of a compound design, noted as remarkable locomotives with a well-balanced design.

The Midi embraced main line electrification early, and among the lines wired by 1929 were its premier route from Bordeaux to the Spanish border at Hendaye and Irun, the line running along the foot of the Pyrénées from a junction at Dax to Toulouse via Pau. The Midi's overhead catenary was distinctive for its curved masts, resembling a tunnel of classic gothic arches. Electricity was generated locally from hydro-electric plants in the Pyrénées. Among the lines not initially wired was the important direct passenger route between Bordeaux and Narbonne.

Midi and P-O's amalgamation in 1934 was a natural union, and a prelude to SNCF's national consolidation four years later.

CHEMINS de FER du MIDI

L'AUVERGNE
VIADUC de GARABIT sur la TRUYÈRE
CIRCUITS d'AUTO-CARS
entre _ S⁺ FLOUR _ MILLAU _ CARCASSONNE

CHEMIN DE FER D'ORLÉANS

BORDEAUX

Train Rapide de Bordeaux

Intérieur d'un Wagon.

DURÉE DU TRAJET
PAR TRAINS RAPIDES, EXPRESS & DE LUXE

Au Départ de Paris (Gare d'Orléans)	8 heures environ
d°.— d'Orléans	7 d°.—
d°.— de Tours	5 d°.—
d°.— de Montluçon	8 d°.—
d°.— de Lyon	15 d°.—
d°.— de Genève	20 d°.—

LITS-TOILETTE, WAGONS-LITS & RESTAURANT

Consulter le Livret-Guide de la Compagnie dont l'envoi
gratuit est fait sur demande adressée à l'Administration
Centrale I, Place Valhubert à PARIS.

J. Hugo d'Alési

AFFICHES SOLEIL-AQUARELLE
Ateliers E.HUGO D'ALÉSI
3, Place Pigalle PARIS

REPRODUCTION INTERDITE

IMPRIMÉ chez F.HERMET

CHEMINS DE FER D'ORLÉANS ET DU MIDI
Trains rapides et de Luxe - 15 heures de PARIS.

Luchon
la Reine des Pyrénées

CASINO

ÉTABLISSEMENT THERMAL

SAISON du 1er JUIN au 1er OCTOBRE

IMP. CANIS-PARIS

CHEMINS DE FER PARIS-ORLÉANS-MIDI

BIARRITZ

CHEMINS DE FER DU MIDI

Côte Basque
SAINT JEAN DE LUZ ET CIBOURE
Saison
toute l'Année
MER ET MONTAGNE ≡ GOLF

CHEMIN DE FER DU NORD

The Gateway to the North

Chemin de Fer du Nord was one of six regional French networks, and, as its name infers, served the north of France. Its principal routes connected Paris with the north Channel port at Calais and with Belgium. As the preferred gateway to Paris, Nord's Calais route was familiar to British travellers as it gave many visitors their first impressions of both the country and French railways. In the late-Victorian era, a typical journey involved boarding an evening train in London, arriving at Dover before midnight and travelling by ship across the Channel. Typically Dover to Calais took about 75 minutes, depending on conditions, with an early morning arrival at Calais. Travellers making their first journey, wide-eyed with excitement upon seeing France for the first time, overcame the unsocial hour, while experienced travellers endured this necessary part of the journey as they made their way from the ferry to the train with their belongings in tow. With sunrise still hours away, the Calais terminal would bustle with activity; as outgoing passengers boarded waiting trains, inbound expresses from across the continent arrived one after another just a few minutes apart.

J.P. Pearson recorded many such journeys on his travels from England to continental destinations. He documented his first crossing in 1888. Upon arriving at Calais, he noted with dismay the 'somewhat dilapidated' carriages waiting to bring him onward. These were 'not altogether free from insanitary smells.' Assessing the terminal he wrote, 'the main tracks of the Nord were thick with weeds, most of the window panes in the engine sheds near Calais were broken.' Based on later travels, he deemed his early impressions unfortunate, and he came to be much enamoured with French railways, finding great pleasure in his subsequent travels on the Nord.

In August 1889 he travelled via Calais to Paris for the Exposition Universelle, or World's Fair, noting that he departed Calais at 3.20 a.m. upon a long consist of '24 mediæval-looking coaches'. His train paused for seven minutes at Amiens for a change of engines, and he arrived at Paris Gare du Nord at 9.08 a.m. In those years, a run of six hours was typical for limited express trains running between the port and Paris. On an 1897 journey via Calais to Brussels, Pearson described crossing the

CALAIS - L'Arrivée du rapide Calais-Bâle en gare maritime

Environs de Dieppe. — PETIT APPEVILLE. — La Gare

CFN posters: The New Golden Arrow Pullman, 1929 (opposite top); Vers l'Angleterre via Calais–Douvre, c.1930 (opposite bottom); Boulogne sur Mer, 1889 (above); Étoile du Nord Pullman, 1927 (right).

At Calais, travellers from England transfer from train to boat, 1910 (far left).

Appeville, near Dieppe, 1906 (left).

low country of northern France with mists clinging to the fields while the moon and stars glimmered brightly above. His train, typical of the Nord, kept good time, and offered 'some fast running on the French side of the border'. This route took him via Lille and across the Belgian frontier near Tournai. On another journey, returning from the Gare du Nord, Pearson wrote of witnessing a 'glorious sunset' that 'lit up the western sky' and remarking of the surreal afterglow that 'filled the air for long after the sun had gone down and against which trees, house and all other objects stood out silhouetted in the most wonderful manner. The almost common-place scenery of the Nord route was quite transfigured.'

FRENCH EXPRESSES

Luxury Unlimited

CH. de Fer du NORD ★ CH. de Fer NEERLANDAIS
CH. de Fer BELGES ★ Cie des WAGONS-LITS

ÉTOILE du NORD
(NORTH STAR)
PULLMAN I & II Classe
PARIS - BRUXELLES - AMSTERDAM

Paris served as a prime continental hub for many famous named trains de-luxe — the finest of the crop reserved for influential and wealthy international travellers. Calais was a popular place to board continental expresses. In the 1880s the Compagnie Internationale des Wagons-Lits established its reputation with a network of luxurious international express trains exemplified by the *Orient Express*.

Yet this was only one of many French-based de-luxe trains. In 1889 Wagons-Lits procured a pair of specially built 'Club Trains' for its luxury London–Paris service. One train was built to British standards for service from London; this consisted of three classy saloon carriages, a smoking lounge, and a luggage van (necessary to accommodate the heavy trunks preferred by wealthy holiday makers). The French section was similar, but built to the larger continental standard loading gauge. This also carried a dining car and kitchen car.

A Club Train novelty was the battery-operated electric lights which sparkled with modernity. In 1892 Wagons-Lits introduced a weekly *Peninsula & Orient Express* between Calais and the Italian Adriatic port at Brindisi. Designed to cater to British travellers, this train was also famous for conveying the Royal Mail destined for India. Passengers and mail would transfer to steamers at Brindisi for Oriental destinations from India to Singapore and Hong Kong.

The best-remembered of the cross-channel services was the *Golden Arrow*, a de-luxe train introduced in 1925. Including the channel crossing, *Golden Arrow* put London within six hours of the French capital. Like the earlier Club Trains, this required a pair of similarly-decorated trains working on either side of the channel. Passengers embarking on a continental journey at London's Victoria Station would settle into the plush brown and cream *Golden Arrow* pullmans by 11 a.m. for the 124 km trip via the Southern Railway to Dover. The steamer *Canterbury* forwarded *Golden Arrow* passengers across the channel in style. Upon arrival at Calais, passengers and luggage were expedited onto Wagons-Lits' specially-appointed brown and cream pullmans for the express to Paris Gare du Nord. Attached to the back of *Golden Arrow* trains were Wagons-Lits' elegant adorned blue sleeping cars, working through services to Rome. Upon arrival at Gare du Nord, the sleepers were uncoupled and whisked across Paris to the Gare de Lyon, where they were attached to PLM's waiting *Paris–Rome Express* operating via the Mont Cenis tunnel.

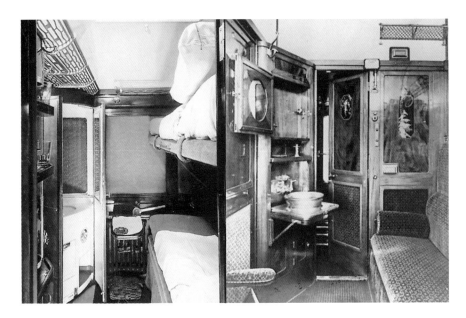

Luxury interior of a 1929 sleeping compartment on *Le Train Bleu* (above).

Nord posters: *Étoile du Nord*, 1927 (opposite); *L'Oiseau Bleu*, Train Pullman, 1929 (right).

Life on board a 1930s luxury train on the Côte d'Azur route, early 1940s (below).

Nord's famous expresses included the *Etoile du Nord (North Star)*, the premier daily train on the 539 km Paris–Brussels–Amsterdam run, and the daily Paris–Antwerp *Oiseau Blue (Blue Bird)*. The *Oiseau Blue* was one of the fastest expresses in Europe, in the 1930s boasting end-to-end speeds of more than 103 km/h, with much higher top running speeds necessary to maintain such a high average. Like Nord's other fast trains, these were routinely hauled by Super Pacifics, large and powerful super-heated compound four-cylinder 4–6–2 locomotives.

South of Paris, PLM's *Côte d'Azur Pullman* worked the 1,109 km Paris–Nice–Mentone route on special extra-fast schedules. Nord and PLM cooperated in the *Calais–Mediterranée Express* — popularly known as *Le Train Bleu* — which connected the north Channel port with choice destinations on the French Riviera, thus avoiding the complexities of transferring between Paris terminals with heavy luggage.

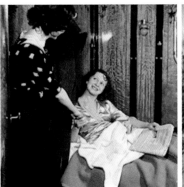

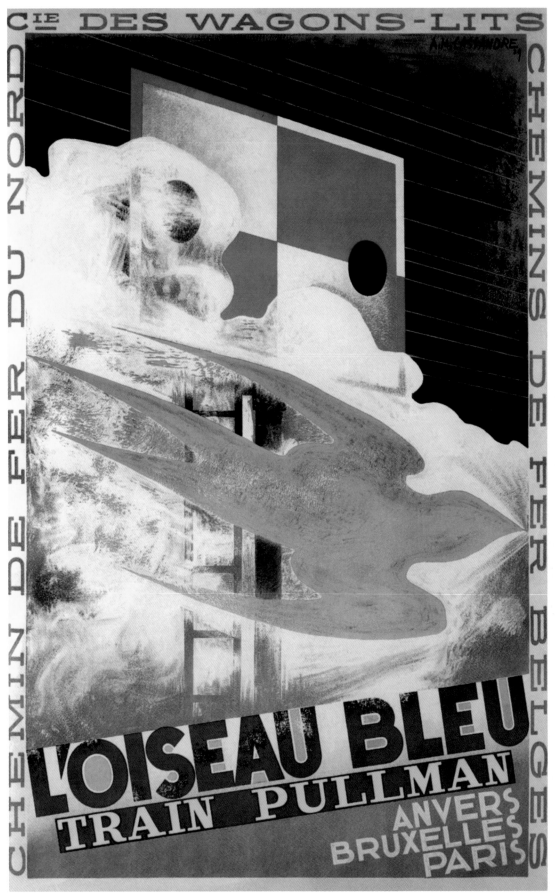

Cᴵᴱ DES WAGONS-LITS

CHEMIN DE FER DU NORD

CHEMINS DE FER BELGES

L'OISEAU BLEU
TRAIN PULLMAN
ANVERS
BRUXELLES
PARIS

PARIS'S MAIN STATIONS

A Ring of Memorable Termini

One of the murals by Albert Maignan decorating the interior of 'Le Train Bleu' restaurant at the Gare de Lyon, the Paris terminus of the Paris–Lyon–Mediterranée (above).

The distinctive façade of the Gare du Nord, opened in 1846 (right).

The Gare de l'Est, designed by architect François Duquesnay and opened in 1849; it was doubled in size in 1931 (below).

Paris, like London, Vienna, and several other large European capitals, was ringed by impressive railway terminals with railway lines radiating out like the spokes of a wheel.

The Gare du Nord, opened in 1846, served its namesake Nord Company, with trains for Calais, Lille, and beyond to Brussels, Amsterdam and Germany. A short distance to the east of the Gare du Nord was the Gare de l'Est, built in 1852 and described by authors Jeffrey Richards and John Mackenzie in their opus *The Railway Station: A Social History* as one of the world's finest. Further south was PLM's Gare de Lyon with its impressive façade. P-O's traditional terminal was the Gare d'Austerlitz, a station sharing with London's Waterloo Station the name of a Napoleonic battle. The lines of the État (state railways), running westward towards Brest, were served by the Gare de Montparnasse, while other État routes, notably the former lines of the old Ouest system, terminated at the Gare St Lazare. Owing in part to its location near residences of famous French impressionist painters, and because of the angle of sun that reaches the platforms, Gare St Lazare became famous for its portrayal by French artists, awed by the light filtered through the station roof, wafts of steam, and smoke from the locomotives. Although the Gare St Lazare was later expanded, and the steam locomotives and their chronic effluence are long gone, it is still possible to experience a similar effect if

one visits in winter when the sun burns off the frost, creating swirling shafts of light against ribbons of polished steel.

In 1900 the Quai d'Orsay station opened in conjunction with the Paris Exposition. Quai d'Orsay redefined the arrangement of the railway station. Prior to Orsay, most big-city terminals were characterised by a headhouse–shed arrangement, as typified by the existing Parisian terminals. The glorious Quai d'Orsay terminal was served by third-rail electric lines running below ground; thus the need for shed was obviated and the trains came directly into the station — a spectacle in its own right. This inspired emulation elsewhere, notably in New York, where the colossal Pennsylvania Station expanded on Orsay on a grand scale.

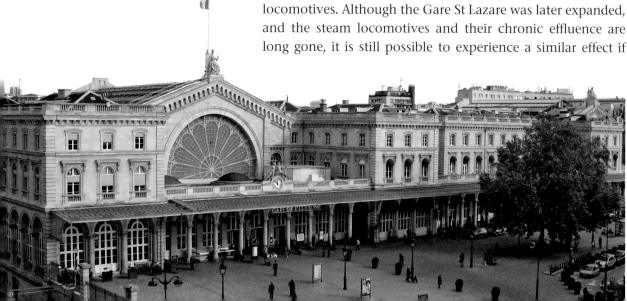

A train wreck at the Gare Montparnasse, 1895 (above).

Claude Monet, *Gare Saint-Lazare*, 1877 (above left).

The interior of the Quai d'Orsay, 1905 (bottom left).

The Gare d'Austerlitz in 1910 (bottom middle).

The Gare de Lyon, with its magnificent clocktower, 1912 (below).

BRUGES · Ruremonde · Gladbach · Neuss · DUSSELDORF · Bloemendaol · Aeltre · Lokeren · ANVERS · Herensthals · Siegen · Thielt · GAND · Termonde · Malines · Diest · Deutz · COLOGNE · Deynze · Alost · Vilvorde · Aerschot · HASSELT · MAESTRICHT · Kerkrade · Siegburg · Ypres · Audenarde · Louvain · St Trond · Tongres · Haaren · Betzdorf · Courtrai · Turlemont · AIX LA CHAPELLE · Born · Tourcoing · Mouscron · BRUXELLES · Langen · St Trond · Ans · Dolhain · Herbesthal · Enskirchen · We · Roubaix · Braine-le-Comte · Varemme · Herbesthal · DUCHÉ · LILLE · Tournay · Brugelette · Nivelles · LIEGE · Verviers · Call · DE · Don · Seclin · Ath · Pignies · Q · Vesservaux · Repinster · Schleyden · NASSA · Carvin · Manage · Huy · Spa · Limbourg · COBLENTZ · MONS · Gosselies · U · NAMUR · E · Lahnstein · Douai · Valenciennes · Marchiennes · Tamines · Marche · Boppard · Vitry · Bouchain · Maubeuge · Charleroy · Doreffe · VIESBADEN · Raeux · NORD · Hautemont · Erquelines · Florenne · Dinant · Bieberic · Cambrai · Caudry · Landrecies · Chimay · Philippeville · Rochefort · Audernach · Bapaume · le Cateau · Avesnes · Givet · St Hubert · Rudesheim · Bohain · Bussigny · Momignies · Couvin · Vireux · Bingen · Péronne · Fresnay le Gd · Hirson · Fumay · Dielkirch · Kreuznach · St Quentin · Essigny le P · Vervins · Revin · Deville · Neufchâteau · TRÈVES · Ham · Rocroi · Montherme · Oberstein · Montescourt · Braux · Charleville · Al · Flavy · la Fère · MEZIÈRES · Nouzon · Mézieres · Mohon · Nouzon · Donchery · LUXEMBOURG · Birkenfeld · Tergnier · Crépy · AISNE · Launoy · Poix · Sedan · Pouru · Appilly · Coucy les Sepes · Puiseux · Boutzicourt · Carignan · ARLON · BAVIÈRE · Noyon · Chauny · Rethel · Doury · Sarrebourg · Ourscamps · St Gobain · Amagne · Chauvency · Margut · Lamouilly · Rottembourg · Kaiserslautern · Ludw · Compiègne · LAON · Anizy · St Erme · ARDENNES · le Châtelet · Montmédy · Longwy · Esch · Rumelange · Thouroite · Crouy · Guignicourt · Vouziers · Verin · Pierrepont · Hettange · Sierck · Sarrelouis · Homburg · Neustao · Marginal · Cirey · Baxancourt · Joppecour · Havange · Thionville · RHENANE · Soissons · Loivre · Witry · Audun · Fontoy · Uckange · Sarrebruck · Deux Ponts · Berzy · Witry · Moyeuvre · Hagandange · Forbach · Cocher · Landau · Perches · Cotterets · Seine · Reims · Sillery · Briey · Maizières · MOSELLE · Sarrebrucken · Berzgabern · Château Thierry · Port à Binson · Rilly · Mourmelon · Hombourg · Forbach · Meau · Varennes · Avenay · la Veuve · Valmy · Verdun · Devant les Ponts · METZ · St Avold · Farschviller · Sarreguemines · Wissembourg · Dormans · Ai · Somme B. · Ars · Noveant · Courcelles · Faulquemont · Epernay · Viry · Jaalons · Ste Menehould · MEUSE · Pagny · Remilly · Herny · Niederbronn · Coulommiers · CHÂLONS sur Marne · Revigny · Mussey · Commercy · Dieulouard · Pont à Mousson · MEURTHE · Sarrebourg · Lutzelburg · Saverne · Haguenau · MARNE · Vitry la Ville · Pargny · Langeville · Lerouville · Sorcy · Pagny · Château Salins · Dieuze · Rechicourt · Heming · SEINE · Vitry le François · BAR le Duc · Void · NANCY · Marbache · Frouard

St.LO

Coutances

CALVADOS

Granville
Vire
Vieussoix
Falaise
Coulibœuf
Fresnay la Mère

St Pierre sur Dives
Vandœuvres

Mexidon
Mault
Menil Mauger

 St Mards Orbec
Beaumont le Roger
Vernon

EVREUX
Bonnières
Rosny
Mantes

Romilly
Conches
la Bonneville
Boisset
Bueil
Bréval

Pontoise

Versailles
PARIS

St Malo
Cancale
M.St Michel
la Fresnais

Avranches
Monserrel
Flers
les Foulons
Messey
Briouse
Almenêches
Argentan

Montabart
Econché
Laigle
Aube
Bourth
St Hilaire
Verneuil
Nonancourt
Dreux

Tilliéres
St Rémy

Rambouillet
Epernon
Limours

Dinan
Bonnemain
St Pierre de Plesguen
Mortain
Domfront

Vingthanaps
Nonant
Sées
ORNE
Montagne

la Loupe
Pontgouin
Courville
Maintenon
Jouy
SEINE ET OISE

Hiniac
Plénée Jugon
Combourg
Broons
Caulnes

ILLE ET VILAINE

MAYENNE

Prez en Pail
ALENCON
Condé

Bretoncelles
CHARTRES
Ablis
Auneau
Etampes

Montreuil
Montauban
Dompierre
Mayenne
Bourg le Roi
Mamers

Nogent le Rotrou
Voves
Santeuil
Angerville
Baigneville
Monerville

Montfort sur Meu
L'Hermitage
St Germain
Port Brillet
Louverné
Fresnay
la Hutte

Vivoin
le Theil
la Ferté Bernard
EURE ET LOIR
Bonneval
Toury
Malesherbes
Nemours
FONTAINEBLEAU

RENNES
Vitré
Chateaubourg
le Genest
Montsurs
Voutré
Rouesse
Sillé
Conlie
Montbixot
la Guerche la Neuville
Sceaux
Connerré
Pont de Gennes

Châteaudun
Ch.au Gaillard
Pithiviers
Beaumont
Fontenay

Brutz
Noyal
LAVAL
Domfront St Saturnin
St Mars
Yvré l'Eveque

Cloyes
St Hilaire
Chevilly
Cercottes
ORLÉANS
LOIRET

Ploermel
Guichen
Bourg-des-Comptes
LE MANS
Noyen
la Suze
Vaiges
St Calais
Fretéval
Meung
St Ay
Beaugency

Messac
Chateau Gontier
Juigné
Avoise
Laigne
Ecommoy
Mayet
Pezou
Vendôme
Mer
LOIRET

Questembert
Redon
Béslé
Précigny
Morannes
Sablé
SARTHE
Château du Loir
Dissay
St Amand
Ménars
BLOIS
Nouan
la Ferté
Gien

Chateaubriant
Sévérac
Ségré
Tiercé
la Flèche
Aubigné
Vaas
St Paterne
Ch.au Renaud
Lamothe

St Gildas-des-Bois
LOIRE INF.re
MAINE ET LOIRE
ANGERS
Baugé
Neuillé
Limeray
Chouzy
LOIR ET CHER

Dréfeac
Pont-Château
Savenay
St Etienne de Montluc
les Forges
Champtocé
Ingrandes
Anetz
Ecouflant
Trélaxe
la Pointe
la Bohalle
St Mathurin
la Ménitré
St Antoine
Mettray
Vouvray
Onzain
Amboise Blère
Montrichard
Romorantin
Salbris

Montoir
Cordemais
Oudon
Varades
Chalonnes
la Poissonniere
les Rosiers
TOURS
Langeais
Vernou
Bourré
Mennetou
Théillay

Ancenis
Clermont
la Jumelliere
Saumur
Varennes
Port Boulet
Cinq Mars
St Pierre
St Louis
Chenonceaux
St Aignan
Selles
Villefranche
Thenioux
Vierzon

Paimbœuf
Basse Indre
Couëron
Ste Luce
Thouaré
Mauves
NANTES
le Pallet
Chemillé
Trémentines
Chalonnes
INDRE ET LOIRE
la Chapelle
Monts
St Patrice
Chinon
Villeperdue
Ste Maure
Loches
Chéri
Reuilly
BOUR

Chantenay
la Haie
Clisson
Cholet
Maulévrier
les Aubiers
Voultegon
Bressuire
Courlay
Moncoutant
Port de Piles
les Ormes
Orange
Ingrandes
Neuvy Pailloux
Chateauroux
Ste Lizaigne
St Florent sur Cher
Issoudun
Savigny

NAPOLÉON VENDÉE
DEUX SEVRES
Châtellerault
la Tricherie
les Barrés
INDRE
Luant
Bigny
St Amand Mont
CH

VENDÉE
la Motte Achard
Olonne
Breuil Barret
Puy de Serre
St Laurs
Parthenay
Coulon
Dissais
Clan
Chasseneuil
POITIERS
le Blanc
Chabenet
Lothiers
Argenton
Ainay

les Sables

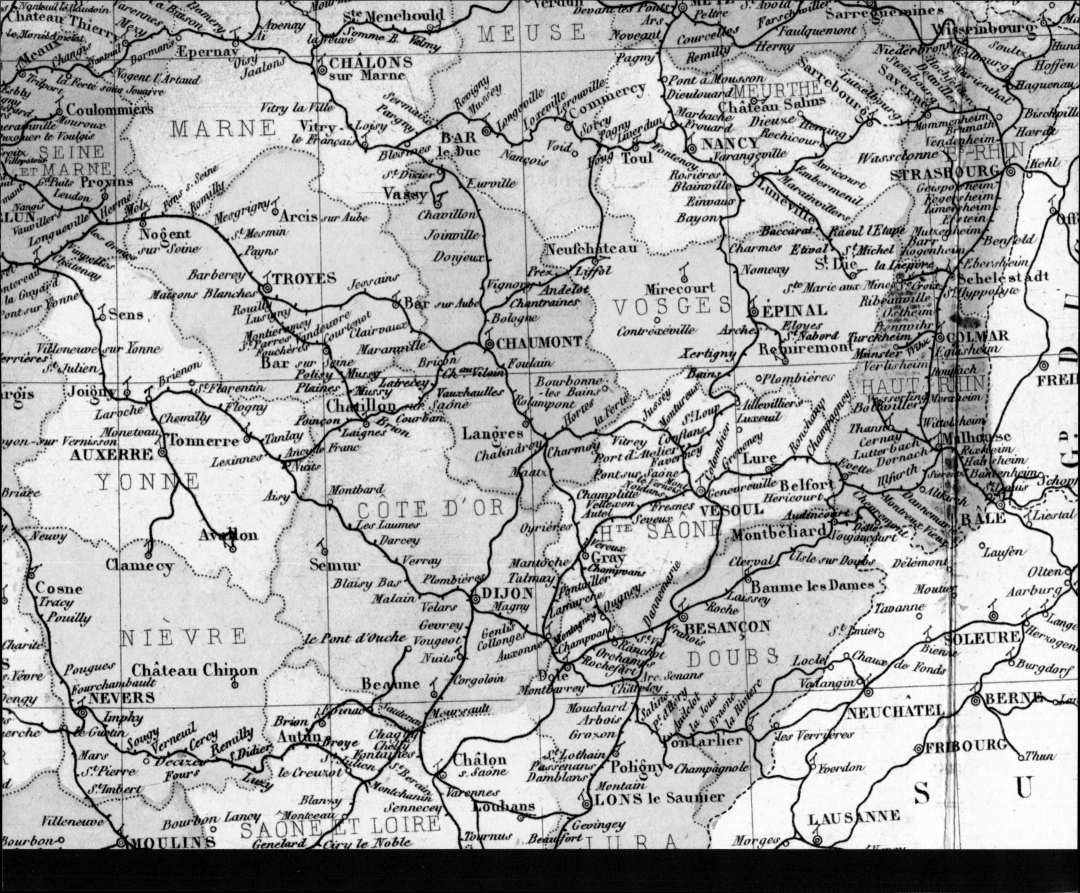

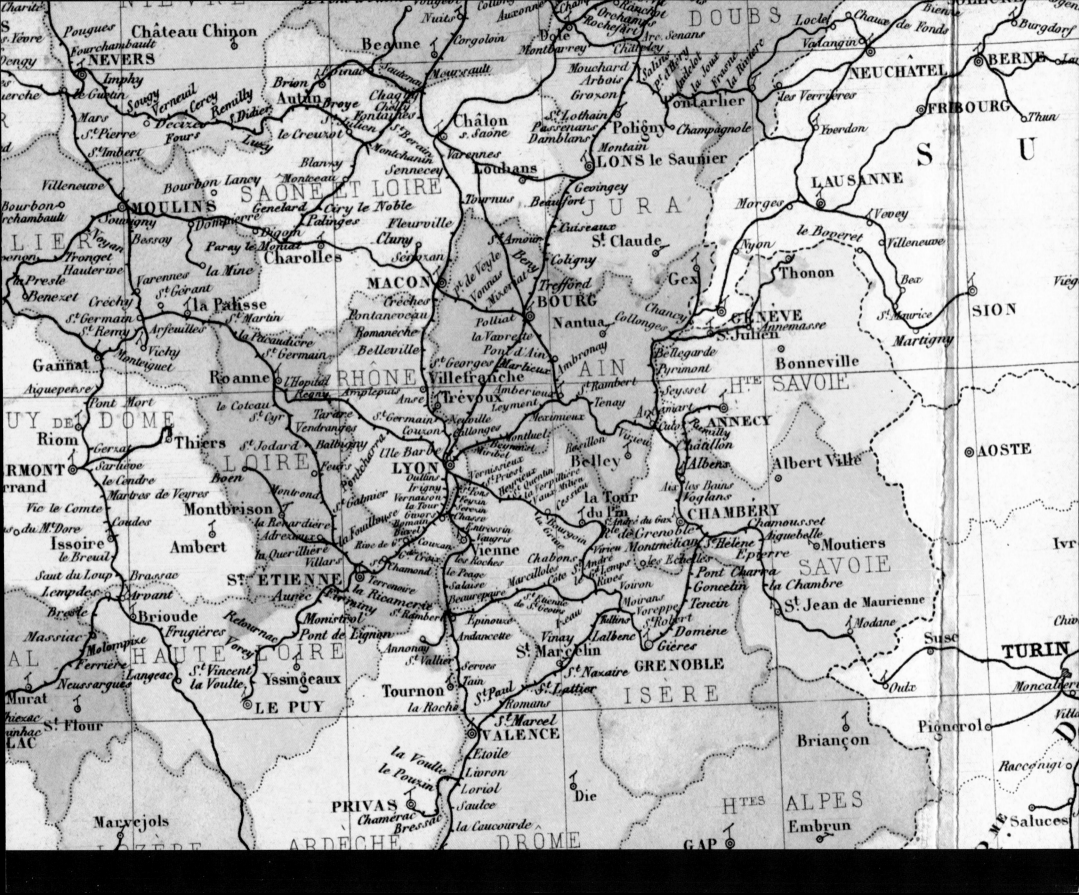

ITALY

Italian railway development predated the modern Italian state by more than two decades, its early railway schemes fulfilling growing demands for efficient regional transport. The steam railway era began with a bang in 1839 with the inauguration of a service operated over the short distance between Naples and Portici. Ferdinand II, King of Naples, was an early railway enthusiast, and ordered construction of the line. On opening day he rode the first trains, admiring the construction as he was given resounding military salutes. In the north, a line connecting Milan northward to Monza opened in 1840, and within a couple of years a more significant route was under way between Milan and Venice.

Italian railway builders faced difficult construction challenges. The great wall of the Alps separated Italy from its northern neighbours, while the spine of the Apennines limited railway penetration of the Italian peninsula, especially between the east and west coasts. The most intensive early construction took place in northern Italy, in the broad Po valley, while north–south main lines tended to hug the coast.

Like elsewhere on the continent, Italian railways vacillated between state and private operation, with varying degrees of state involvement from an early date. However, in Italy railways were early recognised as a unifying force, and following the creation of the Italian state in 1861 the new government invested heavily in railway construction. By 1866 most major cities were connected. During this period five regional railways dominated operations – Upper Italian Railways in the north, Roman Railways in central Italy, Southern Railways and the Victor Emmanuel Railways in Sicily, and Royal Sardinian Railways on its namesake island.

In 1885 Italian lines were largely reorganised into three principal regional networks. In the north the Mediterranean and Adriatic systems offered overlapping connections to most major cities, while in the south a Sicilian system dominated.

After twenty years of this arrangement, growing traffic and railway congestion was plaguing Italy with famously untimely trains which resulted in great public dissatisfaction with the railway network. The solution was a nationalised operation, and in 1905 most lines were assigned to the newly created Ferrovie dello Stato (FS).

In its first decade, FS was directed by the visionary Riccardo Bianchi, who implemented significant improvements which helped secure Italian railways their place on the European map. He ordered widescale electrification of main lines, made important equipment purchases, and began the construction of new highly-engineered routes. Although progress was slow, Italy continued to make massive investment to improve its network, undertaking major construction in the 1920s and 1930s which included many new routes and stations.

Two contemporary interpretations of the opening of the Naples–Portici Railway (above and below).

Naples station in 1880 (opposite).

87

TURIN VIA MONT CENIS

A Spectacular Mountain Crossing

Northern Italy is ringed by towering Alpine peaks which present formidable terrain for railway construction. Yet the Alpine region produced some of Europe's most spectacular main lines, including the famed crossing at the Mont Cenis Pass (Monte Cenisio in Italian). This is a low pass between France and Italy, where decades earlier Napoleon constructed a road over the mountains, and where conjectural historians speculate that two thousand years ago Hannibal marched his army and famed war elephants on his assault against the Roman Empire. In the 1860s this bold railway route was the first main line to connect Italy directly with France. The Mont Cenis Railway Tunnel, also known as the Fréjus Tunnel, was among the first very long railway bores, measuring 13.7 km in length. It remains the crowning engineering landmark of the crossing which includes 29 tunnels on 60 km of double track through exceptionally rugged Alpine terrain. Not only do the grades reach 3 per cent, steeper than most standard gauge Swiss Alpine main lines and steeper than most standard gauge lines in the American Rockies, but the railway is beleaguered by heavy snowfall in winter. For a few years, prior to completion of the Mont Cenis Tunnel, the lightly built Mont Cenis Railway, known colloquially as the 'Devil's Ladder', crossed the mountains roughly on the alignment of the Napoleonic road.

The Mont Cenis crossing is the most spectacular part of the international journey between Turin and Paris, and the premier route used by overnight sleeping car trains such as the *Rome Express*. The Mont Cenis route also hosted Peninsular & Orient's long-distance trains between the North Sea port of Calais and Brindisi on the Italian Adriatic coast — a preferred route for British mail trains serving the Middle East and beyond. Most exclusive was the once-weekly *Péninsulaire Express* operated in conjunction with France's Nord Company, intended for British passengers travelling to southern Italy.

Leaving Turin for Paris, the line crosses a broad plain, roughly following the Po's tributary the Dora Riparia, negotiating the confines of the Chiuse Pass and offering a prelude to the Alpine scenery ahead. Passengers heading toward Paris on the right-hand side were afforded the best views of the ascent of Mont Cenis. After passing through the wild gorge of Le Gorgie near Exilles — location of a picturesque fortress — the line reaches 770 m above sea level. From here the difficult climb begins as the line winds its way up toward the top of the Dora Riparia valley.

The first Mont Cenis Railway in a print from 1865 (below).

Boring the Mont Cenis Tunnel, from an engineering magazine article of 1868 (bottom right).

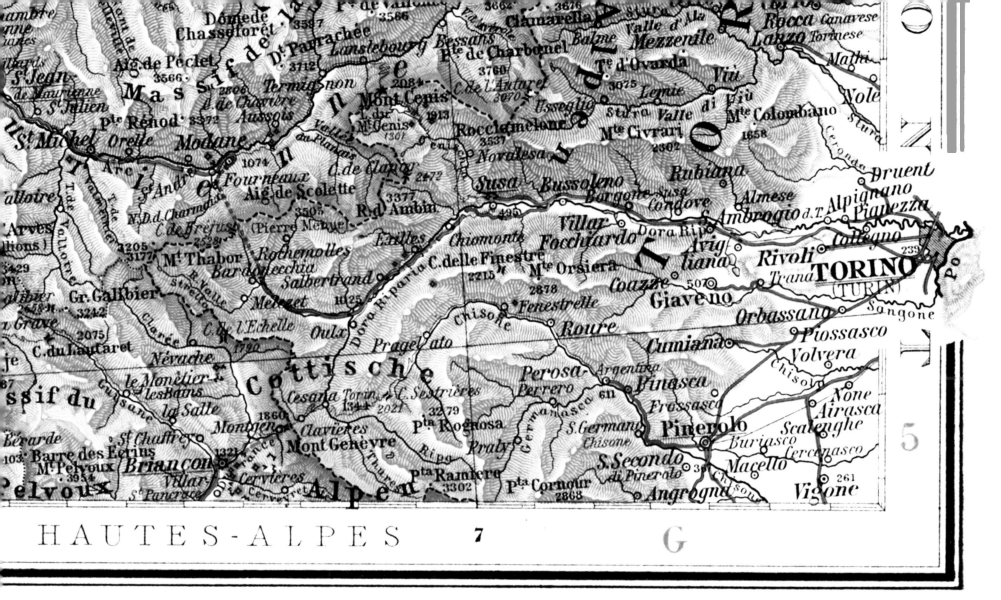

After passing through numerous short tunnels, the line passes the ornamented south portal of Mont Cenis Tunnel at Bardonnèche (elevation 1,257 m). Passage through the double-track tunnel ('travellers are warned not to protrude their heads or arms from the carriage windows during the transit,' warns *Baedeker*) was anticlimactic compared with the stunning scenery on the approach to the pass, a particularly surreal scene when viewed nocturnally from a sleeper in winter, when fluffy blankets of effervescent snow glistening by moonlight. The line continues to climb inside the mountain, finally cresting at 1,295 m, a low crossing compared with the old road's 2,083 m summit and the nearby peak of Mont Cenis which scrapes the sky at 3,320 m.

The railway crosses into France inside the tunnel, thus spanning the divide between the Cottian and Graian Alps. Beyond the north portal the line descends into the Arc Valley to Modane, historically the location of French–Italian customs and the base of railway operations. The difficult nature of this Alpine crossing encouraged electrification to simplify operations, lower costs, increase line capacity and eliminate smoke from the tunnels. It was wired between 1912 and 1915, originally using the peculiar Italian three-phase high-voltage system requiring dual overhead contact wires.

MONT CENIS TUNNEL

TURIN–MILAN–ROME–NAPLES

Italy's Main North-South Route

Rugged central Italian geography required heavily engineered railways, and by the 1950s Italian railways boasted nearly 1,850 tunnels and more than 43,000 bridges and viaducts. While the broad, comparatively level Po Valley facilitated relatively easy construction, many early lines, including the original route from between Bologna and Florence, suffered from difficult grades, tight curvature, and constraints due to a single track.

Through the 1870s maximum train speed was a mere 65 km/h, with many trains operating much slower; in the late Victorian era Italian passenger trains were notoriously slow, while time-keeping was liberally interpreted, much to the annoyance of international travellers who had grown accustomed to relatively fast European express trains.

Though Italy's main routes were slow, they were also heavily used. In his 1910 book *Transportation in Europe*, Logan McPherson wrote this description which sums up a crowded Italian suburban service: 'Early morning and late evening trains that carry working men into and out of the large cities, the third class cars have hard wooden benches up which their occupants may be seen huddling together, each passenger supporting the person next to him as they smoke and sleep in the stifling atmosphere.' Yet, not all was crowds and gloom.

Bradshaw's Guide of 1912 highlighted the Milan–Bologna–Florence–Rome route, noting that south of Milan the 'line passes through a flat but highly cultivated district', while, 'eight miles beyond Codogno is characterised by vineyards and mulberry trees.' Running across the plains brought the line to the foothills of the Apennines, clearly viewed from the train. At Borgo San Donnino, passengers could glimpse a twelfth century cathedral, and near Castel Guelfo the ruins of a medieval fortress. Beyond Bologna, the railway's easy running ended as it began its ascent of the Apennines, where it followed the River Reno, crossing it repeatedly as it gained elevation. After cresting a mountain pass, the descent to Florence passed through a heavily industrialised area which, although not picturesque, undoubtedly supplied the railway with ample goods traffic to balance receipts from loss-making passenger business. South from Florence, the railway followed the River Arno. Ancient architecture near the line includes ruins of a Roman atrium at Arezzo, 88 km south of Florence.

TRENI RAPIDI

MILANO

FIRENZE

BOLOGNA

ROMA

NAPOLI

Bologna - Stazione principale

An FS *Treni Rapidi* poster from the late 1930s (left).

Bologna, 1914; Florence, 1905; Siena, 1919; Rome, 1886; Naples, 1956.

Firenze - Stazione - Sala d'a

SIENA - Stazione ferroviaria

Saluti da Roma

Napoli - Stazione Ferroviaria.

91

MILANO CENTRALE

Northern Italy's Flagship Station

Milano Centrale, 1935 (above).

Details of the 1931 station – statues, mosaic, portico (below and right).

The first Milano Centrale station opened in 1864 in the area now occupied by the Piazza della Repubblica. It was designed by the French architect Louis-Jules Bouchot, and its architectural style was reminiscent of Parisian buildings of the period. The station was designed to replace Porta Tosa Station, opened in 1846 as the terminus of the line to Treviglio and Venice, and Porta Nuova Station, opened in 1850 as the terminus of the line to Monza and Chiasso. It remained in operation until June 1931, when the current station was opened.

The colossal façade of the new Stazione Centrale faces the city's Piazza Andrea Doria, one of the largest open public squares in central Europe. Behind the building, trains serve a massive five-span shed 7.6 m above street level, while street trams grind along the western flank to deliver passengers across the city. The concourse is among the largest of any railway station in the world – 215 m long, 22 m wide, and 25 m high. Enormous skylights illuminate the hall with filtered rays of sun, although there is subdued sensation of gloom resulting from the hall's tremendous verticality coupled with the cavernous train sheds beyond.

The design of the new Milano Centrale was the work of architect Ulisse Stacchini. Planning began before the First World War, but construction did not begin until 1925. Its grandiose classically-inspired style and monumental scale appealed to aesthetic ideas of Italian Fascism under the regime of Benito Mussolini. The gargantuan frontal colonnade offers an effect of the Italian State swallowing the mass of humanity entering its doors. Completed a generation after most traditional European terminals, Milano Stazione Centrale was one of the last terminals executed with classic flare. In stark contrast, postwar structures have tended toward austerity and raw functionality.

The booking hall of the 1931 station (left).

The first Milano Centrale of 1864, in a painting by
Angelo Morbelli of 1889 (below).

THE FLORENCE–BOLOGNA DIRETTISSIMA

A Key Link in Italy's Pioneering High-Speed Network

Building the Florence–Bologna *direttissima* (below).

Italian trunk lines suffered from difficult geography with primitive engineering that resulted in tortuous steep lines, often limited to single track. Despite difficult profiles, by the early years of the twentieth century key north–south routes were saturated with freight and passenger traffic. To solve this problem, FS under the administration of Riccardo Bianchi planned all-new high-capacity lines on key routes.

The Florence–Bologna line was a special problem. The original route built between 1856 and 1862, known as the Porretta line, ran via Pistoia over a 616 m summit at Pracchia. Key portions of the line were single track and noted for exceptional steep gradients, where long-boiler eight-coupled locomotives were required to move heavy trains. Steam-hauled express passenger trains required 2 hours 45 minutes to make the 132 km run, while freight trains took even longer and tended to clog line capacity, occupying passing stations waiting for faster trains to overtake or pass them. Although initial approval for a new line was approved in 1908, complexities of locating and building the Great Apennine Tunnel combined with the onset of the First World War delayed construction for decades.

In the meantime, other congested routes were improved. The Rome–Naples corridor was the first route to benefit from opening of a highly engineered *Direttissima* – which loosely translated means a 'low-graded, direct railway', similar to what American railways describe as a 'cut-off'. Key to the *Direttissima* was a low-graded double-track line free from level crossings with highways or other railway lines, with gentle, broad-radius curvature. Complicating the execution of this concept was the planning of lines in mountainous terrain, requiring massive engineering to overcome natural obstacles. The *Direttissima* was characterised by long stretches of high fills and deep cuttings combined with frequent viaducts and tunnels.

The Rome–Naples *Direttissima* opened in 1927, setting important precedents for later high-speed railway construction across Europe. Where the old route was 296.6 km long with a 332 m mountain summit, the *Direttissima* required just 216.5 km following an alignment closer to the coast, and cresting at just 126 m above sea level.

The Florence–Bologna *Direttissima* opened seven years later, having overcome myriad difficulties constructing the Great Apennine tunnel, which at 18.5 km was second only to the Simplon Tunnel in length. Construction began in 1920, but was slowed by discovery of vast quantities of water in the rock. This double-track tunnel featured a below-ground passing station, a novel feature for such a long tunnel. The tunnel was the new line's crowning engineering feature, one of 31 tunnels on the new line that helped trim more than 300 m from the Apennine summit, and nearly 34 km from the Florence–Bologna run, cutting travel time for express trains to just over an hour. Like many Italian lines, the Florence–Bologna was electrified at 3,000 volts direct current, using electricity produced locally by hydro-power.

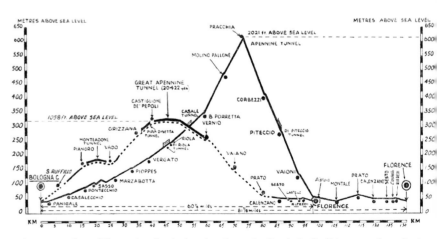

A cross-section of the route, clearly showing the reduction in both distance and gradient.

The Setta Viaduct at Vado, south of Bologna, with (insets) photographs taken during its construction.

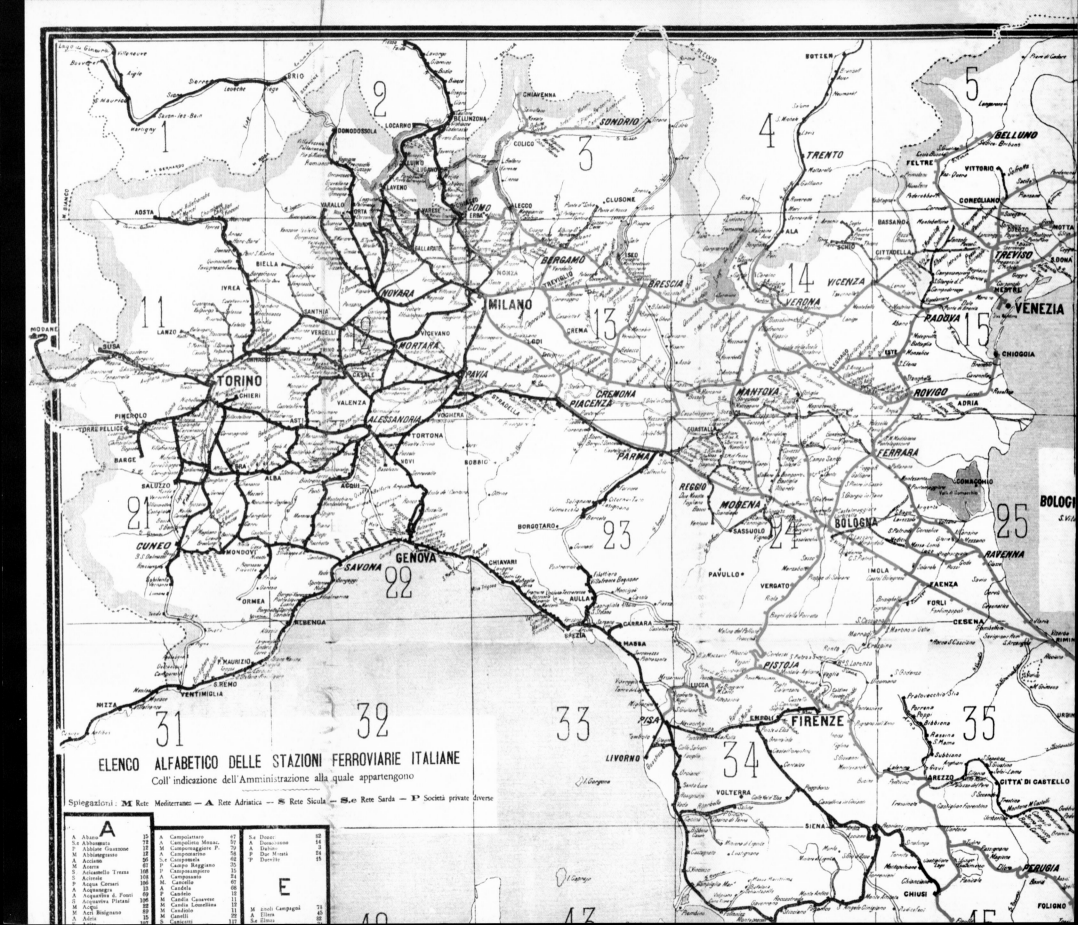

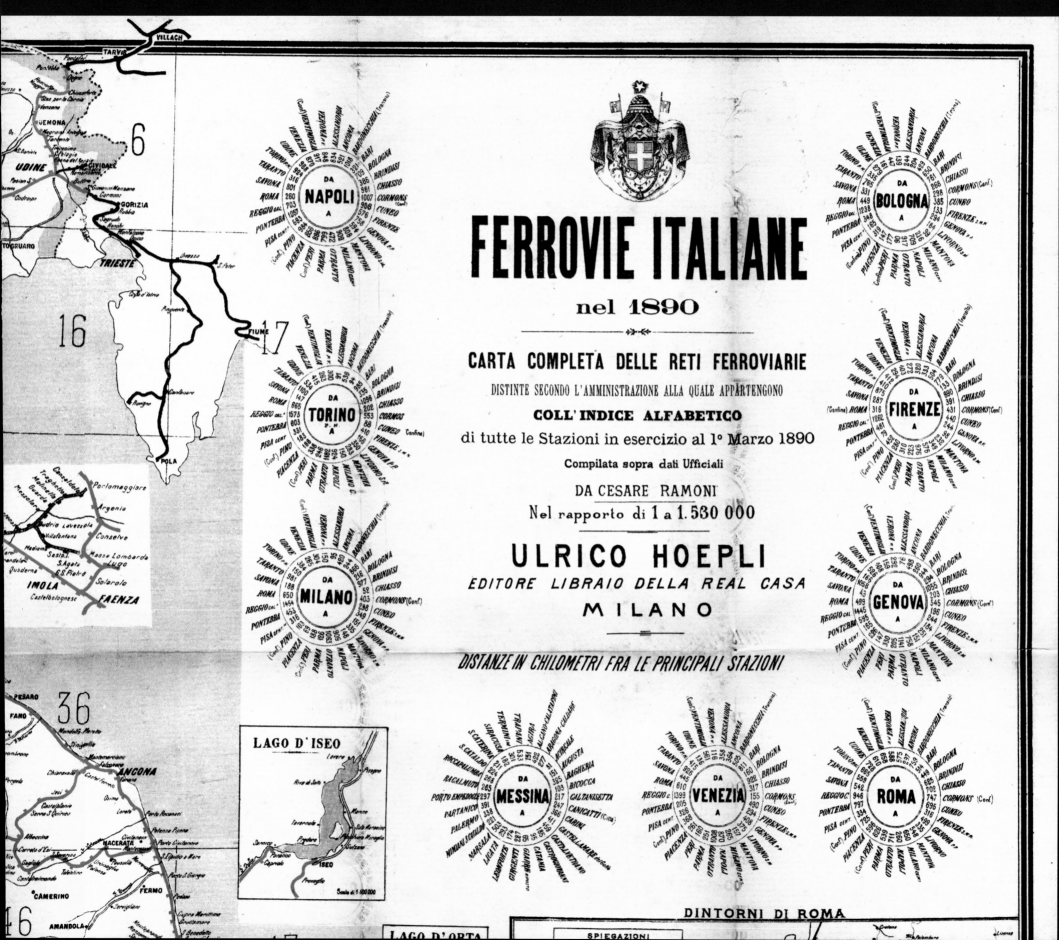

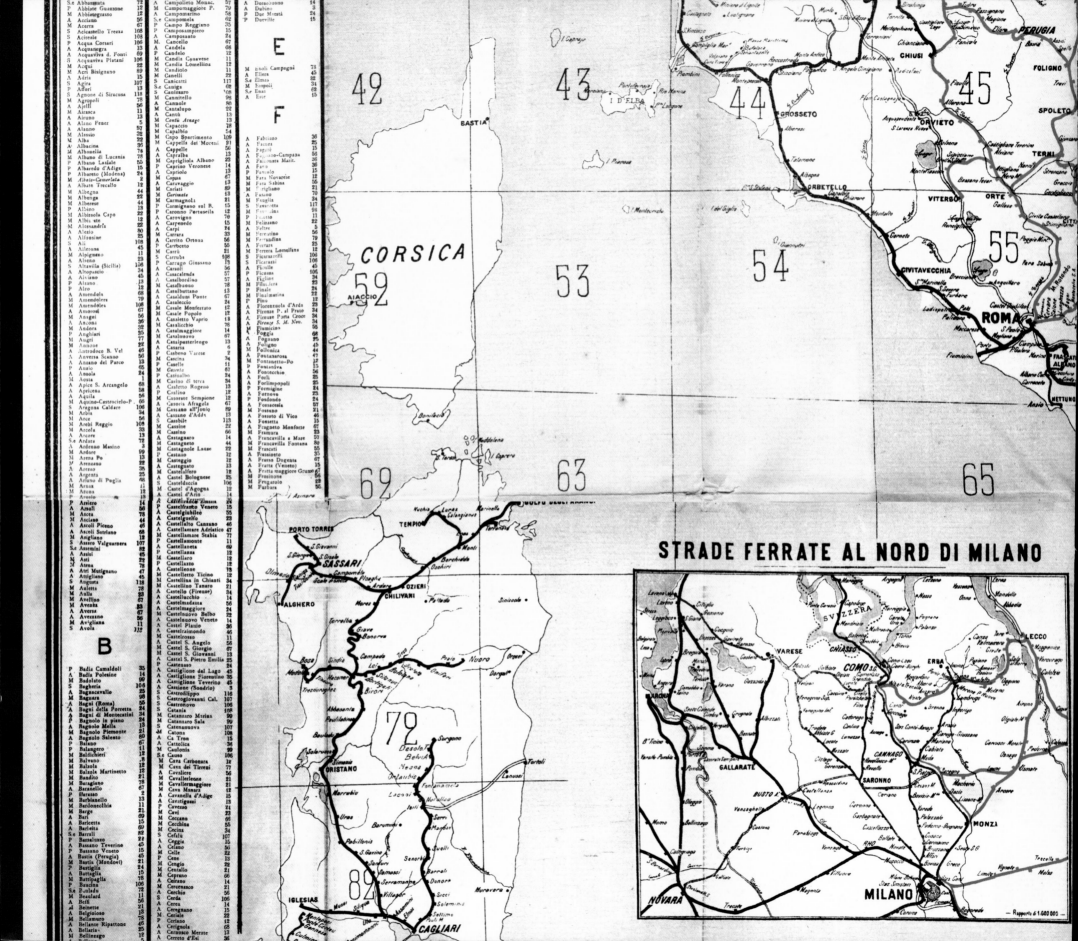

S.e	Abbassanta	
A	Abbiate Guazzone	72
M	Abbiategrasso	12
A	Acciano	55
M	Acerra	67
A	Aciacastello Trezza	108
S	Acireale	108
S	Acqua Corsari	106
A	Acquanegra	13
A	Acquaviva d. Fonti	69
A	Acquaviva Platani	106
M	Acqui	22
A	Acri Bisignano	89
S	Adria	15
S	Agira	107
S	Affori	22
S	Agnone di Siracusa	118
P	Agropoli	78
M	Ajelli	13
M	Airasca	13
A	Airuno	13
A	Alano Feno	5
A	Alanno	57
M	Alassio	32
M	Alba	26
M	Albacina	36
A	Albanella	78
M	Albano di Lucania	78
M	Albano Laziale	56
P	Albaredo d'Adige	24
P	Albareto (Modena)	24
A	Albate-Camerlato	
A	Albate Trecallo	44
M	Albenga	22
A	Alberese	44
M	Albino	7
M	Albissola Capo	22
M	Albis ste	12
A	Alessandria	22
A	Alezio	80
A	Alfonsine	108
S	Ali	45
A	Ailetona	11
M	Alpignano	23
A	Alseno	136
S	Altavilla (Sicilia)	
A	Altopascio	45
A	Alviano	45
M	Alzano	7
A	Alzo	68
A	Amendola	79
M	Amendolea	108
A	Amarosi	76
A	Anagni	36
M	Ancona	36
M	Andora	22
P	Anghiari	77
M	Augri	13
A	Annone	42
A	Antrodoco B. Vel	46
A	Anversa Scanno	56
A	Anzano del Parco	13
A	Anzio	65
A	Aosola	79
A	Aosta	1
S	Apice S. Arcangelo	68
A	Apricena	56
A	Aquila	56
P	Aquino-Castrociclo-P.	66
A	Aragona Caldare	106
A	Arbia	34
A	Arce	34
A	Aredi Reggio	108
A	Arcola	33
A	Arcore	13
S.e	Ardara	72
A	Ardenno Masino	3
A	Ardore	99
M	Arena Po	13
M	Arenzano	22
A	Arezzo	35
A	Argenta	108
A	Ariano di Puglia	68
M	Aroas	13
A	Arona	13
P	Arosio	13

P	Arsiero	14
A	Azoli	56
A	Ascea	78
A	Ascoli Piceno	46
A	Ascoli Satriano	68
A	Asigliano	12
A	Assoro Valguarnera	107
S.e	Assemini	
A	Assisi	45
A	Asti	22
A	Atri Mutignano	47
A	Attigliano	45
A	Augusta	118
A	Auletta	78
A	Aulla	33
M	Avellino	67
A	Aventa	83
A	Aversa	67
A	Averzano	11
A	Avigliana	
S	Avola	118

B

P	Badia Camaldoli	35
P	Badia Polesine	14
M	Badolato	99
S	Bagheria	106
A	Bagnacavallo	
M	Bagnara	98
M	Bagni (Roma)	55
A	Bagni della Porretta	24
A	Bagni di Montecatini	34
M	Bagnolo in piano	24
M	Bagnolo Mella	13
M	Bagnolo Piemonte	21
A	Bagnolo Salento	80
P	Bagnone	13
P	Baiano	
M	Balangero	11
M	Baldichieri	8
M	Balvano	78
M	Balzola	22
M	Balzola Martinetto	21
A	Bandito	21
A	Baragiano	78
A	Baranello	67
M	Barasso	2
A	Barbanello	11
P	Barge	21
A	Bari	69
A	Baricetta	13
A	Barletta	69
S.e	Barrali	82
P	Bassaluzzo	22
P	Bassano Teverino	45
P	Bassano Veneto	15
P	Bastia (Perugia)	35
M	Bastia (Mondovì)	21
P	Battiglia	24
A	Battaglia	78
M	Battipaglia	78
A	Baucina	106
S.e	Bauladu	72
M	Beaulard	11
S.e	Beffi	21
Al	Beinette	13
M	Belgioioso	13
M	Bellamo	78
M	Bellante Ripattone	46
P	Bellaria	13
A	Bellizzi	
A	Bellinzago	15

S.e	Campolieto Monac.	57
A	Campomaggiore P.	79
A	Campomarino	79
S.e	Campomorino	79
P	Campo Reggiano	35
M	Camposampiero	
A	Camposanto	67
M	Cancello	67
P	Candela	12
A	Candia Canavese	12
A	Candia Lomellina	11
M	Candiolo	11
A	Canelli	22
M	Canicatti	117
S.e	Caniga	62
M	Canizzaro	'08
M	Cannitello	98
A	Cannole	80
A	Cantalupo	13
M	Contù Arnage	13
A	Cantù	13
A	Capaccio	13
M	Capalbio	54
M	Capo Spartimento	109
M	Cappella dei Moreni	21
A	Cappelle	
A	Capralba	23
A	Capriglia Albano	23
A	Caprino Veronese	24
A	Capriolo	13
M	Capua	67
A	Caravaggio	13
M	Cariati	89
A	Carimate	13
M	Carmagnola	15
A	Carmignano sul R.	15
A	Caronno Pertusella	70
A	Carovigno	70
A	Carpenedo	15
M	Carpi	13
A	Carrara	33
A	Carrito Ortona	21
A	Carroceto	55
A	Carrù	21
S	Carrago Giussano	108
A	Carsoli	56
M	Casacalenda	
P	Casalbordino	57
P	Casalbuono	13
M	Casalbuttano	13
A	Casaleccio	67
A	Casalduni Ponte	67
M	Casaletto	
A	Casale Monferrato	12
A	Casale Popolo	13
A	Casaletto Vaprio	13
M	Casalicchio	
A	Casalmaggiore	
M	Casalnuovo	67
A	Casalpusterlengo	13
P	Casarsa	
M	Casbeno Varese	2
A	Cascina	34
A	Caselle	11
M	Casino di terra	34
A	Casletto Rogeno	12
A	Coslino	12
A	Casorate Sempione	
A	Casoria Afragola	
M	Cassano all'Jonio	89
A	Cassano d'Adda	
S	Cassibile	113
M	Cassine	22
M	Cassino	
A	Castagnaro	14
M	Castagneto	12
A	Castagnole Lanze	12
P	Castasio	12
A	Casteggio	13
A	Castegnato	13
M	Castellafero	12
A	Castel Bolognese	25
M	Castel d'Agogna	12
M	Castel d'Ario	12
M	Castelfranco Emilia	
A	Castelfranco Veneto	55
M	Castelgiubileo	55
A	Castelguelfo	
A	Castelfalto Canzano	46
M	Castellammare Adriatico	34
A	Castellammare Stabia	77
A	Castellamonte	11
A	Castellaneta	
P	Castellana	13
A	Castellaro	12
A	Castellazzo	13
M	Castelleone	18
M	Castelletto Ticino	13
A	Castellina in Chianti	34
M	Castellino Tanaro	13
A	Castello (Firenze)	13
A	Castellucchio	14
A	Castelmadama	56
M	Castelmaggiore	24
A	Castelnuovo Belbo	12
A	Castelnuovo Veneto	
A	Castel Plaino	36
A	Castelraimondo	46
A	Castelrosso	13
M	Castel S. Angelo	56
A	Castel S. Giorgio	07
M	Castel S. Giovanni	13
M	Castel S. Pietro Emilia	25
A	Castenaso	
S	Castiglione del Lago	45
A	Castiglione Fiorentino	35
S	Castiglione Teverino	
A	Gastione (Sondrio)	3
S	Castrofilippo	13
S	Castrogiovanni Cal.	107
A	Castronovo	106
M	Catania	116
A	Catanzaro Marina	99
M	Catanzaro Sala	
A	Catanzaro	107
A	Catona	108
A	Ca Tron	15
S.e	Cauna	106
A	Cava Carbonara	
A	Cava dei Tirreni	77
A	Cavaliere	
A	Cavalleleone	21
A	Cavallermaggiore	21
A	Cavanella d'Adige	15
A	Cavatigozzi	12
A	Caveno	14
A	Cavi	24
A	Ceccano	66
A	Cecchina	56
A	Cecina	34
S	Cefalù	107
A	Ceggia	
A	Celano	56
A	Celle	22
A	Cene	7
A	Cengio	22
A	Ceutallo	21
A	Ceprano	66
A	Cerano	14
A	Cercenasco	21
A	Cerchio	56
A	Cercino	
A	Cerea	15
A	Ceregnano	
A	Cereseto	
A	Ceriale	22
A	Ceriano	
A	Cerignola	68
A	Cernusco Merate	13
A	Cerreto d'Esi	36

A	Dosso-buono	14
P	Dubino	3
A	Due Mestà	
P	Dueville	15

E

M	noli Campagnà	73
A	Ellera	45
S.e	Elmas	82
M	Empoli	34
S.e	Enas	62
A	Este	15

F

A	Fabriano	36
A	Fagnano	25
A	Pagatè	
A	Fagnano-Campana	36
A	Falconara Marit.	36
A	Faro	26
A	Fanzolo	
A	Fara Novarese	12
M	Fara Sabina	21
A	Fasano	70
A	Faugiia	34
S	Favarotta	117
M	Favallina	98
A	Feletto	11
A	Felizzano	
A	Feltre	6
A	Ferentino	56
A	Ferrandina	79
A	Ferrara	14
S	Ferrera Lomellina	106
S	Ficarazzi	106
A	Ficulle	36
A	Figline	34
A	Ficusano	105
A	Filacciano	21
P	Finale	24
P	Finalmarina	24
A	Fino	
P	Florenzuola d'Arda	23
A	Firenze P. al Prato	34
A	Firenze Porta Croce	34
A	Firenze S. M. Nov.	34
M	Fiumicino	
A	Foggia	68
A	Fognano	75
A	Foligno	
M	Follonica	44
A	Fontanarosa	47
A	Fontanetto-Po	12
A	Fontaniva	
A	Fontecchio	56
A	Fontechio	13
A	Forli	56
A	Forlimpopoli	
M	Formigine	24
A	Fornovo	23
P	Fosdondo	24
A	Fossacesia	57
A	Fossato	91
A	Fossato di Vico	46
A	Fossetta	15
A	Fragagto Monforte	67
A	Framura	23
A	Francavilla a Mare	57
A	Francavilla Fontana	80
M	Frascati	35
A	Frassineto	34
A	Frasso Dogana	67
A	Fratta (Veneto)	15
A	Frattamaggiore Grumo	64
A	Frosinone	66
A	Frugarolo	
A	Furbara	55

STRADE FERRATE AL NORD DI MILANO

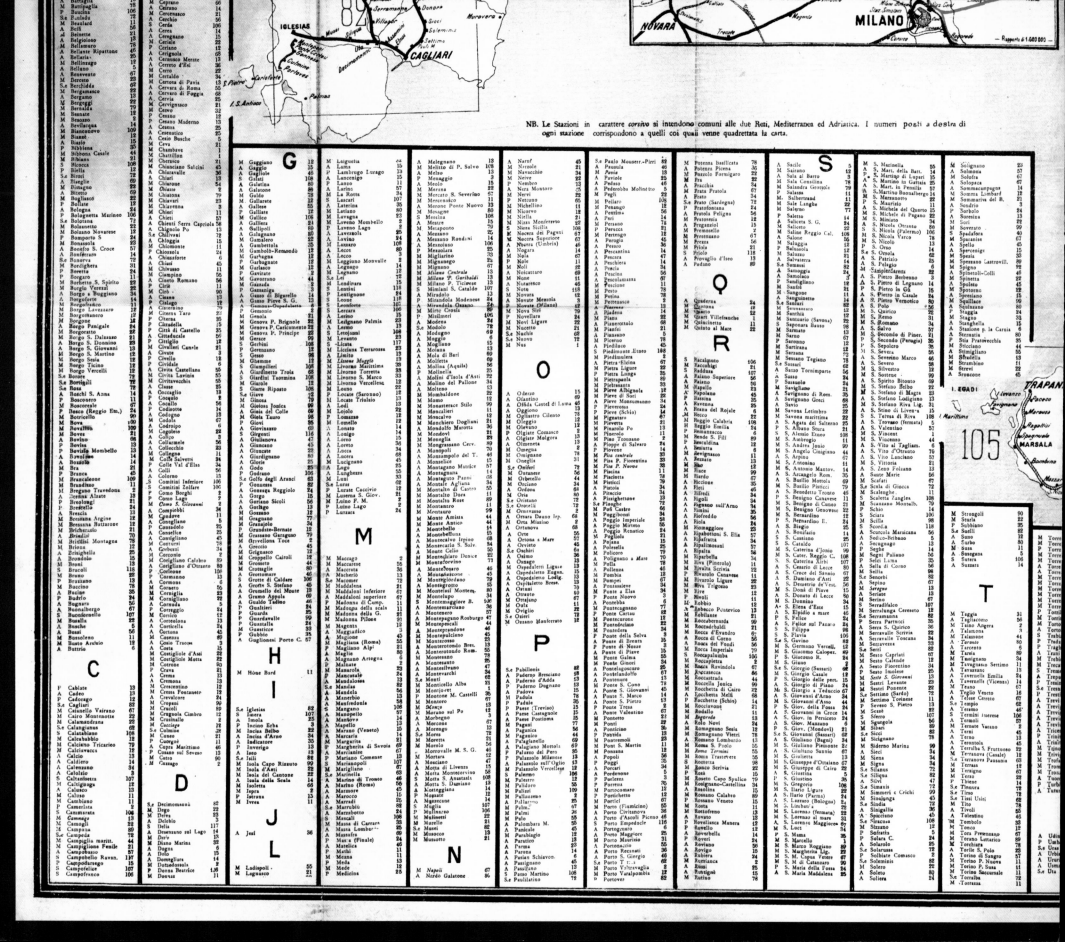

NB. Le Stazioni in carattere *corsivo* si intendono comuni alle due Reti, Mediterranea ed Adriatica. I numeri posti a destra di ogni stazione corrispondono a quelli coi quali venne quadrettata la carta.

Rapporto di 1.000.000

105

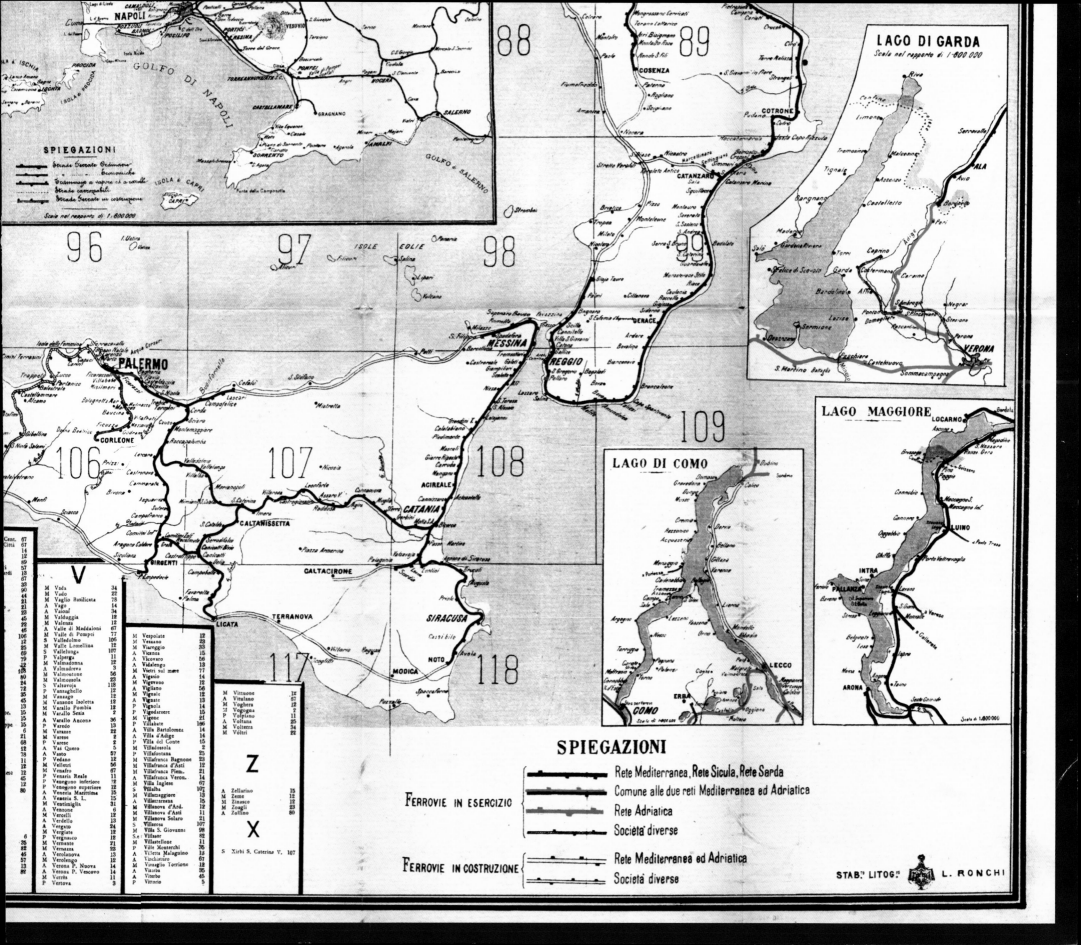

GOLFO DI NAPOLI

NAPOLI

GOLFO di SALERNO

88

89
COSENZA
COTRONE
CATANZARO

LAGO DI GARDA
Scala nel rapporto di 1:600.000

VERONA

96   97   ISOLE EOLIE   98   99
GERACE

PALERMO
MESSINA
REGGIO

CORLEONE

106   107   108
ACIREALE
CATANIA
CALTANISSETTA

109

LAGO DI COMO

LAGO MAGGIORE
LOCARNO
LUINO
INTRA
PALLANZA
ARONA
COMO
LECCO
ERBA

GIRGENTI
TERRANOVA
LICATA

CALTAGIRONE
SIRACUSA
MODICA
NOTO

117   118

ΘΕΣΣΑΛΙΑ - ΒΟΛΟΣ   Volo

ΦΑΡΜΑΚΕΙΟΝ

ΕΛΛΑΣ 1

ΛΕΠΤΟΝ   ΛΕΠΤΟΝ

THE BALKANS AND GREECE

For centuries the Balkan peninsula suffered the trials of a complex history, where occidental and oriental collided and faced the unfortunate three-way friction between Islamic, Roman Catholic and Orthodox Christian beliefs. Here imperial Russian, Habsburg and Ottoman Turk Empires vied for power, often at the expense of the local population. Yet still this rugged, beautiful and mysterious part of Europe compelled the railway traveller. When the intrepid Victorian boarded the famed *Orient Express* at Paris, he viewed with anticipation the experiences east of Vienna, where the train left the ways of the West behind.

Balkan routes were completed decades later than main routes elsewhere in Europe. Just as heavy works on key routes got under way, the Balkan War of 1912 and 1913, followed by the Great War, further delayed progress. After the ravages of these wars, Balkan railways finally came into their own.

Designed to avoid the historic route via Germany and Austria, the postwar *Simplon Orient Express* followed a southerly course via Zagreb and Belgrade. While one section continued toward its historic destination at Istanbul, another meandered south through Macedonia and Greece to Athens.

A postcard from 1911 shows the Volos–Larissa train in Greece running down the middle of the main street (opposite).

The Trieste–Opcina Tramway, 1905 (left).

The Sava River Bridge, Zagreb, 1935 (bottom left).

The Diakofto–Kalavryta Railway (below).

New borders and newly established nations added new complexities. Politics and wars aside, the region's difficult geography, especially near the Adriatic coast, demanded costly and heavily engineered routes, often constructed as single track, with numerous tunnels and tall bridges. In addition to standard gauge lines, various narrow gauge systems reached remote areas for the benefit of tourists.

Greece's Peloponnesian narrow gauge extended from Athens to a focal point at Corinth, where its routes encircled the island, while the steeply-graded Diakofto–Kalavryta Railway on the Corinthian coast connected these two towns. It was fitted with the Abt rack system, which allowed locomotives to claw their difficult ascent through rugged mountain ravines deemed beyond the means of conventional adhesion. The main attraction at the destination of Kalavryta was, and still is, the ancient Monastery of Megaspelion, with its chambers carved out the cliff-side.

ZAGREB TO SPLIT

Southwards into the Heart of Dalmatia

The Habsburg monarchy's imperial desires directed nineteenth century railway building in the territory occupied by Yugoslavia after the First World War, and today by Slovenia and Croatia. The region's railways were largely administered by the Royal Hungarian Railways, while Austrian engineers and financing had provided resources for construction. Routes were a function of Habsburg domination, which dictated both location and direction as well as predominant traffic flow.

Zagreb station, 1901 (top right).

Karlovac station, 1899 (bottom right).

Steinbrück (Zadani Most), 1914 (below).

Steinbrück.

In 1873 a route from southern Austria reached Zagreb via the picturesque junction of Zidani Most (Steinbrück in German), located deep in the valley of the River Sava. Zagreb dates from Roman times, when it was believed that Emperor Tiberius established a strategic fort along the Sava near the foot of forested Medvednica mountains. This flourished in the Middle Ages, and developed as an important industrial centre after the First World War. In 1865 another railway was built connecting Zagreb with Karlovac (Karlstadt in German and Károlyváros in Hungarian). By 1873, this route reached the

Adriatic port of Fiume, now the Croatian city of Rijeka — in the twentieth century this was variously in Austro-Hungarian, Italian and Yugoslavian territory.

Construction of the Hungarian–Dalmatian railway began in 1912 on the eve of the Great War, which redrew international borders. Initially this extended from a junction near Ogulin (on the Zagreb–Rijeka trunk line) to Knin, to link an existing line to the scenically spectacular Adriatic port at Split. Construction was interrupted by the war, and the line was not completed until after the formation of the pan-national Yugoslavia in 1918. Passenger trains covered the Zagreb–Split route in 19$\frac{1}{2}$ hours, passing through colourful and spectacular mountain scenery to reach the Dalmatian coast.

The beer brewing centre at Karlovac (the Croatian equivalent of Czech Republic's Plzen) is 56 km south-west of Zagreb. The town takes its name from Archduke Karl, credited with its founding in the mid-sixteenth century. The strategic location of Castle Dubovac on the River Kupa was designed to protect river trade. Further south, trains to Split and central Dalmatia diverge north of Ogulin at Ostarije. The line turns south-east, running via Plaški and Vrhovine toward Knin. Difficult terrain required exceptional engineering, making for a stunning if slow railway journey. Among the engineering wonders is the 2,270 m Sinac Tunnel, and impressive bridges over the Rivers Lika and Ričice.

During the interwar period the newly-formed Yugoslavian State Railway faced the challenges of rebuilding and integrating railway lines inherited from former Habsburg domains along with those in Serbia and Montenegro, while reorienting traffic flows to reflect the needs of the new country. During this time the route to Split was particularly important, as it served as a principle Yugoslavian port. The popularity of the Dalmatian coast encouraged travel on the route, and passenger trains carried through carriages from major European centres including Bucharest, Budapest, Krakow, Prague and Vienna. The 1930s compendium *Railway Wonders of the World* featured Yugoslavian railways, highlighting its creative means of attracting traffic, including offering honeymooning couples half fare (providing they travelled within two weeks of their wedding).

Traversing the Zagreb–Split railway, 1976 (top).

Building the Zagreb–Split railway; one of the first trains on the line; Sinj and Kliš stations (above).

HELLENIC STATE RAILWAYS

The Railways of Early Modern Greece

The lore of ancient Greece is core to Western culture, while for centuries Greece was firmly under the yoke of the Ottoman Turks. The Greek cause for freedom inspired Western romantics, with poet Lord Byron leading the charge (and perishing from fever before completing his crusade). The modern Greek state emerged in 1832 at the dawn of the railway age, yet Greece was the last major nation in Europe to embrace the iron horse, its first railway only completed in 1869. This line, just over 10 km long, connected Athens and the port of Piraeus on Phaleron Bay. The route was electrified in 1904, and offered a frequent passenger service.

Greece's first railway, Athens–Piraeus, 1869 (above).

The Athens–Piraeus Railway being built through Omonia (right top).

The goods yard at Thessalonika, 1936 (right bottom).

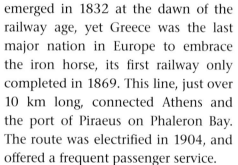

Main lines were even slower to gain ground, partly because of Greece's exceptionally difficult geography, its relative isolation from the rest of Europe, and its historic dependence on maritime transport. By 1904 a standard gauge line had been built north from Piraeus and Athens to Chakis. Gradually this route was extended via Thebes, Larissa and Platy. It was finally connected with the rest of the European network in 1916.

For many years Greece's primary international link was near the Yugoslavian frontier at Ghevgheli (now the Macedonian town of Gevgelija). This sinuous steeply-graded line formed the backbone of the Greek network, which became the Hellenic State Railways in 1920. Secondary lines reached from Gefyra west to Kalabaka, and east to Velestino, Volos and Milies. More extensive railways were constructed in northern Greece, reaching eastwards towards Constantinople (Istanbul) via Drama and Alexandropoulos.

By the mid-1930s Greece had more than 2,500 km of track, including narrow gauge railways, but it never developed

an extensive overlapping network with parallel or redundant routes. One of the few areas of parallel infrastructure was on the original route near Athens. In its latter steam days, Greek railways operated some of the largest locomotives in Europe, massive 2–10–0s built near to American proportions.

Greek State Railways 2–8–2 No. 721 at Megara station between Athens and Corinth, early 1940s (top).

The original Athens–Piraeus railway running along St Panteleimon Street on the outskirts of Athens, 1899 (left).

Marina, one of the original Athens–Piraeus locomotives, which worked the line up to electrification in 1904 (above middle).

Nauplion station in the Peleponnese, 1911 (above right).

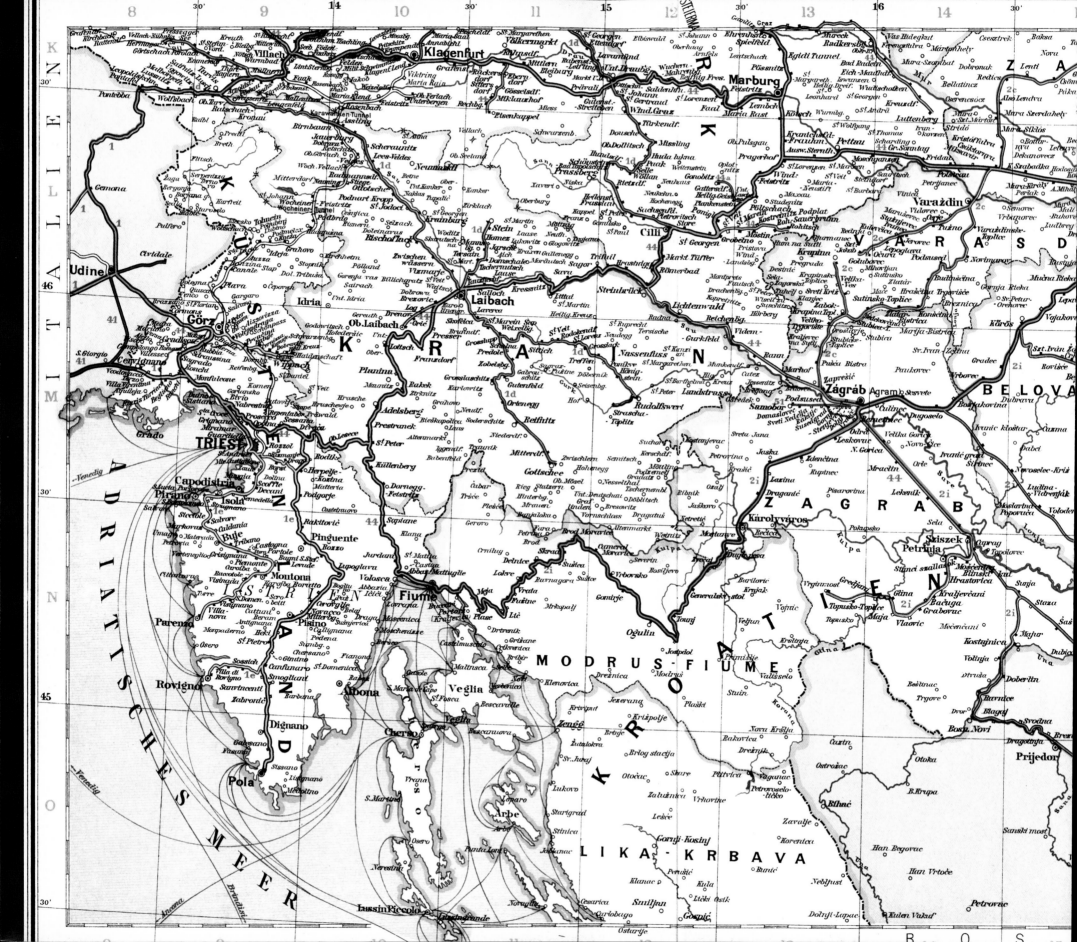

IBERIA

Spain's pioneer railway was a short Mediterranean coastal line connecting Barcelona with Materó. Planned in 1843, and built three years later, it was for several years an isolated curiosity. Spanish railways were largely financed by French investors, and like the French network primary lines radiated from the capital to provincial centres. In 1844 routes were planned connecting Madrid with Cadiz, Alicante and Leon. In contrast with typical continental railways, which embraced the British standard 4 feet 8½ inch (1.44 m) track gauge, Spanish railways opted for a broad standard, close to 5 feet 6 inches (originally about 1.67 m, later narrowed slightly) between the

rails. By 1923, there were 11,379 km of Iberian broad gauge operating in Spain, with additional routes in Portugal.

Regional narrow gauge networks were also developed, and numerous small railway companies operated short routes, largely in northern Spain and Andalusia. By 1923 narrow gauge routes totalled some 3,540 km. These quaint and colourful lines not only operated some of the most unusual equipment, but traversed some of the most spectacular and difficult territory, which attracted visitors from far afield.

By the end of the nineteenth century Spain's primary railways were operated by overlapping regional companies. The Norte Company (Compañia de los Caminos de Hierro del Norte) connected Madrid with Irun at the French frontier, along with routes reaching Oviedo, Bilbao, Valencia, Tarragonia and Barcelona. The Madrid, Saragossa and Alicante (officially Compañia de los Ferrocarriles de Madrid a Zaragoza y a Alicante, known as the MZA) connected its namesakes with myriad points in southern Spain, reaching from French to Portugese frontiers. The Madrid, Caceres and Portugal, and Andalusian Railways served their respective regions.

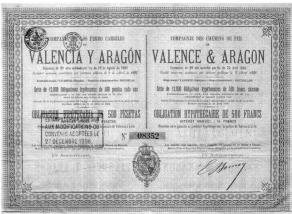

Never prosperous, Spanish broad gauge railways were ravaged during the Spanish Civil War (1936–39); most routes were nationalised in 1941 as the Red Nacional de los Ferrocarriles Españoles (universally known by its initials RENFE), while many narrow gauge lines continued in private operation. At the dawn of the twentieth century Spain's railways were considered among the most primitive in Europe, yet by the 1990s they were operating some of the most modern, fastest and most punctual trains on the continent.

Spain's first railway, the short line between Barcelona and Materó: the line's first locomotive and Barcelona station, 1843 (left above and below).

Barcelona station in 1900 (above top).

A share certificate for the Valencia and Aragon Railway, 1880 (above).

Pancorbo: Passing Train, by Darío de Regoyos y Valdés, 1901 (Museu Nacional d'Art de Catalunya) (opposite).

FROM THE FRENCH BORDER TO MADRID

Through the Cantabrian Mountains

The International Bridge and station at Irún (below); top photograph c.1932, bottom photograph 1912.

The *Sud Express* in southern France, hauled by Midi 2–4–2 locomotive No. 343, 1886 (right).

Inauguration of the Northern Railway in San Sebastián, August 1864 (far right).

Many visitors' first Spanish railway experience was crossing the French–Spanish frontier between Hendaye and Irun, then continuing southwards via Norte Company's line toward Madrid. To facilitate international movements, the famed international bridge connecting Hendaye and Irun carried both Spanish broad gauge and French standard gauge tracks (with a parallel narrow gauge line on a separate span). This was the route of the famed *Sud Express* from Paris to Madrid (and for a time to Lisbon), which until the First World War was a luxurious long distance limited deemed one of the 'world's most comfortable trains'.

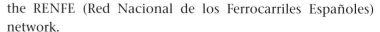

Not all of Norte's trains were so salubrious. In Victorian times, visitors arriving from France by local trains were aghast at the sorry state of Norte's second and third class carriages. As late as the 1960s Spanish railways continued to offer three classes of travel – the last in Europe to do so. In 1950, the Madrid–Irun route was first to use new streamlined lightweight TALGO trains. These flashy trains operated on expedited schedules making them emblematic of modern improvements to the RENFE (Red Nacional de los Ferrocarriles Españoles) network.

The Irun to Madrid route initially featured oceanside running, and from San Sebastian offered stunning views of the semicircular Bay of La Concha, yet craggy summits alluded to difficult mountainous trackage beyond. This route featured a saw-tooth profile with summits at Cegama (668 m above sea level), Quintanapalla (909 m), and the highest west of Espinar (1,292 m). Steep climbs resulted in slow running; trains working toward Madrid would take a helper locomotive at Beasain. Weaving its way toward the high summit the line would then repeatedly cross the river Oria, while passing through numerous short tunnels. The famed Pancorbo Pass was a scenic highlight; here the line was engineered on a high shelf above the river gorge.

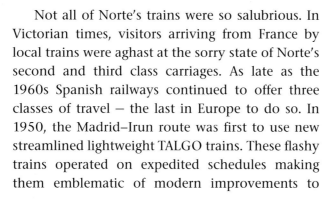

The dramatic
Pancorbo Pass –
1856, 1963, and
today.

MADRID TO BARCELONA

Early Spanish Long-Distance Expresses

The roof of Madrid's Atocha Station, still proudly proclaiming its MZA roots (above top).

Port-Bou in 1936 (above).

Two of MZA's famed Garratts; a workhorse locomotive in the late 1940s, and restored ex-RENFE 282F-0421 hauling a tourist passanger train between Lleida and La Pobla de Segur (right).

After the Norte Company, the MZA or Compañia de los Ferrocarriles de Madrid a Zaragoza y a Alicante (Madrid, Saragossa and Alicante Railway Company) was the second largest of Spain's traditional railways. It dated from 1857, when it was envisioned as a system connecting its namesakes. In 1898 it absorbed the 'Red Catalana' system, which provided a through route from Madrid to Barcelona and beyond by skirting the southern Pyrenees to the French frontier at Port-Bou.

At first a separate station was maintained at Barcelona for trains to France, but in the 1920s this was deemed inadequate and a new station took its place. The wall of the Pyrenees precluded extensive railway construction, and until new lines were built in the 1920s MZA's southern connection with the French network was the only other direct outlet with the continental system after Norte's connection at Irun. As at Irun, this involved a gauge change for through traffic, and most passengers switched trains at the border. By the 1930s MZA's network reached more than 695 km, connecting important cities in the south of Spain including Seville, Alicante, Toledo, and the Portugese frontier town of Badajoz.

In its later years, MZA's expresses were noted for their compound 4–6–2 Pacific steam locomotives built by the German firms of Maffei and Henschel & Son. Following the formation of RENFE in 1941, the longest passenger run in Spain was the 1,133 km service between Barcelona and Seville, travelling over lines formerly operated by both Norte and MZA. It ran via Valencia and Alcazar de San Juan, which until the 1960s famously operated Garratt steam locomotives between Tarragona and Valencia. The Garratt was an abnormally large articulated type featuring a suspended boiler, and was popular on British imperial lines; the RENFE service was a rare example of its use in passenger operation in Western Europe.

Mataró station, 1914 (above left).

Barcelona, Estació de França (France Station) under construction, 1929 (above).

Alicante station, *c.*1930 (right).

Cartagena station, 1897 (left).

MADRID TO ALICANTE

The Slowest 'Expresses' in Europe

The terminals of MZA's Madrid-Alicante route – Madrid Atocha Station in the early 1930s and Alicante c.1911 (above).

MZA's Madrid to Alicante route opened in 1858, the first of Spain's railway lines to connect Madrid with the Mediterranean coast. This line ran due south from the capital, running 49 km to the junction at Aranjuez, where the line toward Alicante diverged from the route toward Cuerna, later extended as a direct route from Madrid to Valencia. On its way, MZA's Alicante route passed Alcazar de San Juan, famous for the massive windmills of Cervantes' fictional *Don Quixote*. Alcazar de San Juan was also an important junction where one route diverged south-westerly toward Cordoba and Seville, also carrying traffic for Lisbon via the junction at Manzanares. The line to Alicante continued south via Albacete, beyond which was the junction at Chinchilla for a route to Murcia.

From Victorian times, and well into the twentieth century, Spain's long-distance trains were notoriously some of the slowest 'express' trains in Western Europe. The most important trains connecting Madrid with coastal destinations tended to be scheduled nocturnally. In his 1923 book *The Railways of Spain,* George L. Boag explains: 'The dweller on the coast, with business in the Capital, gets into his sleeping car in the afternoon or evening, dines in the restaurant car … smokes and chats with his fellow travellers and sleeps through the rest of the journey until he awakes in Madrid.'

Intercity travel was viewed as much a social event as a journey, so there was little incentive to speed up trains. At that

time the 64 km per hour sprint from Madrid to Aranjuez was among the fastest on the Madrid–Alicante run. By comparison, today's AVE races overland at speeds reaching 300 km/h, connecting Madrid with Seville, Malaga, Barcelona and other destinations. Unlike most Spanish broad gauge lines, AVE routes were constructed to the 4 foot $8^1/_2$ inch standard, making them compatible for eventual connection with the rest of the European network.

Two views of the busy station and yard at Alcazar de San Juan; a bird's-eye of the station in 1941, and the main platforms in 1908 (opposite right).

The MZA station at Colonia Santa Eulalia, 1900 (left).

MADRID TO PORTUGAL

Lisbon's Elegant Stations and Traditional Trams

Spanish railways had a variety of gateways with its Iberian neighbour, with which it shared the Iberian broad gauge, thus facilitating through train operation. Among the direct routes between Madrid and Lisbon was the route historically operated by the Sociedad de los Ferrocarriles de Madrid a Caceres y a Portugal (the Madrid, Caceres and Portugal) — among the lines nationalised as RENFE after the Spanish Civil War. Running due west from Madrid toward Lisbon, the company also operated connecting routes from Plasencia to Salamanca, Zamora and Astorga, and a short branch to Caceres. It crossed the Spanish–Portugese frontier at Marvao, with the natural continuation of the route in Portugal via Abrantes, Entroncamento (a junction with a route to Porto), and on to Lisbon. Alternative cross-border routes included the MZA line running west from Ciudad Real via Merida and Aljucen to the border crossing at Badajos, a pair of border crossings west of Salamanca, and a north-west crossing at Valença de Minho.

Lisbon is spectacularly situated on seven hills rising above the River Tagus,

The opening ceremony of the Avila–Salamanca Railway, 1926 (above).

Rossio Station, Lisbon: under construction, 1886; signs at the station entrance, 1910; street scene in front of the station, 1900 (right).

and features a plethora of interesting railways. Where most Iberian cities abandoned their tram networks between the 1950s and 1970s, Lisbon retained its trams and inclined railways, at the same time preserving the historic character of the cars and lines. The city has several railway terminals, of which Rossio with its elegant façade featuring oval doorways is largely used for local and suburban services. Santa Apolonia station was preferred for long-distance services as well as

118

serving suburban traffic. From the Cais do Sodré station, trains depart westward along the north shore of the river toward the coastal towns of Estoril and Cascais on a line opened in 1895 as the Estoril Railway. This route was electrified with 1,500 volts direct current overhead wires in 1926.

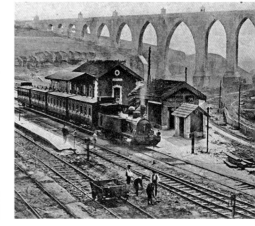

Madrid's Santa Apolonia Station, 1865 (top left).

Campolide, an important junction north of Madrid, 1901 (above).

Madrid trams: an overfull tram, 1940s; trams on the Avenida 24 de Julho, 1910 (bottom left).

SPAIN'S NORTH COAST

Railways of a Mountainous Coastline

Spain's north coast faces the Bay of Biscay, an area of exceptional scenic beauty with some of the country's most memorable railways. Historically, the broad gauge routes were the domain of Norte Company (part of RENFE after 1941), which, in addition to its primary Madrid to Irun main line, operated routes running from Zaragoza via Castejon and Pamplona to San Sebastian, and from Castejon via Miranda (with a junction on the Madrid–Irun line) to Bilbao. Additional routes ran northward from a junction on the Madrid–Irun line at Venta de Banos and dividing at Palencia. One line ran to Santander (among Spain's finest ports); another to Leon, Oviedo, and beyond to Gijon; a third followed a circuitous route via the historic Roman cities of Astorga and Lugo before climbing a 1,000 m summit on a 2 per cent twisting climb at Brañuelas to reach the scenically stunning port at Coruna.

Even more spectacular were northern Spain's narrow gauge routes, traditionally operated by a myriad of small railway companies. The oldest, the Langreo Railway, began as a coal-hauling line, running from mines at Sama de Langreo to the port of Gijon. Its tracks, at 4 feet 8½ inches (1.44 m), would be considered the standard

width in most countries, but in Spain it is lumped in with the other 'slim gauge' lines. Among its highlights was the exceptionally steep Florida Incline, operated with cables instead of locomotives. The incline survived until 1963, when it was finally replaced by line-relocation using a locomotive-worked grade with a tunnel.

Better known was the sinuous narrow gauge line running from Santander to Bilboa, featuring spectacular seaside running at Santander with stunning views of the mountains beyond. J.P. Pearson travelled the route in April 1897; he described his eastward journey from the Bay of Santander behind a tiny outside-cylinder 4–4–0 tank engine. This chuffed along at a leisurely 32 km/h with 'blue rippling water everywhere around us, the train running on a causeway for good distance'. He noted that the line crossed four causeways before beginning its ascent of the mountains. 'At Hoz de Anero, a ridgy mountain and a cone appear behind, and the line leaves the rich valleys and ascends to hillier ground.' He noted that passing Trento the line curved around and navigated a tunnel and some rock cuts, before a gorgeous bay was seen in the distance on the

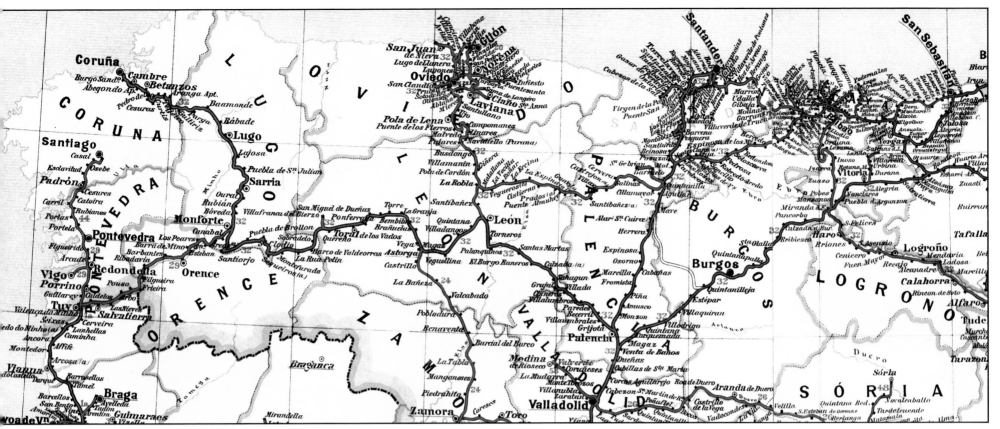

3. PUENTE VIESGO.—Estación.

Puerto de Pajares.—Túnel de La Cabeza

Librería de M. Albira, Santander
ASTILLERO: LA ESTACIÓN

left-hand side of the train. Reaching the famed Carranzo River Gorge, the scenery reached a crescendo, deemed the most spectacular on the Bilboa route, passing the rocking window of the train like a panorama; Pearson commented, 'threading a tunnel, grand crags appear in front, splendid side gorges open off the main one very frequently'. The precipitous walls of the gorge were punctuated by waterfalls.

Scenes from early twentieth century northern Spanish railways: Puente Viesgo on the Palencia–Santander line, 1904; Puerto de Pajares between León and Gijón, 1900; Astillero on the Santander–Bilbao line, 1898 (above).

Two views of Santander station in 1920: a general view of the station, and the Soto-Iruz Express leaving eastbound, headed by Engine No. 21 (opposite left).

Sama station on the Langreo Railway, 1905 (opposite right).

ANDALUSIAN RAILWAYS

To the Far South of Spain

SEVILLA — Estación del ferrocarril a Córdoba

Andalusia in the south-west is one of Spain's most colourful and fascinating regions, reaching from the Mediterranean coastal cities of Huelva, Cadiz, Algeciras, Malaga and Almeria to the rugged Sierra Nevada mountains and windswept deserts often used as settings for 'spaghetti western' films notionally set in the western United States. It is Europe's southernmost area, and represents a melding of European and northern African cultures, where Moorish presence distinguishes local architecture and customs.

Connecting Andalusia with Madrid and other regions were MZA's broad gauge main lines, later integral to the RENFE network. A premier train was the Madrid–Seville *Andalusian Express*. Seville served as an Andalusian gateway, and its locomotive shops at San Jeronimo featured a complete roundhouse with forty stalls which was the region's largest. This was the base for some of Europe's antique locomotives. Engines seen as antique before the First World War were still active more than fifty years later, some working daily with more than a century of service behind them.

Jerez station (left top), and the first train from Jerez to El Puerto, 1845 (left middle).

Seville station, 1898 (above).

The busy station at Bobadilla; 1940s, 1920, and 1900 (below).

122

The majority of Andalusian broad gauge lines, extending to 1,614 km, were historically operated by Compañia de los Ferrocarriles Andaluces (Andalusian Railways), which secured a near-monopoly on intercity traffic in the region. Its lines connected Seville with Cadiz, Algecirus, Grenada and Almeria among many other towns. As with most broad gauge companies this was melded into RENFE after the Spanish Civil War.

The crossroads of the region was the sleepy junction town of Bobadilla, where trains would converge from all directions several times daily allowing passengers to make connections, and perhaps grab a hasty meal. To the south was the spectacular line to Malaga which traversed the rugged El Chorro Gorge. Less known were some privately-operated narrow gauge lines built largely to tap mineral resources, among which were the British-owned Rio Tinto Company, and the 180-km-long Zafra–Huelva Railway, famed for using steam railcars in the 1930s.

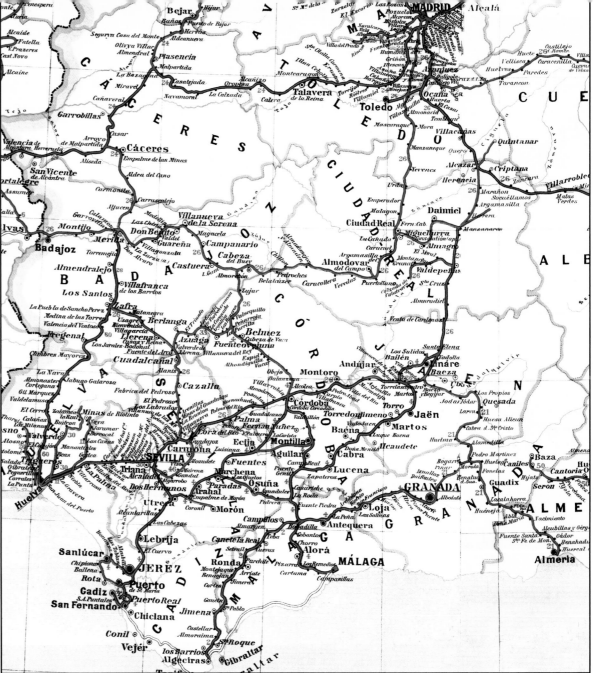

El Chorro station on the Granada–Malaga line, 1903 (far left).

Garratt locomotive No. 145 on the Rio Tinto railway, late 1940s (left).

2 · 1 · 0 · 1 · 2 · 3 · 4

44

TOULOUSE

F · R · A · N · C · E

GULF OF LYON

Dax
Orthés
Bayonne
Adour R.
S.Jean de Luz
Pau
Oléron
43
Narbonne
Tran
Oyarzun
Fuenterrabia
S. Sebastian
Pasages
Durango
bao
Tolosa
Hernani
Villabona
S. Juan Pied de Port
S.Bertrand
S.Gaudens
Perpignan
GASCONIA
Salete
S.A.Arlaban
Roncesvalles
Pic du Midi
Maladetta
Arambra
Olazaguttia
Vitoria
Salvatierra
Pamplona
Mont Perdu
Maladetta
Bellegarde
C. Cerbera
Estella
Monreal
R. Aragon
Broto
ANDORRA
C. de Greus
Peñacerrada
Sanguesa
R. Cinca
Tor
Rosas
Viana
Tafalla
S.Juan de la Peña
Urgel
CERDA
Ripoll
El Ampurdan
Ampurias
Varia
Olite
Jaca
R.Essera
R.Noguera
Ongardya
Berga
Torruella
rono
R.Gallego
Averbe
Gradu
R.Noguera
Sol sona
Cardona
Vich
Gerona
42
Corella
Tudela
Guarga
Barbastro
R.Segre
Manresa
Caldas
Palamos
Tarazona
Borja
Zueta
Almudebar
Peñusa
Isona
Montserrat
Feliu de Guixols
CATALUÑA
Granollers
Rostalrich
Tordera
Pozuelo
Alagon
Huesca
Monzon
Balaguer
Guisona
Cervera
Igualada
Tarrasa
S. Celoni
Blanes
Epila
Zaragoza
Sa.
R.Suda
Lerida
Urgessabadell
La Roca
Calella
Villa de Muel Ru.
de Alcubierre
Peñalva
Martorell
Mataro
Arenys de Mar
Caurinena
Ielsa
La Graria
Montblanch
Molins
Villa Franca
Badalona
Belchite
R.Ebro
Mequinenza
Montblanch
San Boy
Guermeda Ru.
Ixar
Fayon
Bebrus
Reus
Vendrel
BARCELONA
41
Daroca
Caspe
Mora
Falset
Arcos
Monaspe
Tarragona
Medinaceli
Bello
Tornos
Alcaniz
Cambrils
Molina
Calanda
Submarine Telegraph
Val-conchon
Calamocha
Tortosa
G. de Amposta
Montalban
R.Guadalupe
Zurita
Ebro R.
I. Buda
Mezquita
Amposta
Puerto de los Alfaques
Forcall
Morella
Albarracin
S. Matheo
Vinaroz
Teruel
Beniarlo
BALEARIC ISLANDS
Cuevas
Peñiscola
MENORCA (MINORCA)
MALLORCA (MAJORCA)
C. Cavalaria
C. Sella
40
Cuenca
R.Mijares
Oropesa
Ciudadela
Mahon
P. Mahon
Pajaron
Viver
Castellon de la Plana
C. Formenton
C. Dartuch
Ayre I.
Columbretes I.s
Pollenza
Jerica
Villareal
Aleudia
Sineu
C. Pera
NUEVA
Segorbe
Palma
Manacor
Liria
Murviedro
Drayonera I.

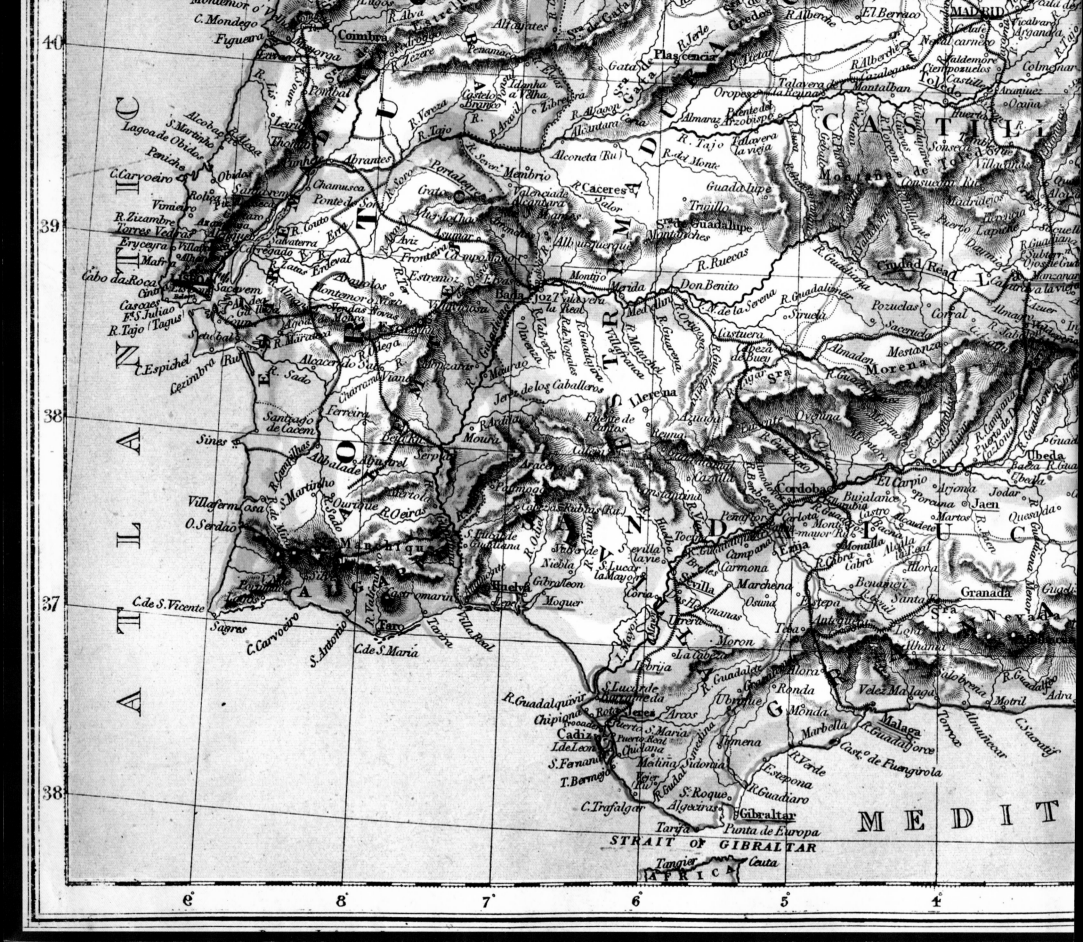

LETTS'S POPULAR ATLAS.

RAILWAY & STATISTICAL MAP OF

SPAIN & PORTUGAL

Scale 55 Miles to the Inch.

Railways ‹‹‹‹‹

C. *Cape.* I. *Island.* M. *Mount.* R. *River.* S. *San.* Sᵗᵃ *Saint.*
Sᵗᵃ *Sierra Mountain.* T. *Tower.* (Ru) *Ruins.*

THE PORTION OF THE MAP TINTED GREEN INDICATES THE WINE GROWING DISTRICTS OF THE COUNTRY; THE PLACES UNDERLINED YELLOW BEING CENTRES OF THE WHITE WINE, RED THE RED WINE, AND ORANGE THE LIQUEUR TRADE.

COMPARATIVE AREA and POPULATION:—

	English Square Miles.	Population.	Population per Sq. Mile.
England and Wales	58,320	22,712,266	389
Spain	182,758	16,625,860	90
Portugal ...	36,510	3,995,152	108

Cities with population exceeding 100,000   MADRID.

The famous historical divisions of Spain and Portugal are retained in this Map; the present divisions are named after their chief towns and the latter are underlined.

2 West of 1 Greenwich. 0 East of 1 Greenwich. 2 3

CENTRAL EUROPE

The Ludwigsbahn and the Origins of German Railways

In 1834 King Ludwig I of Bavaria gave royal approval to construction of a short railway connecting Nuremberg and Fürth. On 7 December 1835, history was made when the Robert Stephenson & Company-built Patentee-type locomotive *Der Adler* (*The Eagle*) hauled the first public train on German soil. The pioneer railway, known as the Ludwigsbahn — named in honour of the king — set the wheels turning for railways across Germany. The inspiration for the commissioning of the line is widely attributed to German-born Friedrich List, an early railway visionary, who had emigrated to America where he worked building anthracite lines in Pennsylvania before returning home in 1832 to work on Germany's first practical steam railways.

The Ludwigsbahn's original facilities were constructed on a small scale: railway historian Hamilton Ellis described Nuremberg's station as 'a modest facility', explaining that in its early days the Ludwigsbahn was almost exclusively a passenger line, its first freight shipment appropriately being casks of beer. Ninety years after the line opened it was closed as a steam-powered railway, re-opening five years later as an interurban electric line.

At the dawn of its railway age, German unification was still more than three decades away, so instead of a centrally focused system, such as those in France or Spain, Germany built railways from multiple origins, each serving the needs of an individual German state, its cities and territories. Within five years of opening of the first line, railway schemes were under way in several German states. Although in the early years German railways were hampered by the lack of central planning, because Germany had multiple nodes its railways rapidly developed into a complex interconnecting network.

This arrangement was well suited to industrialisation, and facilitated rapid travel between cities and across the country. Berlin, Dresden, Frankfurt, Hamburg, Munich and Stuttgart all benefited as important railway centres.

Early German railway building was largely the result of private development, but by the 1850s the strategic importance of an efficient and uniform railway system was seen as a state concern. The first significant state railway system began in Bavaria in 1846, and by the 1880s Royal Bavarian Railways operated more than 4,100 route km. Prince Otto Von Bismarck, who unified Germany in the early 1870s, anticipated the unified state control of German railways. Though this took a half a century to be realised, the Royal Prussian State Railways, formed in 1850, aggressively acquired private railways throughout the 1870s and 1880s, at the same time extending control to adjacent states.

The process of state control took decades. Clement Edwards, in his 1898 book *Railway Nationalization*, noted that in Bavaria state railways comprised 3,170 miles (5,101 km) in comparison with 548 miles (882 km) of private lines. By that time Prussia's railways were largely under state control, with only 1,712 km in private operation, compared with 24,422 km operated by the state railways.

Despite these regional differences, German railways benefited from uniform methods of operation and exceptionally high service standards. In the early 1900s a British commentator noted that German second class carriages provided decidedly better accommodation than those of British first class.

The First World War brought decades of chaos to Germany's railways. As a result of the war Germany lost considerable territory and a much scaled back network. In the early 1920s the Weimar government consolidated most of Germany's state railways as the Reichbahn.

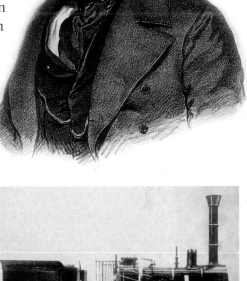

Economist and early German railway visionary Friedrich List (above top).

A photograph of *Der Adler* locomotive taken in the 1850s (above).

Der Adler (*The Eagle*) on its first run on the Ludwigsbahn on 7 December 1835 (opposite).

BERLIN-DRESDEN-PRAGUE

Railways through Saxony

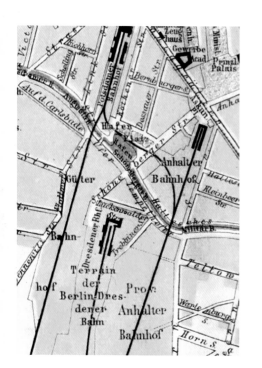

As the Prussian capital, Berlin rapidly emerged as Germany's greatest railway hub, and by mid-century was ringed by terminal stations. By 1838 Berlin had two short railways, one running to Zehlendorf, the other to Potsdam, and longer inter-city lines were not very far behind.

One of the most important longer lines linked Berlin and Dresden; Dresden trains were traditionally served by the aptly named Dresdener Bahnhof, although services were later shifted to the Anhalter Bahnhof. The Dresden–Leipzig route, opened in 1839, was among Germany's earliest main lines, and notably included Germany's first railway tunnel, near Oberau, which was 513 metres long. The Dresden and Leipzig Railway also developed Germany's pioneer domestically-built steam engine in 1839 (Germany's earliest locomotives were British and American imports). Patriotically named *Saxonia*, this locomotive featured a non-standard 0–4–2 wheel arrangement.

The capital of Saxony, Dresden had a population in 1914 of approximately 548,000; it was the region's cultural centre, described in *Bradshaw's Guide* as known for its 'art, music, and good society'. It was served by two primary stations – Dresden Hauptbahnhof in the Alt Stadt (old city), and Dresden Neustadt (in the

newer city developed opposite the Elbe from the historic centre). Writing in *The Railway Magazine*, George A. Wade remarked that Dresden Hauptbahnhof lent an appearance of 'dignity and beauty' to the traveller, with the tracks covered by twin-arched train sheds, the interior offering 'a light and airy appearance'. The arrangement featured elevated through tracks above street level, with lower level central stub terminal tracks. Construction began in 1892 and was completed by 1898.

The magnificent Friedrich August Brücke, built in 1910, spanned the Elbe connecting the two stations. In 1912, the 180 km run from Berlin to Dresden could be completed in two and a half hours.

While the railways connecting Berlin, Leipzig and Dresden were constructed over the easy terrain of open river plains, Saxony State Railway's route running south-east from Dresden toward Prague followed the sinuous Elbe River gorge through Sächsische Schweiz, or 'Saxon Switzerland'. It passed through

the picturesque resort towns of Königstein, Bad Schandau and Schöna, whose stratified cliffs made a stunning backdrop. At Tetschen, then a Bohemian town and today the Czech town of Decín, the railway emerged from the confines of the gorge and divided to follow parallel lines on both sides of the river toward Ústí nad Labem. The main route to Prague then moved away from the Elbe, following the Ohre and then the Vltava. A 1914 schedule reveals that the 6 a.m. train from Dresden Hauptbahnhof paused at Schandau at 7.18 and at Tetschen at 8.35, arriving in Prague at 11.50.

Among Saxony State Railway's named trains was the famed *Karlsbad Express*, which included a section running from Berlin to Dresden, then via Tetschen to the renowned Bohemian health spa at Karlsbad (now Karlovy Vary in the Czech Republic). Karlsbad's popularity with wealthy travellers meant it was worthwhile to run seasonal through carriages to Brussels, Paris, Vienna and Warsaw.

Dresdner and Anhalter stations on an 1875 plan of Berlin (opposite top left).

Anhalter Bahnhof, 1900 (opposite right).

Dresden Hauptbahnhof, *c*.1900 (opposite bottom left).

Saxonia, the first German locomotive; built in Übigau by Johann Schubert for the Leipzig–Dresden line, 1838–9 (below).

Bridge over the Elbe on the Saxon-Bohemian railway in Dresden (above right).

The first train on the Leipzig–Dresden railway in 1837 (right).

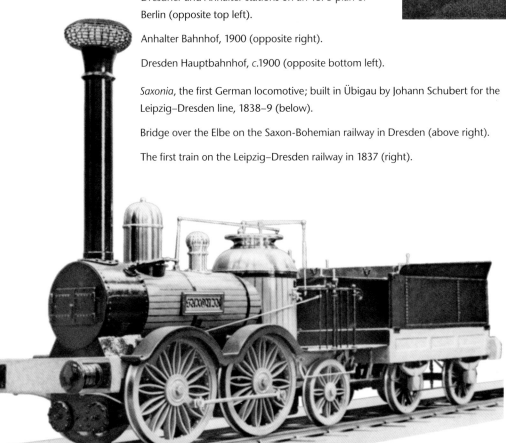

HAMBURG TO BERLIN

Germany's First High-Speed Link

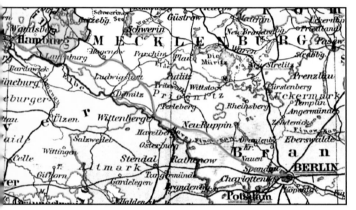

Hamburg and Berlin were and still are two of the most important cities in Germany, Hamburg being the largest German port and one of Europe's principal commercial centres, as well as historically the largest of three free Hanseatic towns of the German Empire, and Berlin emerged as the capital city following Bismarck's unification of Germany. Railway lines radiated from both cities across Germany, but the most important by far was the route that connected them.

From the traveller's point of view, the most noteworthy aspect of this route was its high-speed service. Even in the 1890s this was a very fast line, and the 286 km run was accomplished by express trains in less than four hours, including station stops and a pause for up to six minutes at Wittenberge to change locomotives, with end-to-end speeds averaging 80 km/h. The swift run was a blessing in more ways than one; speed was a novelty in itself, amusing the traveller while minimising journey time, but also there was not a lot to see on the way. In his 1932 memoir *Railways and Scenery*, the avid railway traveller J.P. Pearson made this quite clear, writing that 'no one would be likely to describe the scenery of the Berlin to Hamburg Line in very high terms,' an especially poignant statement from a man who, having

travelled widely in Germany, believed that the country was 'a virtual Mecca for the railway enthusiast.' Much of the journey consisted of relatively flat and monotonous terrain, occasionally punctuated by pine forests and river crossings.

Before Hamburg consolidated its railway terminals in 1906, trains for Berlin departed the aptly named Berliner Bahnhof, located in the east of the city. The new Hamburg Hauptbahnhof, built to replace four earlier stations, was a twentieth-century marvel, among the last big terminal stations built in Germany during the classic era.

Among places of interest along the line was Bergedorf, just a few miles outside Hamburg, where *Baedeker's Guide* of 1900 for Northern Germany noted that 'the peasant-women of the *Vierlande,* wearing a peculiar and picturesque costume, offer fruit and flowers for sale.' Further along at Friedrichsruh, where Germany's unifier, Bismarck, took his last painful breaths on 30 July 1898. After a rapid sprint eastward, the line crossed the River Havel, and then the Spree near Spandau just five miles from Berlin.

After the closure of the older Hamburger Bahnhof in the 1880s, Hamburg trains used the Lehrter Bahnhof located alongside the Spree north-west of the Königsplatz. Unlike smaller German cities in the twentieth century, Berlin never benefited from a centrally unified Hauptbahnhof, and continued to be served by a variety of terminals interconnected by its famous Ringbahn urban railway. Berlin's long-discussed Hauptbahnhof was finally completed in 2006 — a century after Hamburg's magnificent terminal.

The Berlin–Hamburg line in 1893 (opposite top left).

Lehrter Bahnhof, Berlin, 1900 (opposite bottom left).

The *Fliegender Hamburger*, which ran regularly between Berlin (Lehrter Bahnhof) and Hamburg Hauptbahnhof (opposite bottom middle). In 1933 the train travelled the 286 km in 138 minutes, averaging 124 km/h.

On 21 June 1931 the propeller-driven *Schienenzeppelin* experimental railcar ran the 257 km route between Hamburg Bergedorf and Berlin Lehrter in Berlin in 98 minutes, reaching a top speed of 230 km/h, a world record for rail vehicles that was not broken until 1955 (opposite bottom right).

An ICE-T high-speed train passes through Paulinenaue on the Berlin–Hamburg high-speed line (opposite right).

Hamburg Hauptbahnhof in 2009, among the last big terminal stations built in Germany during the classic era – the inset shows a postcard from 1906, the year construction was completed (top right).

Berlin's Hauptbahnhof, completed in 2006 (right).

THE RHINE VALLEY

Germany's Classic Riverside Route

The Rhine Valley is one of the continent's great trans-European corridors. Because it reaches the North Sea closer to the Atlantic than most other major European navigable waterways, it has historically carried a tide of freight and passenger trade. *Bradshaw's Continental Guide* of August 1914, published on the eve of the Great War, informs travellers that 'The River Rhine is abundantly interesting from its impetuous source to its sluggish meeting with the sea.'

Railway development quickly augmented this well-established thoroughfare as new lines reached Köln from a variety of North Sea ports, funnelling traffic down the river's parallel railways built on each side of the river toward Frankfurt. These busy double-track lines, mirroring each other on the Rhein's 'left' (west) and 'right' (east) banks, traverse some of the most colourful and picturesque scenery in central Europe. Each bend in the river reveals a medieval castle, fortress or church, often precariously clinging to rocks and cliffs high above the water, while vineyards, villages, farmland and forest roll by in an unending tapestry of nature and human activity.

Long considered one of Europe's great railway journeys, the traverse of the Rhine between Köln and Frankfurt was often conceived as part of a greater adventure, part of the premier route for travellers from Britain, the low countries, and northern France, to Bavaria, Switzerland, the Mediterranean, the Balkans and beyond. At Köln the lengthy balloon-shed of the Hauptbahnhof is situated on the left bank of the river, which is spanned by the nearby Hohenzollern Bridge. This massive structure was constructed between 1907 and 1911; originally it carried four railway tracks, plus a road and tram lines. It was almost completely destroyed during the Second World War, and rebuilt with six tracks and the road and trams relocated. Looming above the station and bridge is Köln's famous Dom, a cathedral deemed to be the ultimate execution of the Gothic style in Germany.

In addition to the two main line railways connecting Köln and Bonn, there was the Vorgebirgsbahn, named for the coal-rich hills west of the river, and the interurban electric Rheinuferbahn. Bonn is best known as the birthplace of the German classical composer Ludwig van Beethoven. A few miles south of Bonn the right bank railway passes Königswinter; here a short rack and pinion railway ascended the Drachenfels (Dragon Rock), where legend has it Siegfried slew his dragon. Originally a steam-powered line, this was later converted to electric operation.

At Koblenz, where the town dates from Roman times, the Rhein meets the Mosel. Across the river, on the right bank, the Ehrenbreitstein fortress sits more than 85 m above the railway.

The most scenic stretch of the Rhine journey greeted travellers south of Koblenz – this is the 'Mittel-Rhein', where the gorge narrows and the river twists and turns wildly. Boppard, located on the left bank near an elbow bend, has long been a popular resort. Near Kaub, on the right bank, the famed Pfalzgrafenstein sits mid-river, built as a fourteenth-century toll gate by Holy Roman Emperor Ludwig. A few miles beyond on the left bank is Oberwesel, a historic walled town where the railway bisects its medieval towers. Toward Mainz the river valley broadens again; at Mainz, a major junction, some trains ran eastward along the Main to Frankfurt, while others continued southward toward Switzerland.

Burg Pfalzgrafenstein with Burg Gutenfels in the background, c.1900 (opposite top left).

Opening of the Cologne–Bonn railway at Augustusburg Palace, Brühl in 1844, painted by Nikolaus Christian Hohe (opposite bottom left).

Button from Bonn–Cölner Eisenbahn staff uniform (opposite bottom right).

Frankfurt am Main Hauptbahnhof (top two photographs).

Pfaffendorfer railway bridge in Koblenz, 1895. The former palace of the Kürfürst of Trier is in the background (right).

Ehrenbreitstein Fortress in Koblenz (below).

A Rheine panorama souvenir from 1905 (next two pages).

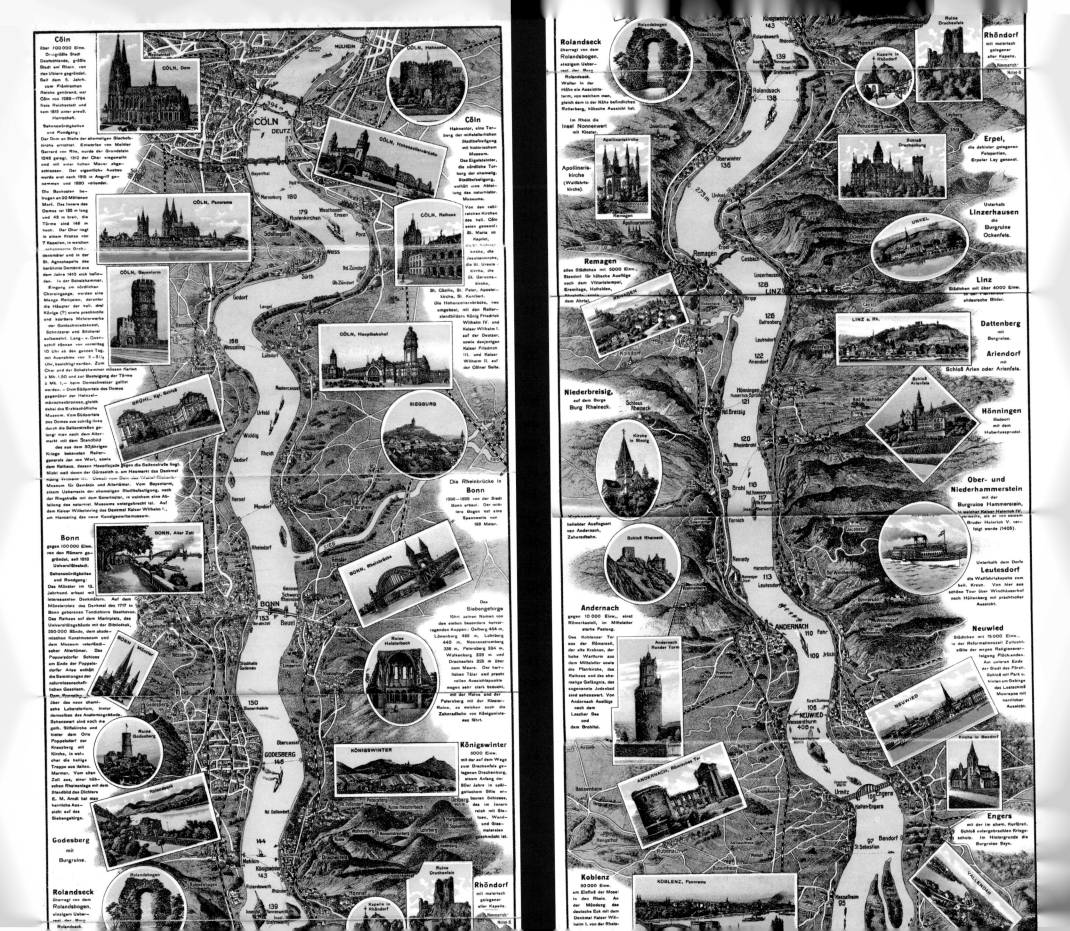

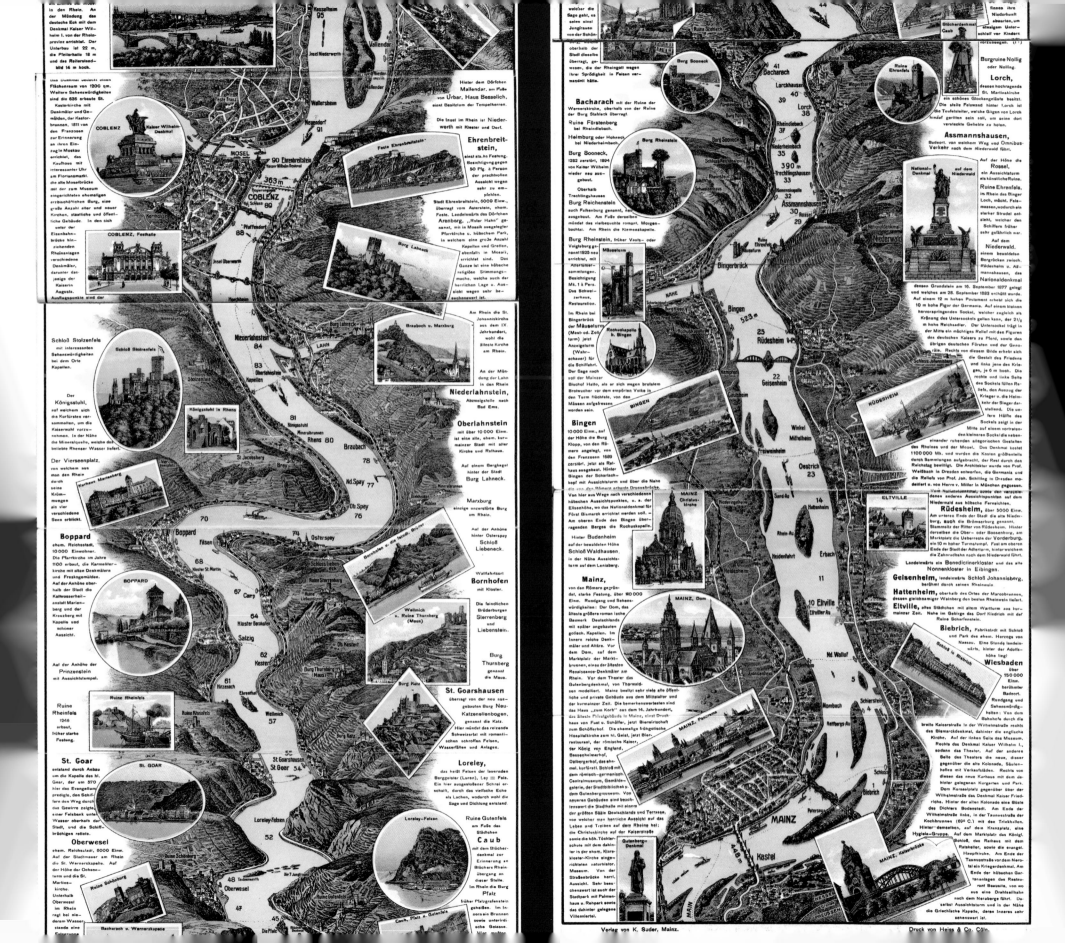

VIENNA–BRATISLAVA–BUDAPEST

Early Railways in Hungary

Hungary first considered railway development in the 1830s, and viewed early railway schemes as ways of improving its international standing. Following its failed revolution of 1848–49, its railway plans were invariably linked with Austria's, and for the next sixty-five years the two nations' affairs were integrated under the reign of the Habsburg emperor Franz Joseph.

The earliest of Hungary's railways was the Pozsony (now the Slovakian capital Bratislava) to Nagyszombat (now Slovakian Trnava) horse railway, a short suburban line that commenced operation in 1840. More significant was the Hungarian Central Railway between Pozsony (now the Slovakian capital Bratislava) and Pest, authorised in 1844 and constructed in sections over the next seven years. The first section to open was the 54 km line between Pest and Vác, which began operations in July 1846. An imported steam locomotive thrilled onlookers and passengers, and the 23 July 1846 *Budapest Híradó* newspaper described its first departure from the Pest terminal (near the location of the present day Nyugati Station): 'With a whinny or a whistle, the steam engine *Buda* and *Pest*, decked with flowers and flags, pulled the royal coach and seven passenger coaches out of the station to the great amazement of the assembled crowd.' Scheduled steam train services soon put Budapest less than an hour's travel from Vác.

Completion of the Hungarian Central route to Pozsony, and its link with Austria's Kaiser Ferdinands Nordbahn

via Marchegg, offered a through railway route between the principal Habsburg capitals. It rapidly emerged as one of Hungary's most important lines, and from the 1880s until the First World War it served as the preferred route for the famed *Orient Express* between Vienna and Budapest.

During their first few decades, Hungarian railways vacillated between private and state control. In 1868 most railways were consolidated under the banner of the Royal Hungarian State Railway, which continued to build new lines until the onset of the First World War. Following the war, the Treaty of Trianon fragmented the former Habsburg domains, stripping Hungary of much of its former territory. As a result Hungary lost an estimated 38 per cent of its railway network, and new international frontiers cut across its lines at forty-nine locations. New railway centres emerged at frontier towns, many of which had previously had little importance for railway operations.

Hungary's first railway tunnel was located immediately west of Pozsony's main station. This terminal has even greater significance today, being the primary station for Bratislava — capital of independent Slovakia. Leaving the curving terminal, the line toward Budapest runs high above Bratislava, gradually curving around the city, passing industry and goods yards. Much of the run stays far north of the Danube, which follows a winding southerly course ill-suited to a direct railway line. J.P. Pearson travelled the route in 1896, the 'golden age' of Hungarian railways. He marvelled at the peculiarities of the Hungarian language and admired the scenery, noting that 'from Naymaros, we had splendid mountains and valleys opposite us on the far bank and, before Zebegeny, a grand view ahead to a range of mountains, with two cones rising above the sweep of the river.'

Hungarian 4–8–0 locomotive at Budapest West, 1972 (opposite top).

Kaiser Ferdinand's insignia on the station in Bielsko-Biala (opposite middle).

Kaiser Ferdinand Nordbahnhof, Vienna, 1908 – departure point for trains to Hungary (opposite bottom).

Western Railway Station (Nyugati Pályaudvar) in Budapest, Hungary, 2006 (right) and 1896 (bottom right).

Bratislava – the original station building from 1848 (below).

Pécs railway station, built in 1900 by Ferenc Pfaff, featuring reliefs depicting James Watt and George Stephenson (bottom).

KAISER FERDINAND'S NORDBAHN

The Beginning of Austria's Railways

Kaiser Ferdinand (above).

The patriotically-named Robert Stephenson-built locomotive *Austria* (below).

Jubilant citizens and gun salutes greet the arrival of the first train at Glöggnitz on 5 May 1842 (above right).

Austria's first major railway route was authorised in the 1830s under the reign of Kaiser Ferdinand, establishing a tradition of naming Austrian railways after key members of the Habsburg monarchy. Although Austria was initially hesitant to invest in railways, the strategic value of fast and reliable transport links soon urged the emperor forward.

Austria's Nordbahn was envisioned as linking Vienna, at the heart of the Habsburg Empire, with Austrian Galicia, then within Austria's domains near the frontier with Czarist Russia. The first section, between Floridsdorf and Deutsch Wagram, was opened in November 1837; Vienna was reached in 1838, and the extension to Brünn was completed in 1839.

Austria had yet to develop a railway supply industry, so it imported Robert Stephenson locomotives from Britain. The first three were symbolically named *Austria*, *Moravia* and *Vindobona* (the Roman name for Vienna), reflecting the places connected by the line. The railway reached Vienna from the north-east across eastern Moravia, connecting Lundenburg (now the Czech town of Breclav), to Prerau (Prerov), Ostrau (Ostrava) and Oderburg (Bohumín). The Nordbahn itself did not reach further north-east to reach Kraków directly, but its connection with other lines allowed for through Vienna–Kraków services, and beyond to Austrian Lemberg (now L'viv in the Ukraine). Secondary routes connected the principal cities of Brünn (Brno), and Olmutz (Olomouc), the historic capital of Moravia famed for its exceptional architecture.

During the nationalistic uprisings of 1848, the Habsburg royal family retreated from Vienna to Olmutz to avoid public hostility. Both Brünn and Olmutz later developed as major railway centres. An important link was constructed to reach Warsaw, then under Russian administration, so by 1845 there was a through railway corridor, which included the Nordbahn, running between Vienna and Warsaw.

Austria developed its primary railway network in the mid-nineteenth century, railway construction being hastened by the events of 1848–49 which demonstrated the urgent need to knit the Austro-Hungarian Empire together. The Südbahn reached south over the Alps to the Adriatic; the Kaiserin Elisabeth Bahn, built in the late 1850s, linked Vienna and Salzburg with later connections through the Inn valley to Innsbrück. In 1867 a second Alpine crossing to Italy was opened over the Brenner Pass. During the 1870s the Kaiser

Deutsch-Wagram station, 1830 (left).

The bridge at Emms on the Kaiserin-Elisabeth-Bahn, c.1860 (below).

Franz Josef Bahn reached north-west from Vienna, providing connections to Pilsen (Plsen) and Prague. In the 1880s the Vorarlberg Bahn was carved west from Innsbruck over difficult Alpine terrain to the Swiss frontier.

Compared with the Alpine railways and their necessary engineering, the Nordbahn offered a relatively simple route which angled across the lowlands of the Moravian plain on long sections of comparatively level tangent track. The October 1882 *Bradshaw's Guide* lists an express train making the 416.4 km run from Vienna to Kraków as departing at 8 a.m. and arriving at 9.42 p.m. By 1914 times were notably faster – the 7.28 a.m. express from Vienna Nord took a little more than 7 hours to make the run, and this with 12 minutes for a connection from Berlin via Breslau at Oderburg. Although scenically unimpressive, the Nordbahn's strategic importance ensured that it was a busy railway carrying freight and passengers to the northern reaches of the Habsburg Empire.

THE SÜDBAHN – THE SEMMERING ROUTE

A Pioneering Trans-Alpine Route

Karl Ritter von Ghega (above).

Steam locomotive at the Badelwand, 1954 (below).

Gallery at Weinzettelwand (right below).

Austria's Südbahn, spanning the Alps via the Semmering Pass, is undoubtedly one of the continent's most famous trunk routes. It was the first main line European railway built over difficult mountainous terrain, and set important engineering precedents for future construction. This sinuous line through forested Alpine scenery has long been one of central Europe's most enjoyable main lines for travellers. Envisioned as early as 1838, when American railways demonstrated the capabilities of mountain railways, it took another decade before construction began.

The section between Trieste and Mürzzuschlag, on the south slope of the Semmering, was finished first. The difficult alignment over the spine of the Semmering Pass was only completed in 1853, and the route opened in July 1854.

American influence was very evident in the early years of the Südbahn; not only had its engineers visited American railways to study construction techniques, but its early locomotives were built by Philadelphia builder William Norris and shipped to Austria, starting with a 4–2–0 type appropriately named *Philadelphia*. This set a technological precedent, and locomotives built in Austria during its formative railway years emulated the Norris design.

On a modern map the Südbahn seems to follow an odd route, yet at the time of its inception this made complete sense – it connected Vienna with Austria's Adriatic port at Trieste by way of Graz, the historic capital of Styria, and Laibach, now Ljubljana, capital of Slovenia, thus offering both strategic military and commercial benefits. When it was built the whole route was in Habsburg territory; today it spans three different countries – Trieste was ceded to Italy following the First World War – so the line no longer functions as a through corridor.

The Alpine Semmering crossing is the scenic highlight of the Südbahn; the most difficult engineering is on the north slope between Gloggnitz and the Semmering summit tunnel. On the climb from Gloggnitz, the line follows the Schwarza River. At Payerbach the line loops over an impressive curved arched viaduct to double back up the valley, gaining elevation. Passengers on the left side of an ascending train are afforded stunning views down the valley they have just travelled, where careful eyes looking down upon the line might spot a following train.

At Eichberg the line turns south as it climbs toward the top of the pass, transiting several tunnels and magnificent multiple-arch viaducts, several of which, such as the famed Bollerswand Viaduct, were built in Roman style, with one set of arches atop another. The winter resort at Semmering is the site of a handsome station and the stone-faced south portal of the 1,399 m summit tunnel. While still pleasant, the descent toward Mürzzuschlag is anticlimactic compared with the north slope.

Other highlights include the scenic pastoral scenery south of Pragerhof (Pragersko), and the Sava valley between the junction at Zidani Most and Laibach (Ljubljana). In October 1881 *Bradshaw's Guide* noted that a train departing Vienna at 7 a.m. passed Semmering at 9.45 a.m., but did not arrive in Trieste for another 12 hours.

The building of the viaduct over the Kalte Rinne, 1854 (above).

A painting by A. Werner of an heroic railway incident on the Semmering route in 1859. An Austrian soldier, knowing the tracks ahead have been sabotaged, manages to climb aboard the train to attract enough attention to get the driver to stop, thus preventing a catastrophic derailment (right).

Panorama of the Semmering route, engraved by Imre Benkert and published in 1856 (next two pages).

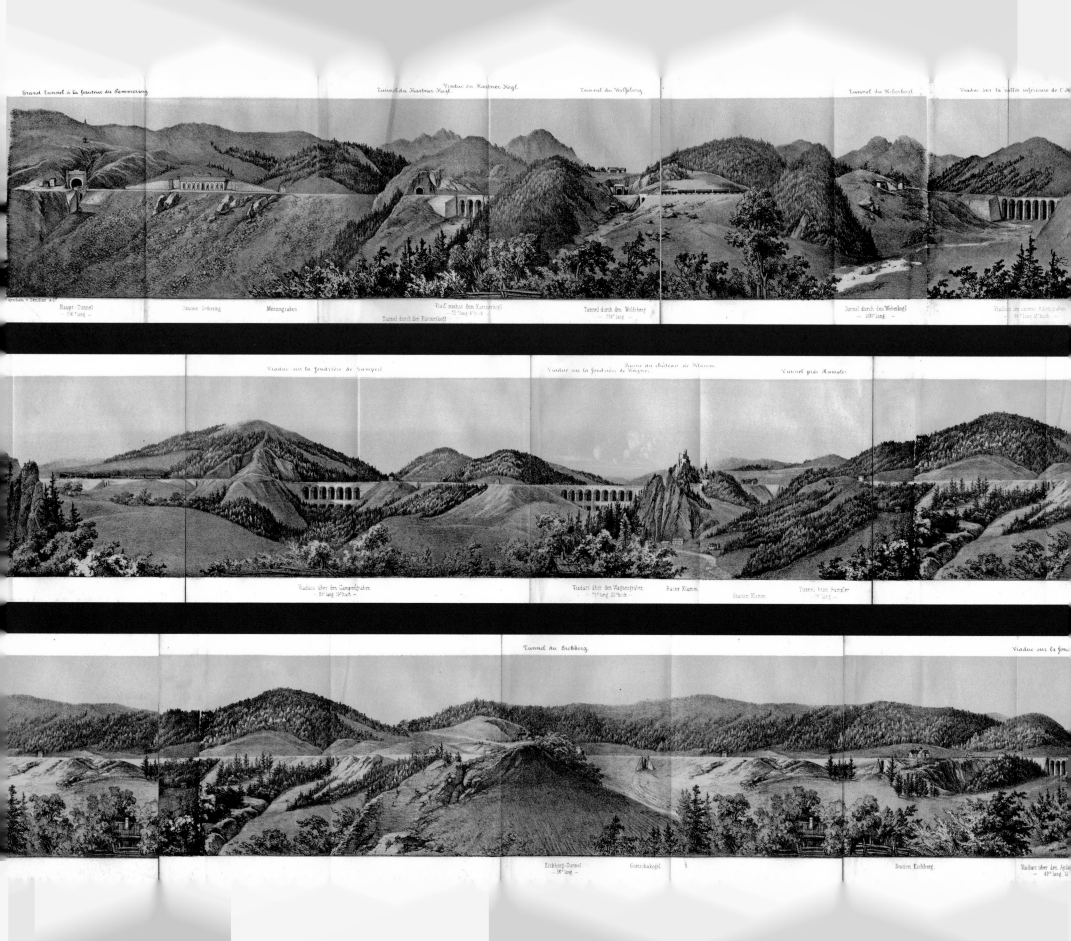

Grand Tunnel à la hauteur du Semmering   Tunnel du Kartner Kogl.   Viaduc du Kartner Kogl.   Tunnel du Wolfsberg   Tunnel du Weberkogl.   Viaduc sur la vallée inférieure de l'A...

Haupt-Tunnel   Station Sethering   Meriengraben   Viad. nächst dem Kartnerkogl   Tunnel durch den Wolfsberg   Tunnel durch den Weberkogl   Viaduct im untern A...graben
750 lang   Tunnel durch den Kartnerkogl   72 lang 8 hoch   234 lang   200 lang   50 lang 18 hoch

Viaduc sur la fondrière de Gamperl   Ruine du château de Klamm   Tunnel près Rumpler
    Viaduc sur la fondrière de Wagner

Viaduct über den Gamperlgraben   Viaduct über den Wagnergraben   Ruine Klamm   Station Klamm   Tunnel beim Rumpler
53 lang 19 hoch   75 lang 30 hoch   54 lang

Tunnel du Eichberg.   Viaduc sur la fon...

Eichberg-Tunnel   Gortschakogel   Station Eichberg.   Viaduct über den Ayda...
50 lang   40 lang 16...

Viad. über die Kalte Rinne   Viad. über die Kranzelklaufe   Tunnel am Weinzettlfeld   Weinzettel-Wand   Viaduct
— 57m lang 24 6m hoch —   46m lang 19m hoch —   Gallop Freitenstein   — 119m lang —   3ter Tunnel   Gallerie   2ter Tunnel   1ter Tunnel
Tunnel durch die Bollerswand

Tunnel du Eichberg   Tunnel du Eichberg

Eichberg-Tunnel   Gortschakogel   Eichberg-Tunnel   Gortschakogel
— 56m lang —   — 56m lang —

Pottenbach-Tunnel   Peyerbach   Schwarza-Viaduct
— 85m lang —   Viaduct über den Peyerbachgraben   — 170m lang 25m hoch —

Gez. u. lith.

THE BRENNER PASS

Through the Alps from Innsbruck to Verona

The arrival of the train carrying German Kaiser Wilhelm to meet with Austrian Emperor Franz Josef, Innsbruck station, 1889 (above).

Tracks on the west side of Innsbruck Hauptbahnhof, with a stunning mountain backdrop (top right).

A cartoon from 1900 in which a Tyrolese farmer suggests that horses travelling on the new Brennerbahn can get to their destination by themselves (bottom right).

Innsbruck's Haupbahnhof has one of the most stunning backdrops of any major railway terminal in Europe – snow-crested peaks loom in the distance both north and south of the station. While those to the north represent an almost impenetrable wall, separating Austria from Germany, the mountains to the south are more forgiving. South of Innsbruck, the Brenner Pass boasted a Roman road, putting it among the oldest of the Alpine trade routes. Completed in 1867, the railway over the pass was Austria's second major Alpine crossing after the Südbahn's Semmering route, connecting Innsbruck with Verona in Italy.

Following a deep narrow gorge south of Innsbruck, the line first reaches Matrei, the village just a short walk south of the station and a popular stopover. Beyond Matrei the line climbs steeply, maintaining a steady gradient without the need for racks or other aids. It loops around the valley at St Jodok, where it negotiates a tight horseshoe curve and a tunnel, encircling the village as it gains elevation. As a train climbs, passengers might gaze with awe, looking back down the valley of the Sill. As the line ascends the Brenner, it passes a thickly forested area, traversing another short tunnel near Ritten. The Brenner Pass is a natural saddle in the mountains, 1,370 m above sea level. Prior to the First World War this was entirely within the Austrian Tyrol, but after the war Austria ceded the south Tyrol to Italy, and the border was moved to the top of the pass. Since then the south slope has been in Italian territory, and in Italian the pass is called Passo del Brennero.

The change of national borders resulted in changes to operations, and all trains required a change of locomotive. The electrification of the route resulted in more complications, since Austria's ÖBB and Italian system used different electric standards.

South of the summit the line descends sharply. In modern times an expensive realignment has reduced the curvature, but historically the south slope involved a spectacular drop. Further down the pass the route passes historic castles perched atop the lower mountain peaks, then descends through the narrow gorge at Fortezza where the scenery is stark and impressive.

Die neue Brennerbahn.

Tiroler Bauer: „J hob mir's glei denkt, daß fie's ohne Roß nit dermachen können."

St Jodok, a village at the beginning of Valsertal on the route of the Brennerbahn (top).

Innsbruck railway station (far left).

Sigmundskron on the Bozen–Merance railway, 1883 (left).

A freight train traversing the Brenner Pass in winter (bottom).

147

THE WESTBAHN AND THE ARLBERG ROUTE

The Alpine Route to Switzerland

Construction of Austria's Kaiserin Elisabeth Bahn started westwards from Vienna in 1856. Known as the Westbahn in later years, the line was served by Vienna's Westbahnhof, one of six historic terminals ringing the Austrian capital, and was the principal domestic trunk line connecting Vienna with the important cities of Linz and Salzburg, and thence to Worgl, Innsbruck and beyond via the Arlberg Route to Switzerland or the Brenner Pass to Italy. West from Salzburg, via connections to the German railways, the Kaiserin Elisabeth Bahn/Westbahn formed part of the key Vienna–Munich route. Although not as scenic as Austria's Alpine crossings, the line offered pleasant views of the rolling country along the Danube, notably east of Ybbs where the line closely followed the south bank of the river.

West of Innsbruck, engineers faced the difficult challenge of constructing a railway over the Austrian Vorarlberg to connect Austria with Switzerland and south-western Bavaria. This longitudinal trough in the western Austrian Alps follows the upper reaches of the River Inn, and is part of the Danube watershed. While offering a natural gateway to the west, it also contains some of the most rugged territory crossed by a main line international railway. The engineer Julius Lott directed construction, having previously worked on the route over the Brenner Pass.

Among the Arlberg's highlights are near Landeck, where the line clings to one side of a deep valley while on the far side castles cling to precipitously steep cliffs. At Weisberg the railway spans the darkened recesses of Trianna Gorge against

Julius Lott, builder of the Arlbergbahn (above).

Nordwestbahnhof, Vienna, painted by Karl Karger, 1875 (right).

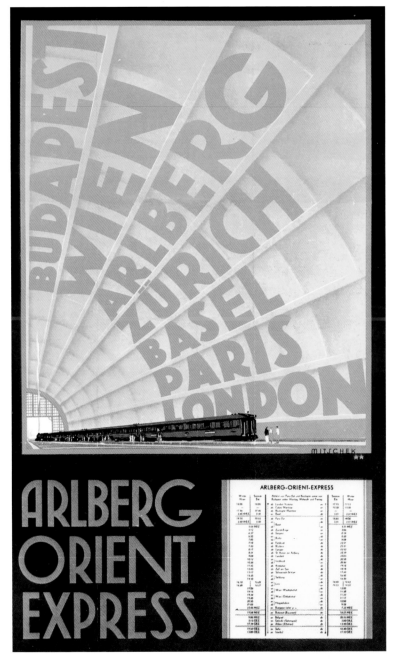

the backdrop of the historic Schloss Weisberg, considered one of the most stunning railway settings in Europe.

Construction was particularly difficult near the summit of the pass, where a series of tunnels were required, the longest being the 10.25 km Arlberg Tunnel, opened in November 1883. At the time it was constructed it was the third longest tunnel in the world. Beyond the tunnel the line descends through avalanche country toward Bludenz, 136 km from Innsbruck. The line required special protection where it crossed known avalanche runs, while elsewhere snow fences and large capacity rotary snow ploughs helped to keep the line clear in the winter. The route to Switzerland skirts a corner of Liechtenstein, while another branch angles north-west toward Germany, where it follows the shore of Lake Constance.

The Trisanna Viaduct and Castle Weisberg (far left)

Arlberg Orient Express poster, Mitschek, 1931 (left).

The break-up of the Habsburg Empire after the First World War deprived Austria of considerable domestic coal reserves. As a result, it turned to electrification as a means of powering its railways, and the Arlberg route was among the early lines to be wired. Austria adopted the same high-voltage alternating current overhead standard used in Germany and Switzerland, which has aided through services between these countries.

THE CLASSIC EUROPEAN SLEEPING CAR ROUTES

Speed with Luxury and Comfort On Board

The Orient Express, Paris–Constantinople, c.1900 (above). The locomotive is a Series 170 express built by Karl Gölsdorfs, chief mechanical engineer with the Austrian State Railways; note the distinctive connecting pipe between the two steam domes.

European railways began as local schemes, gradually coalescing into national and regional systems. Until the 1870s, however, railways were poorly suited to international travel. Even where lines connected at international frontiers, facilities were primarily designed for the interchange of freight rather than for handling through international passenger trains. A host of technical and bureaucratic difficulties precluded long-distance travel across national frontiers.

It was the relaxation of customs and border restrictions following the Franco-Prussian War that started to facilitate improvements to international railway services in Europe. Georges Nagelmackers' Wagons-Lits International Sleeping Car Company, formed in 1872, quickly emerged as the leader in international services. Significantly, Wagons-Lits owned and maintained its own passenger carriages, carefully designed to meet all the various railway standards in their intended operating territory. To attract the best classes of passengers, carriages were designed and decorated with a high standard of comfort and taste. Wagons-Lits neither owned nor operated its own locomotives, relying exclusively upon host railways to supply operating crews and equipment. By the 1880s Wagons-Lits was famous for its network of sleeping car routes across the continent, the best known being its de-luxe *Exprés d'Orient* (*Orient Express*), introduced in October 1883, providing a link between Paris and Istanbul via Vienna.

Overnight international expresses were the preferred means of travel of the affluent, influential, privileged passenger. Travellers could transcend time and space by boarding a luxury evening train in their home country, then waking up to a rolling panorama of a place entirely foreign, all the while enjoying the sublime surreal world offered by the fineries of the international express carriages.

France's central location and radial network made Paris an ideal hub for international routes and overnight services. The *Sud Express* (Paris–Madrid–Lisbon), famed as one of Europe's most luxurious trains, began operations in 1883; the *Nord Express* (Paris–Warsaw–St Petersburg), among Europe's most evocative, initiated services in 1896.

Wealthy British travellers were regular patrons of continental trains, as were American tourists, and key connections were offered from North Sea ports across France to continental destinations. Introduced in the same year as the *Orient Express*, although not as well-remembered, was the *Calais–Mediterranean Express*, while from 1897 the *Rome Express* offered an excellent de-luxe service between Calais and the Italian capital via Paris and the Mont Cenis Tunnel. In its early days this carried just two baggage/mail carriages, two Wagons-Lits sleeping carriages, and a well-stocked restaurant car offering passengers 'hors d'oeuvres variés, filets de sole au vin blanc,' and 'côtelettes de mouton á la Mont Cenis', among other dishes. Food for the southward run was stocked by the incoming *Peninsular Express,* itself an important run that reached the Adriatic port of Brindisi to connect with the mail ships serving the Orient.

SÜDBAHNHOTEL
SEMMERING
A U S T R I A

Among the earliest routes carrying international traffic was Austria's Südbahn over the Semmering Pass. Further west, the *Nord–Sud Brenner Express* connected Berlin and Rome/Naples via Munich and the Brenner Pass. Among important seasonal trains were the *Amsterdam–Riviera Express,* the *Engadine Express* (Calais to Chur in Switzerland), and the *Karlsbad Express* (Calais/Ostend/Berlin to Karlsbad). One of the longest and most obscure runs was the *St Petersbourg–Vienna–Cannes Express*, which began service in 1898.

Not all sleeping car routes were the domain of Wagons-Lits; from the 1880s onwards Prussian railways operated their own overnight trains.

A 1930s winter sports travel poster for the Sudbahnhotel at Semmering, Austria, designed by Hermann Kosel for the Vienna Tourist board (above left).

Sleeping car poster by W. Hemming, 1929 (above).

THE ORIENT EXPRESS

The cover of an advertising brochure published in 1898 which carried a full list of agencies of the Wagons-Lits Company.

Europe's *Orient Express* or *Express d'Orient* was a train of legend – surrounded by myths, shrouded in mystique, and glorified in literature and film. Because of the unusual fascination it exerts on the imagination, it has become the best-known train on the Continent, or for that matter, anywhere in the world. This train was associated with diplomats, travelling royalty, adventurers and spies, and was popularised in the mid-twentieth century in novels and films by Agatha Christie, Alfred Hitchcock and Graham Greene, amongst others. Although it has become part of common lore rather than being known only as a simple means of transport, the *Orient Express* was indeed once a genuine, scheduled train, enjoying a long and complex history. It was one of the most influential trains of its day, setting a standard for international express services across the continent.

In the years prior to the First World War, the *Orient Express,* through its guise as a first class, modern conveyance, offered a veneer of civility in a region simmering with discord and ripe for conflict. As well as international borders, it crossed a host of invisible frontiers, transcending long-standing cultural barriers created by differences in language, costume, religion and politics. It connected realms whose written languages were opaque to one another, for on its journey, the western letters of the classical Roman alphabet gave way first to Bulgarian Cyrillic, then to Greek, and finally to the variant Arabic script of the Ottoman Turks. The ability to transcend cultural barriers, while rolling along at speed behind a powerful locomotive, gave travellers an indescribable thrill and a sense of adventure, although the train allowed passengers to view strange lands while insulating them from any real contact. The *Orient Express* offered a cross section of Europe's most diverse Empire, the Habsburg monarchy centred in Austria–Hungary, which held together under fragile unity prior to the war and afterwards spawned a host of cobbled together nation-states.

Yet today the name *Orient Express* is often misinterpreted. To set matters straight: the *Orient Express* was a direct service connecting Paris in France with Constantinople (today Istanbul in Turkey) on the Bosphorus estuary of the Black Sea. While it was best known for its luxury services, during its lifetime it was also used extensively by local people for relatively short

Georges Nagelmackers in his sumptuous office in 1900 with Camille Chouffart, General Director of Wagons-Lits (right top).

The agreement of 17 May 1883 between the Est Railway company and the CIWL permitting the running of through trains between Paris and Constantinople (right below).

journeys, and also by immigrants to western Europe including those planning to travel further west to America by ship.

The meaning of 'Orient' requires some clarification. In the Victorian-era, the Western world used the word 'Orient' to convey its more historic sense, indicating the countries directly to the 'East' of Europe. From Roman times, the eastern half of the Empire carried 'Orient' in its description, and so in the context of the train, 'Orient' referred to those regions covered by the old Eastern Roman Empire, an area that we now call the Balkans. British travellers in the late nineteenth century would have been awed by the colourful costumes of Balkan peasants, and would have considered the whole tourist experience 'Oriental' in nature. Furthermore, Constantinople, the train's eastern terminus, was long viewed as the gateway to Asia, and thus part of the passage to the Middle and Far East. By contrast, today 'Orient' tends to specify the nations of the Far East, which was neither the intended destination of the train, nor the image the name of the train intended to convey in its heyday.

Wagons-Lits

The *Orient Express* was the brainchild of Belgian entrepreneur Georges Nagelmackers (1845–1905). The son of a wealthy banker, trained as an engineer, this inspired, well-travelled man possessed a unique blend of talents and connections that allowed him to pull off the greatest feat associated with Continental railways: the creation of the first luxury, trans-European express. Interestingly, the spark for his quintessentially European train came from his experiences with de-luxe American limited-express sleeping car trains. By the 1870s, these not only connected cities across eastern North America such as Montréal, Washington D.C., New Orleans, Boston, New York, Chicago and St Louis, but also had spanned the continent, allowing for travel all the way to the

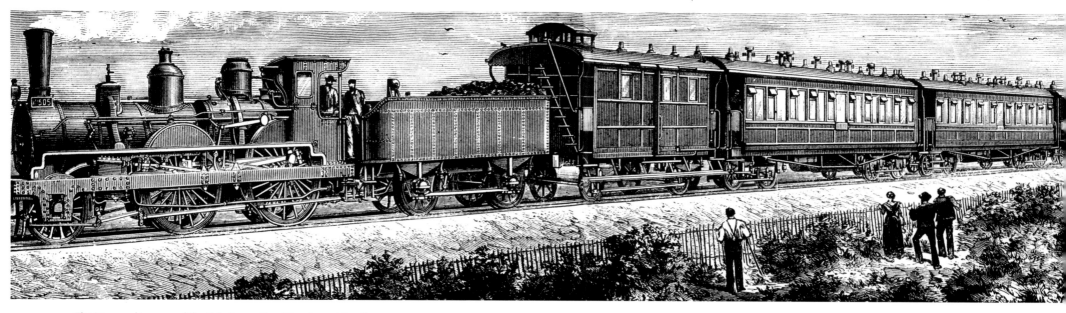

Pacific. Specifically, it was the great trains of the American West, operating with finely outfitted Pullman Palace Cars, that encouraged Nagelmackers in 1872 to launch his own company in Europe called Compagnie Internationale des Wagons-Lits ('International Sleeping Car Company').

As with most new endeavours, Nagelmackers' Wagons-Lits company had to learn to walk before it could run. The organisation initially provided sleeping cars to the Paris–Vienna route under contract. This service was made possible in part as a function of the Treaty of 1871 that concluded the Franco-Prussian War. The business received a significant boost in 1876 when Nagelmackers re-organised Wagons-Lits, including among new shareholders his close friend, King Leopold II of Belgium.

There is little doubt that the king aided Nagelmackers' complex exercise of providing an express, international service across seven national frontiers. This required negotiating with a variety of different railroads, each with their own operational peculiarities. Furthermore, the nations of central Europe eyed each other suspiciously after centuries of warfare and animosity, triggered by myriad claims to overlapping territories, periods of conquest and empire building, and a host of cultural and religious differences. Yet, by the nineteenth century, on an elite level this was largely internecine warfare, since most European rulers shared common blood. Leopold II of Belgium was a classic example: a child of the regal Saxe-Coburg family, he was a nephew of Britain's Queen Victoria, as well as a close relation to Austria's Habsburg dynasty. In short, he was near cousin to most European monarchs. Further aiding the king's influence was Belgium's largely neutral status in contemporary European affairs. This excellent political standing, combined with pan-European influence on the highest level, certainly facilitated Nagelmackers' efforts in establishing co-operation between nations and railways. In addition, furthering his goal were members of his intended clientele: wealthy businessmen, diplomats, and royal travellers, all of whom would benefit most from the service. After all, it was the elite who used the service – the *Orient Express* was never intended as a means of transport for common travellers.

King Leopold II of Belgium, a strong supporter of Georges Nagelmackers' plans for the *Orient Express*.

Debut

Finally, in October 1883, Nagelmackers' Wagons-Lits introduced the famed de-luxe international train: *Exprés d'Orient,* connecting Paris and Constantinople. This was the *grand dame* of European international trains – it was the first classy train to cross multiple frontiers, and in the very finest style of the period. When its inaugural consist backed into the train station Gare de l'Est in Paris in preparation for its pioneer eastward journey, the finery of its specially appointed carriages awed the press, the public, and its honoured passengers. Nothing like it had ever been seen in Europe before. In his book *Orient Express – The Birth, Life, and Death of a Great Train,* published in 1968, Garry Hogg recorded a quote from Edmond About (1828–85), an eminent Parisian journalist who witnessed the train's arrival (and was among the travellers on its inaugural run), and who noted that the cars were 'constructed of teak and glass, brilliantly lit by gas lamps, splendidly windowed, as well appointed and comfortable on immediate view, as any luxury flat in Paris.' The journalist was captivated by the inaugural service – which as it happens shared more with high-end excursions than with the regularly scheduled trains – and wrote a popular report about his experiences. This, along with other early accounts of the *Orient Express,* contributed greatly to its legendary status and public fascination. Nearly as much has been written about its inaugural run as has been written about its next thirty years of operation.

The *Orient Express's* carriages offered several distinctive aspects. While the vast majority of European carriages of the time used the conventional compartmental arrangement that confined passengers to small groups, by contrast the *Orient Express* incorporated much longer, corridor-style cars that allowed passengers to move more freely, and from car to car. Yet its sleeping compartments offered a high degree of privacy, each luxuriously decorated to standards set by the finest European hotels. This was in the ornate, ostentatious styles of the high-Victorian period. While most conventional stock offered little in the way of passenger comfort, the *Orient Express* was relatively spacious. Of special interest were on-board toilets, two in each sleeping car, one exclusively for men, the other for women. These were equipped with both hot and cold running water – the utmost luxury at the time – and were cleaned and prepared by staff after each visit. The train's showcase, and Nagelmackers' pride and joy, was the Wagon-Salon-Restaurant. This was a combined lounge and restaurant, featuring a ladies' drawing room and a men's 'smoking lounge' – smoking was considered improper and unladylike in Victorian times – as well as an elegant dining room.

A colourful poster for the *Orient Express* designed by Raphael de Ochoa y Madrazo in 1895.

Wagons-Lits teak-built sleeping car No. 77 with three axles, built by Rathgeber in 1881–82 (left).

The interior of the *Orient Express* dining car in 1883 (bottom left).

Dining car No. 999 with Italian-style decor by Poteau (bottom right).

As well as being longer than other standard European cars of the time, the sleeping and restaurant cars also offered a much higher quality 'ride'. The reason for this was simple, although it eluded many observers: most carriages that operated on European railways used fixed two- and three-axle designs. These limited the length of the cars and tended to transmit the condition of the track from the wheels into the carriage. However, Nagelmackers had embraced the American standard, with cars riding on pairs of well-suspended four-wheel bogies (or 'trucks' as they are called in America), which allowed for a longer, more substantial (and heavier) car, while greatly smoothing the ride.

Original Routes of the Orient Express

The train's intended route was famous at the time because it crossed no less than seven international frontiers, and operated over eight distinct railway systems. Nagelmackers' operation of the train was a political masterpiece as well as an operational one. Despite his high-placed connections, dealing with railways in countries that, at best, eyed their neighbours with hostile mistrust, could not have been an easy task.

This train was more about the high quality of service than about maintaining a specific route. Over the years, the Wagons-Lits' *Orient Express,* and its various subsidiary and connecting trains, have served a variety of routes, over a multitude of railway lines in a number of countries, connecting myriad end points.

The original train began its journey in the evening twice-weekly at Gare de l'Est in Paris. It worked eastward over France's Compagnie de l'Est to the border with Alsace–Lorraine (which, following the Franco-Prussian War, was under administration by German authorities who ran the railways as well). The *Orient Express* continued east through Strasbourg, then travelled via

A summer 1889 poster advertising the *Orient Express* (above left).

Orient Express routes in 1930–31 (above right).

Germany's various state railways across the Grand Duchy of Baden, the kingdoms of Württemberg and Bavaria, via Karlsruhe, Stuttgart, up the steeply graded incline at Geislingen and beyond to the historic city of Ulm, then via Munich into the Austro-Hungarian Empire. Here the train used two of Austria's competing national railways, running via Salzburg, Vienna, Bratislava and Budapest. East of Budapest, the route became more nebulous and changeable. Not only were Balkan railways far less developed than those in Western nations, but the actual route used by the train varied considerably over the years.

A postcard from 1908 showing the *Orient Express* near Constantinople.

Key to the comfort of its wealthy patrons was simplifying the process at border crossings. This through train minimised delays that could be created by bureaucratic officialdom and customs. The *Orient Express*'s passengers were neither inconvenienced by the need to change trains nor would they have to endure the variances in equipment typically provided by the different railways over this very long route. Initially this process worked well as far as the Romanian frontier, but beyond there it failed to meet expectations. While it was scheduled for a twice-weekly Paris–Constantinople journey taking 75 hours one-way, its original routing suffered from the lack of a bridge over the Danube between Romania and Bulgaria. This required a ferry crossing and a separate train across Bulgaria in rather ordinary carriages. Furthermore, the initial lack of a direct, all-rail route between Europe and the Ottoman capital necessitated a Black Sea voyage from the Bulgarian port of Varna to Constantinople. While Varna was known as the 'Queen of the Black Sea', and was the largest and oldest of Bulgarian ports, its facilities were less than salubrious by the standards of Western travellers, and were not on a par with the type of travel offered by the *Orient Express*.

In 1885, another option was offered to through passengers using a route south from Budapest via Belgrade to the Balkan city of Nis. This ancient and historic crossroads was as an exotic place as any for the train to terminate, but the inconvenience of continuing the overland journey to Constantinople via stagecoach didn't encourage many passengers to make the full journey. Yet, Nagelmackers' early advertising promoted the train on its fabled Paris–Constantinople route, and the

ORIENT EXPRESS
NEAR CONSTANTINOPLE

clever observer would note that the train name shared initials with that of the Ottoman Empire, while early posters used Ottoman symbolism and colouring to entice travellers East. However, until an all-rail route was available, the full voyage from Paris to Constantinople eluded most travellers on the *Orient Express*. Hogg conveyed this uncertainty by reporting on an early *Orient Express* travel brochure which wrote, 'We anxiously await the day when the complete *Orient Express* train will be able to continue the full distance beyond Belgrade.'

Finally, in June 1889, this dream was fulfilled when the necessary railway lines and connections allowed an all-rail Paris–Constantinople *Orient Express*. For the next 25 years, Europe's best-known train connected these terminals carrying its passengers using the very finest scheduled accommodation. Since the train crossed both Eastern and Western fronts during the First World War, service was suspended at the outbreak of the war.

Later Routes

History remembers the *Orient Express* and Wagons-Lits for more than just its peacetime service. The armistice that ended the Great War was signed by Marshal Foch of France in Wagons-Lits restaurant salon or saloon No. 2419. Then, after the war, a new service was introduced called the *Simplon-Orient Express*. While this shared high service standards and end terminals with the pre-war train, it used a completely new routing over much of its journey, only rejoining the classic *Orient Express* route at Belgrade. Animosities against Germany and Austria as a result of the war, as well as extensive damage to railways in those countries and to their national economies, resulted in the *Simplon-Orient Express* following a southerly route via France to Switzerland, Italy and the newly created Yugoslavia. This completely avoided German and Austrian territory and took advantage of the recently opened Simplon Tunnel

A bold *Simplon-Orient Express* and *Taurus Express* poster designed by Andre Wilkin, published in 1930 (above).

The *Simplon-Orient Express* in 1930, passing Chillon Castle in Switzerland (left).

A derailment of the *Orient Express* in eastern France, early 1942 (above).

On 11 November 1918, at the end of the First World War, Marshal Foch (seated in the centre of the photograph) received the German surrender in Wagons-Lits dining car No. 2419 (above right).

A warning notice placed in the dining car of the *Orient Express* during the First World War. Translated it says 'Keep quiet! Be on your guard! The enemies' ears are listening to you.' (above far right).

beneath the Swiss Alps. This route connected Paris with Milan, Venice, Trieste, Zagreb and Belgrade, before continuing on to Constantinople (which by then was often referred to by its modern name, Istanbul). In addition, a separate leg of the service continued on through Greece to Athens.

The more traditional *Orient Express* route was revived by the mid-1920s, and other route variations were added reflecting growing interest in trans-European travel in the wake of the Great War. Beginning in 1932, the *Arlberg-Orient Express* began operation from Paris to Basel and Zürich, then over its namesake Austrian Alpine pass to Innsbruck, where it rejoined the historic route at Salzburg as far as Budapest, then taking a northerly route across Romania. A London connection was afforded by a Wagons-Lits sleeper that operated from Calais with a ferry–rail connection from the British capital. In the post-First World War years, this joined with the main *Orient Express* consist east of Paris. The *Ostend Orient Express* provided a connection from the Belgian port across Germany to Linz and Vienna in Austria.

During the Second World War service was again suspended, due to disruptions caused by Nazi invasions and the subsequent devastation of the European railways. While the *Orient Express* name was revived after the war, the Cold War partition of Europe, combined with the introduction of commercial airline travel, drained the train of its previous prestige and limited its route options. Garry Hogg pinned the 'death' of the train to the ending of through cars to Bucharest in May 1962. After that, an international service with the historic name operated only to Vienna. (However, other authors have suggested other defining moments for the train's ending.)

Today, though no regularly scheduled train completes these journeys, it is possible to retrace the various *Orient Express* routes using a combination of scheduled high-speed EuroCity and InterCity services. In addition, luxurious historic excursions are operated several times annually on various easterly routes in Europe catering to wealthy railway aficionados. In recent years, sleeping car trains have, in general, declined in Western Europe, but a few still ply the rails. Begin at Gare de l'Est in Paris and board a train for either Munich or Vienna. The more interesting journey will take you through Switzerland and then over the Arlberg route via Innsbruck, when awe-inspiring vistas of snow-crested Alpine peaks are among the highlights. At Vienna, head east for Budapest. Where the *Orient Express* continued through Budapest, today this city offers a good opportunity for a stop-over. You can then travel a northerly route across Hungary and Romania to Bucharest and onwards to the Black Sea, although the more adventurous traveller will choose the southerly route via Belgrade and on toward Greece. Crossing the Hungarian–Serbian border still involves on-board immigration and customs checks – passports required! While the Hungarian plains can be relatively unexciting, Belgrade is a fascinating, old-world city worthy of exploration. An old fortress high above the Danube offers magnificent views.

King Boris of Bulgaria, a dedicated train enthusiast, opening a new railway line in northern Bulgaria. He drove the engine on its first run (far left).

Romania's King Carol II in 1935 (left).

Margaretha-Geertruida Zelle, better known as Mata-Hari, often travelled on the *Orient Express* as an agent of the German information services (below).

Characters and Escapades

No chronicle of the *Orient Express* would be complete without some mention of the numerous characters and personalities involved with the train in its classic period. As the premier means of trans-European transport, it attracted more than its fair share of wealthy, regal and famous travellers. Hogg cites the diaries of Wagons-Lits employees as the source for some of his more interesting accounts, although where fact gives way to conjecture will never be known. But even if nothing exciting had ever occurred on the train, the imaginations of writers will have bridged the gaps.

Among the most colourful patrons was Bulgaria's King Boris III (1894–1943), who reigned during the inter-war years. Having travelled by *Orient Express* as a boy, the king became an ardent railway enthusiast. Unlike most prominent travellers, he wasn't content to ride in the carriages and instead preferred the locomotive footplate. While engine rides were not unheard of in the classic days of railway travel, apparently the king not only made numerous trips with this good view of the tracks, but also on several occasions he took the throttle as well. It is believed that his running tended to be more ambitious than that of the normal schedule, and after a few hair-raising trips, the king was gently cautioned and encouraged to leave the job of running trains to the professional men employed for the task. King Boris is best remembered for

his heroic actions in the Second World War when he tried to protect his nation's Jews from the German Nazis. Sadly, Boris died in uncertain circumstances in 1943, leading some of his followers to conclude that he was poisoned by the Nazis.

Romanian royalty was also partial to the train, and E.H. Cookridge in his 1979 book *Orient Express – The Life and Times of the World's Most Famous Train* wrote that Romania's Prince Carol (1893–1953), who became King Carol II in 1930, routinely used the train for holidays in the French Riviera. Later, he used the train for his secret liaisons with women, including Zizi Lambrino, the mother of his child, who was sequestered off to Paris (by *Orient Express*) after their marriage was deemed void by the powers that be. She was not alone, as Prince Carol also had regular liaisons with other women, which continued after he was crowned king. When Stalin and Hitler steamrollered through Romania in 1940, Carol was forced to flee, along with a mistress, using the *Orient Express* as the vehicle of his escape. Happily, although deposed, Carol survived the ravages of the war and eventually married his fellow escapee.

By some accounts, steamy affairs aboard the train seem to have been a routine occurrence, although such goings-on were never as much as alluded to in *Bradshaw's Continental Guides* or other period published literature! Author Nicholas Faith wrote in his 1990 book *The World the Railways Made* that 'The *Orient Express* was a hotbed of sex, mostly the simple, straightforward paid-for variety,' and goes on to infer that the

train's conductors would forward travellers requirements to 'women' further down the line using the railway telegraph. He noted that the passage through Bulgaria was notoriously lusty. No doubt in public Wagons-Lits defended the honour of its employees, denying that anything above the ordinary ever occurred on their trains.

Regardless of whether a passenger entertained illicit liaisons or not, the thrill of travelling on the *Orient Express* through the Balkans region remained the most exciting part of the trip. This region was famous for political strife, wars and banditry. Yet, while the dangers were more often than not illusory, some incidents involving the train did indeed occur. The high-profile operation and its wealthy passengers made the *Orient Express* more of a target than the ordinary goods train or frequently stopping, local passenger run. E.H. Cookridge tells the story of a notorious train robbery. On 31 May 1891, a group of saboteurs, led by a colourful

outlaw known only as Anasthatos, derailed the westward *Orient Express* as it passed through a darkly forested section of line in western Turkey. Unlike American train robbers who were only looking for a cash reward, the tall, bearded Anasthatos appears to have had an unstated political agenda. At the time, Turkey was still under the rule of the Ottomans, whose centuries-old Empire was fraught with political strife and was nearing the end of its reign. No one was killed in the crash caused by the bandits; while some passengers suffered minor injuries, they were more frightened than hurt. As they stumbled from the wreckage, Anasthatos and his gang menaced them, but it has been claimed that he asked them to remain calm, assuring that there would be no violence provided they offered their co-operation. His bandits then bound the train's crew while systematically relieving passengers of their valuables. During this escapade, a few German businessmen were taken hostage, leading to an international

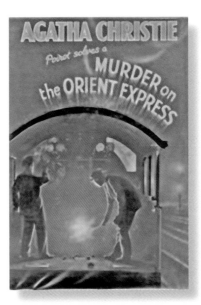

The cover of the first 1934 edition of Agatha Christie's famous Poirot detective novel *Murder on the Orient Express* (above).

Another scene from the filming of *Murder on the Orient Express* (left).

The *Orient Express* in the 1950s, hauled by a 241A 4–8–2 locomotive, passing the outskirts of Dormans on the Paris–Strasbourg stretch of the route (below).

incident between Germany and the Ottomans. While a rescue train raced to collect *Orient's* passengers, Turkish authorities pursued the gang of bandits without result. Ultimately, Anasthatos received his ransom demands and set free the Germans unharmed, and, according to legend, he gave each a gold coin as a gift for their trouble. Anasthatos remained at large, and his true identity and objectives are open to speculation. He was never caught.

Wagons-Lits was undoubtedly horrified at the idea of its flagship train and passengers being treated in such a fashion, though such incidents contributed greatly to the romance and mystique of the train. Like the unfortunate *Titanic* two decades later, it was the combination of luxury and danger that engaged public imagination and enshrined the *Orient Express* in railway lore. Who, after all, recalls a train that always arrived on time, without incident, and with nothing more than a pretty view from the carriage windows?

GERMANY'S MAIN RAILWAY STATIONS

Hanover, Frankfurt, Köln, Hamburg, Leipzig, Stuttgart

German railway station restaurant scene, 1875 (above).

Leipzig Hauptbahnhof, opened in 1915 as a joint terminal for the Royal Saxon State Railways and the Prussian State Railways (right).

In the late nineteenth and early twentieth century, many German cities were unusually progressive, and there was a nationwide move towards combining all of a city's main railway stations into one central, modern, well-planned main station, or Haupbahnhof. This was very much an idea copied from North America's 'Union Stations'. Not only did these new main stations minimise confusion for visitors, they also greatly simplified the process of changing trains. New German terminals were designed for passenger convenience, and anticipated tremendous growth in traffic. As a result most of these stations have withstood the test of time, some serving with little alteration to the present day.

Hanover's Haupbahnhof, built in 1879, set a precedent for a central main terminal. Frankfurt Haupbahnhof, completed in 1888, featured an impressive three-span balloon-shed, covering a large stub-end terminal. Köln's was among the most unusual terminal designs, the station and shed being unified, with the booking office and other facilities located beneath the shed rather than abutting it. Most of Germany's large Hauptbahnhofs are stub-end terminals, but Köln is a through design with access from both ends, even though

many trains terminated there. Located in the virtual shadow of Köln's monumental Gothic cathedral, the station, like the cathedral, was badly damaged in the Second World War.

The culmination of the classic German station was Hamburg, completed in 1906, which authors Jeffrey Richards and John MacKenzie, in their book *The Railway Station: A Social History*, describe as one of the last of the great classic train sheds. Railway travel writer J.P. Pearson visited Hamburg Hauptbahnhof in 1910, a few years after it opened, and described his awe of the new termini and magnificent shed: 'Its great overarching span — so lofty and wide that, when down below on the platforms, one appears to be out in the open — undoubtedly ranks as one of the great railway edifices in the world.' And Pearson would have known, having travelled the world by train. Yet Hamburg was by no means the last of the great German stations.

Germany's largest station is the massive stub-end terminal at Leipzig, which covers an estimated 82,000 square metres. Begun in 1907, it was built in the city centre on the site of the older Thüringer Bahnhof, opposite the Sachsenplatz, the city's main square. It features a shed covering twenty-six tracks, designed by engineers Eiler & Karing using a six-span design that is lower and brighter than the cavernous balloon-style sheds of the earlier large stations.

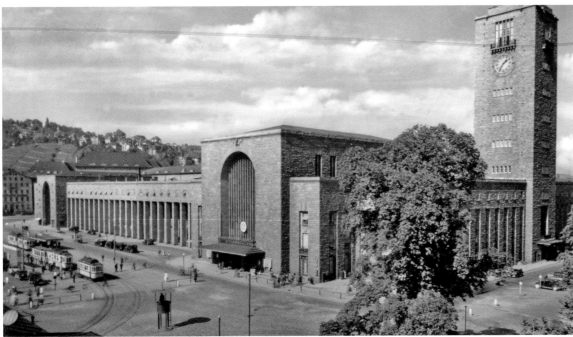

Stuttgart Haupbahnhof shunned the classicism made popular by nineteenth-century station design, embracing blockish simplicity on a monumental scale. It was begun prior to the First World War, but not finished until the mid-1920s.

Vienna Südbahnhof, painted by F. Witt, c.1900 (top left).

Stuttgart Hauptbahnhof in the 1920s (above).

'Grossstadtbahnhof', a painting by Hans Baluschek, 1904 (top right).

Hanover Hauptbahnhof, constructed between 1876 in 1879 and extended in 1910 (right).

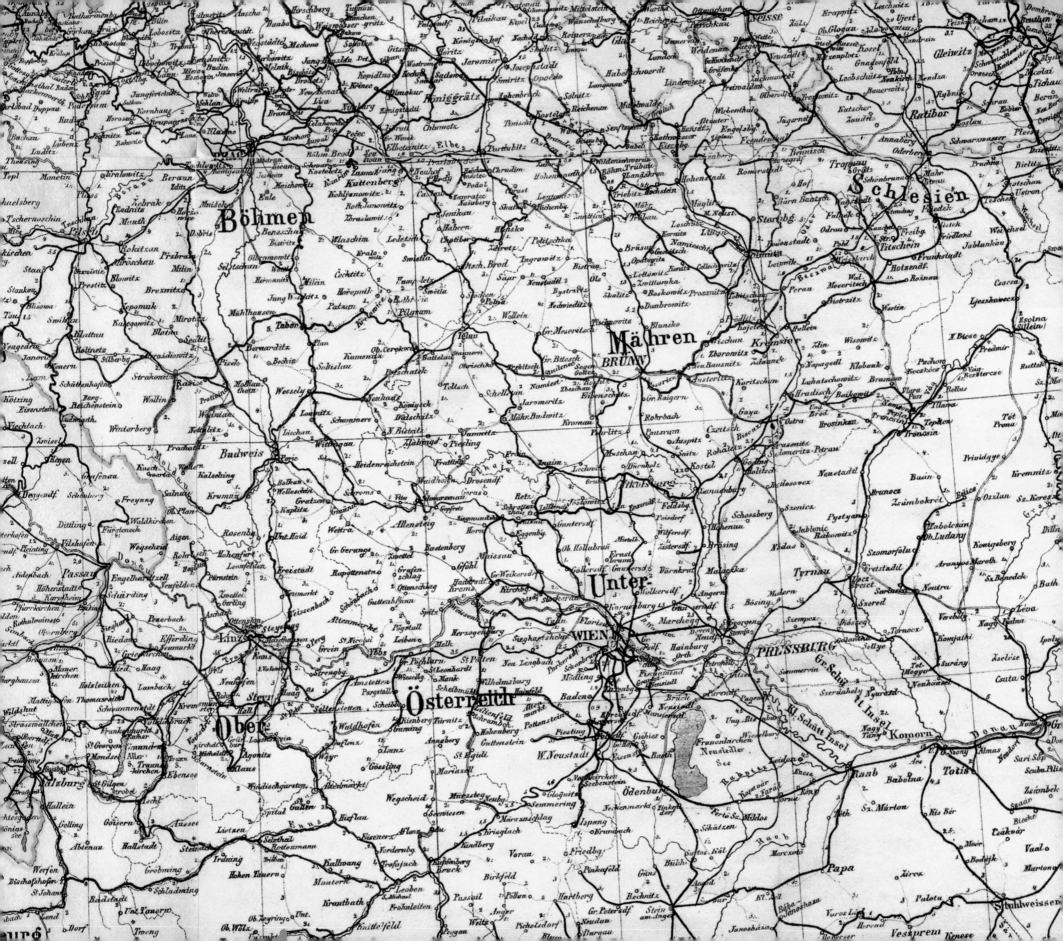

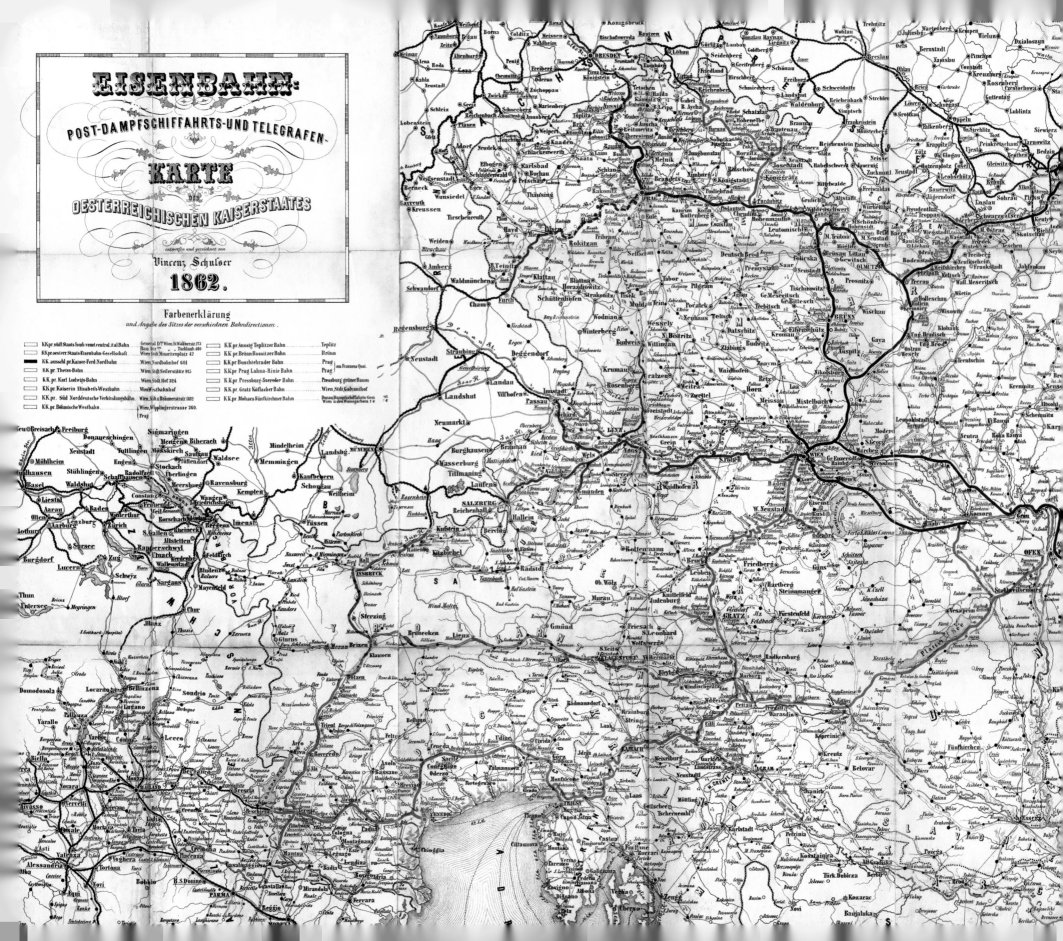

EISENBAHN-

POST-DAMPFSCHIFFAHRTS-UND TELEGRAFEN-

KARTE

DES

OESTERREICHISCHEN KAISERSTAATES

entworfen und gezeichnet von

Vincenz Schulser

1862.

Farbenerklärung
und Angabe des Sitzes der verschiednen Bahndirectionen.

'Express train crossing the Trisanna Bridge at Wiesberg am Arlberg', Austria, a 1900 painting by F. Witt.

SWITZERLAND

Few nations are today more closely associated with their railway networks than Switzerland, yet in its early years Swiss railway development lagged considerably behind that of its European neighbours. Switzerland's early reluctance to embrace the railway has been attributed to the domestic political unrest of the 1840s. The first Swiss railway, built in 1844, was merely a cross-border extension from Strasbourg, and even this formative effort was nearly two decades behind Britain's pioneering Stockton and Darlington line.

The country's first truly domestic railway was the so-called Spanisch-Brötlbahn ('Spanish Bun Railway') between Zürich and Baden, which opened in 1847. While there was little serious Swiss construction for another half dozen years, in the 1850s the Swiss government recognised the strategic value of the railway, and contracted none other than Britain's Robert Stephenson to assist with planning. Based on his advice, Switzerland embarked on rapid construction of routes across its lowland valleys, and starting in the 1870s began ambitious plans to conquer the more difficult Alpine regions.

Swiss railways were initially operated by private companies. In 1898 Switzerland moved to nationalise its primary routes, and in 1902 Swiss Federal Railways (Schwiezerische Bundesbahnen in German; Chemins de Fer Fédéraux Suisse in French), usually known as SBB, assumed operations of five primary Swiss main line networks along with various connecting secondary lines. SBB control extended over most standard gauge lines with the exception of the Berne–Lötschberg–Simplon trunk route, but left the majority of narrow gauge mountain lines and funicular railways to local operators.

Although many of SBB's routes can justly be praised for their scenic highlights and complex engineering, they pale in comparison with the engineering required of Switzerland's famous narrow gauge routes. The spectacular exception to

this rule of thumb is SBB's Gotthard route, with its spiral tunnels and long summit bore piercing the spine of the Alps. It must surely rank among the world's most impressive main line railways.

Britain's Robert Stephenson was contracted to assist with planning Switzerland's railways in the 1850s (above).

Poster for the Berne–Lötschberg–Simplon trunk route by E. Henziross, 1931 (left).

The Aussihler Viaduct near Zürich – an earth dam, stone arch and iron truss construction carrying the Spanisch-Brötlbahn between Zürich and Baden, painted by H. Isenring, late 1850s (opposite).

SBB AND THE ZÜRICH—MUNICH ROUTE

Switzerland's National Network

Viaduct construction near St Gallen, 1925 (above).

The SBB system forms the backbone of the Swiss network, operating key trunk routes and trans-Alpine crossings, and enjoying numerous international connections. By the mid-1950s SBB had more than 2,900 route km of standard gauge, plus another 74 km of narrow gauge lines. The difficult nature of Swiss geography is evident from the fact that SBB's system incorporates 2,970 bridges and nearly 240 tunnels, including no fewer than seven spiral tunnels. Among SBB's improvements was the early electrification of all its primary routes, encouraged by pre-First World War experiments combined with severe wartime fuel shortages.

Two of SBB's important international corridors provide key links with Austria and Germany, running east from Zürich. The first runs to a junction at Winterthur, from where one stem continues to the shore of Lake Constance at Romanshorn, the other following a southerly path via Wil, Gossau and St Gallen to Rorschach and the frontier station at St Margrethen. The single-track Rosenberg Tunnel between St Gallen and St Fiden was a bottleneck until 1912, when a new double-track bore eased capacity constraints.

Rorschach was an important junction, served by two stations, one near the town and the other serving a ferry terminal on Lake Constance. The awkward geography imposed by the lake — also known as the Bodensee — represents the joining point of three nations which, despite commonality of language, had difficult relations from time to time. Trains continuing east of St Margrethen into Germany have to round the head of Lake Constance using 16 km of Austrian railway via Bregenz, reaching German soil at Lindau, where a stub-end terminal requires trains to Munich and beyond to reverse direction.

Historically, SBB routed some of its freight via Romanshorn, ferrying cars across Lake Constance directly to Lindau to avoid the Austrian detour and unnecessary customs duties and delay. Passengers could also avail themselves of steam-ships across Lake Constance, although this was more for the experience than to expedite travel. In 1914 an express train running the 111 km journey from Zürich to St Margrethen would make the journey in two and a half hours.

Seasonally, the route to Bavaria carried through carriages between Berlin, Munich, and choice holiday destinations in Switzerland and France, the necessary connections being made at Zürich Hauptbahnhof. Zürich Hauptbahnhof was Switzerland's busiest railway hub, which *The Railway Magazine* noted in the years following the First World War accommodated 354 passenger trains daily, along with approximately a hundred goods trains. As a stub-end terminal, lines from all directions approached Zürich through a common neck.

SBB's second eastward international line continues southeast from Zürich, hugging the south shores of the Zürichsee and Walensee to Sargens. Here a branch runs south to Chur, where it connects with the narrow gauge Rhaetian Railway system, while the primary route angles northward to Buchs, where the route again divides. One branch offers an alternate route to St Margrethen, with the other runs via Liechtenstein to Feldkirch in Austria, connecting with the Arlberg route to Innsbruck and Vienna.

Bodensee-Toggenburgbahn Poster, Mario Borgini, c.1912 (above).

Station 'atmosphere' at Zürich Hauptbahnhof, 1890 (left).

THE GOTTHARD ROUTE

Switzerland's Mountain Spectacular

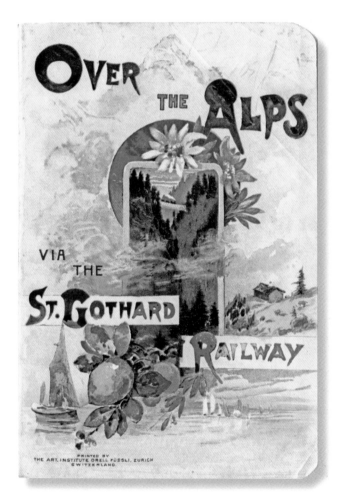

The Swiss Gotthard route is among the most important of European railway corridors. The relatively low saddle of the Gotthard Pass has served for centuries as a trading route, so was a natural choice for an Alpine railway crossing. The railway was conceived from the beginning as an international project, and traverses Switzerland on a north–south axis to connect Germany, Belgium and the Netherlands with Italy and the Adriatic states.

As the first of the two primary Swiss north–south Alpine crossings, the other being the Simplon route, the Gotthardbahn was inspired by the early success of Austria's pioneer Alpine railway via the Semmering Pass, and was a distinct departure from the early Swiss railways, built to hug river valleys at low elevations.

Although planned in the early 1860s, interest in the Gotthardbahn did not gain momentum until an international conference held at Berne in 1869 encouraged funding from Germany and Italy. Construction began in 1872, overcoming a host of technical and logistical hurdles before the exceptionally long Gotthard Tunnel was opened to traffic in 1882. The route was superbly engineered, and despite the difficult Alpine crossing it maintained a maximum gradient of just 2.7 per cent (a climb of 2.7 m for every hundred travelled), which became a Swiss standard for standard gauge mountain grades. Although steep compared with flatland running, the 2.7 per cent ascent offered a relatively gentle climb in contrast with later Alpine narrow gauge routes.

In its original form the Gotthardbahn began at Lucerne, where travellers anticipating a journey over the Alps were greeted by a magnificent railway station. In 1909 the Gotthardbahn was melded into the growing SBB network. As part of SBB, the main lines from Lucerne and Zürich joined at Arth-Goldau for the ascent via the Reuss Valley to the Gotthard Tunnel. The station at Flüelen on Lake Lucerne offered connections with lake steamers, making it a popular place to join the line. South of Erstfeld the line climbs steeply; in just 29 km it rises 634 m to reach the south portal of the Gotthard Tunnel. This required some of the most remarkable engineering to compensate for the valley floor that rose more steeply than the railway's steady 2.7 per cent ascent. To maintain the even gradient necessary for operations, engineers built numerous tunnels and bridges, and more spectacularly used spiral tunnels to gain elevation. The first of these is the helical tunnel at Pfaffensprung, where the line makes a sharp turn directly into the mountainside crossing over itself to

The colourful cover of a 1905 booklet describing the magnificent scenery to be seen along the St Gotthard route (above).

Steam train emerging from the Göschenen portal of the Gotthard Tunnel, 1890s (right).

Gotthardbahn.

emerge 35 m higher on the far side; emerging from the tunnel passengers would gaze down in awe, looking back along the route they had just travelled. A little further up the mountain the line navigates a pair of horseshoe curves as it ascends through more spiral tunnels. Here passengers can gauge their progress as they pass an iconic white church three times, each from a higher level.

The Gotthard Tunnel's south portal is located at Göschenen at an elevation of 1,109 m; in the early days trains paused here for a hasty meal break, while in later times it has served as the junction with the very steeply-graded branch of the narrow gauge rack-equipped Furka–Oberalp line to Andermatt. Passing through the Gotthard Tunnel is somewhat anticlimactic as the train hurtles through the cool moist gloom, cresting the Alps at 1,154 m above sea level, more than 900 m lower than the historic road over the top of the pass.

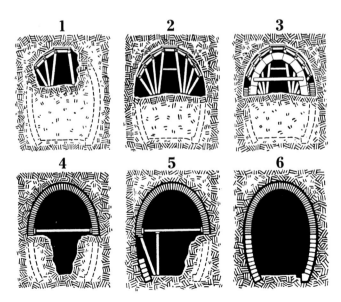

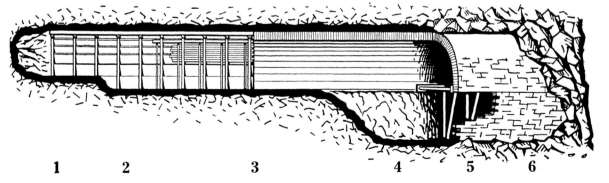

17024 P 2 GOESCHENEN

THE ST GOTTHARD TUNNEL

Through the Alps

In September 1869 representatives from Germany, Switzerland and Italy met in Berne to discuss the building of a railway line through the St Gotthard Pass. It was agreed at the conference to build the line, with all three countries sharing the cost. At the time France objected to this idea, fearing that it would divert traffic from the Mont Cenis route; however, the country's subsequent loss to the Prussians in their 1870–71 conflict silenced this protest.

On 1 November 1871 the Gotthard Rail Company was formed in Lucerne. Louis Favre, who had worked on the Mont Cenis Tunnel, was made its chief engineer. By this time, improvements in drilling equipment made by McKeon and Professor Colladon greatly speeded operations. For blasting purposes black powder was replaced by dynamite, which was ten times more powerful. Later, horses and mules, which transported men and supplies and removed debris, were replaced by compressed air locomotives.

The St Gotthard Tunnel route consists of a series of thirteen tunnels, which extended for a distance of fifteen kilometres. These were described in *Railways: the Pioneer Years*, by Malcolm Fletcher and John Taylor, as follows: 'The main feature of the St Gotthard series of tunnels is the spiral shape of seven of the thirteen. The line rises up the sides of different valleys and eventually reaches the main tunnel at the top. As the valleys get higher, they follow each other in quick succession, with the result that there is no room for the train to turn and it has to cross over a bridge or viaduct to the opposite side of the valley. There it enters a tunnel which rises and turns to emerge at a higher point still. From there, the train crosses another bridge or viaduct and re-enters the hill it has just left.'

With a constant crew of about 2,500 workers excavating from both directions, these tunnels were completed in a little over eight years. However, in the process, 177 lives were lost, including that of the chief engineer. Layers of rock were encountered that were harder than those at Mont Cenis, and interior temperatures were warmer, sometimes reaching 35 degrees centigrade.

The tunnellers finally made contact with each other on 28 February 1880. On 23 December 1881, the tunnel was ceremonially inaugurated, opening for goods traffic on 1 January 1882. Additional space along its route had been provided for double tracking, and soon, as traffic flow increased, this improvement was made. The opening of the tunnel completed construction of the St Gotthard Railway. This line is still in existence and extends from Lucerne to Chiasso at the Italian border, providing a vital link between Italy and Germany. Over its entire length the line has 101 bridges and eighty tunnels.

The lives of many construction workers were lost in the building of the St Gotthard Tunnel, through accident and illness – including that of the chief engineer, Louis Favre (above) in 1879.

This monument to the workers who died is near the station at Airolo, the south portal of the tunnel (left).

Göschenen in a chromolith of 1899 (opposite).

181

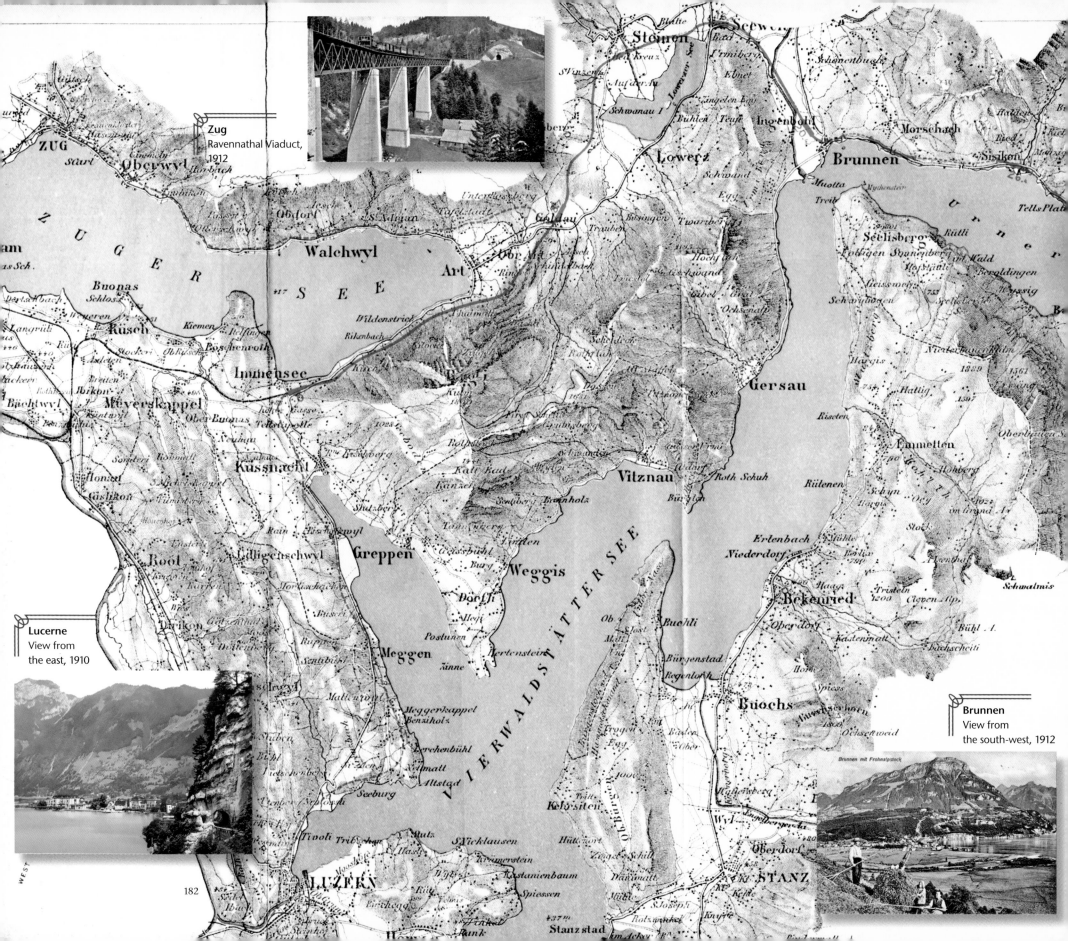

Zug
Ravennathal Viaduct, 1912

Lucerne
View from the east, 1910

Brunnen
View from the south-west, 1912

182

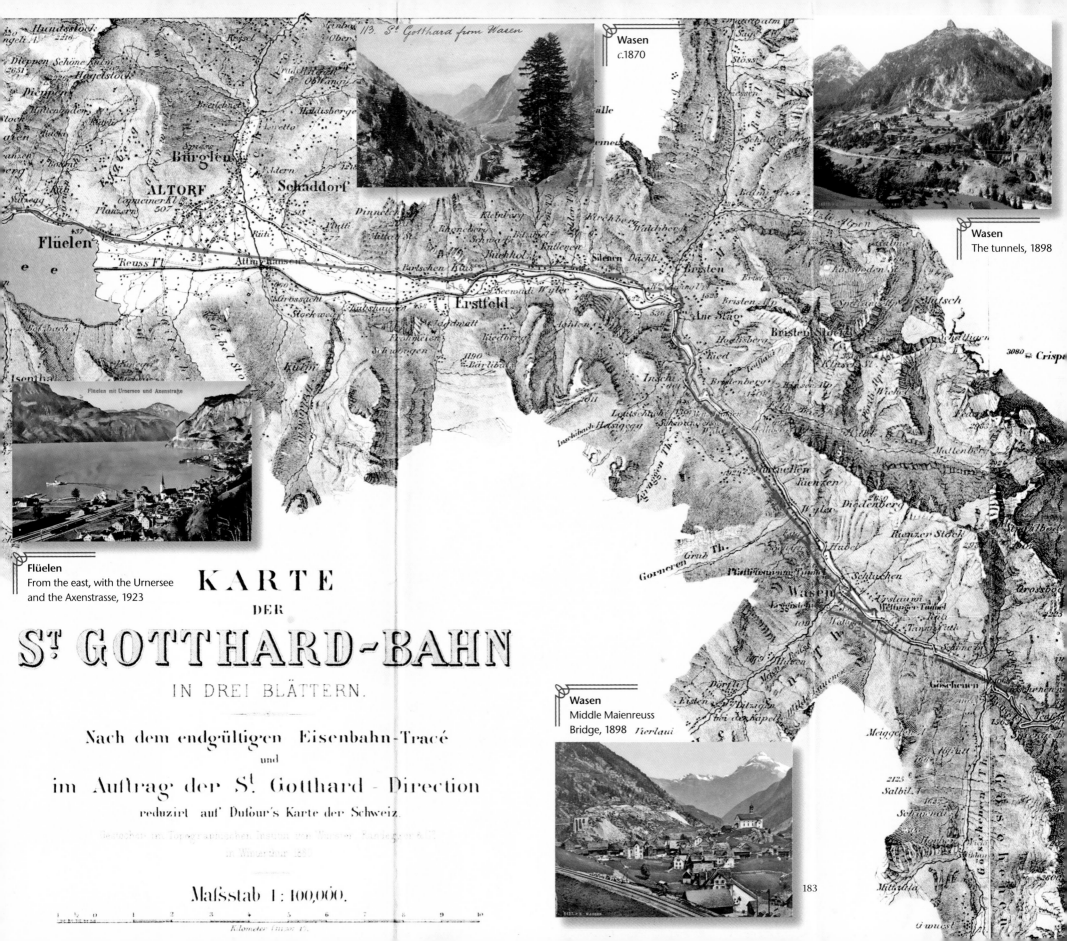

KARTE DER St GOTTHARD-BAHN

IN DREI BLÄTTERN.

Nach dem endgültigen Eisenbahn-Tracé

und

im Auftrag der St. Gotthard - Direction

reduzirt auf Dufour's Karte der Schweiz.

Maßstab 1 : 100,000.

Flüelen
From the east, with the Urnersee and the Axenstrasse, 1923

Wasen
c.1870

Wasen
The tunnels, 1898

Wasen
Middle Maienreuss Bridge, 1898

113. St Gotthard from Wasen

183

Wasen
Three levels of railway track, 1898

Andermatt
General view, 1870s
The Devil's Bridges, 1907

Airolo
View from the north, 1898
Stalvedro Gorge, 1898

Gotthard-Tunnel 14,900 Meter Länge

184

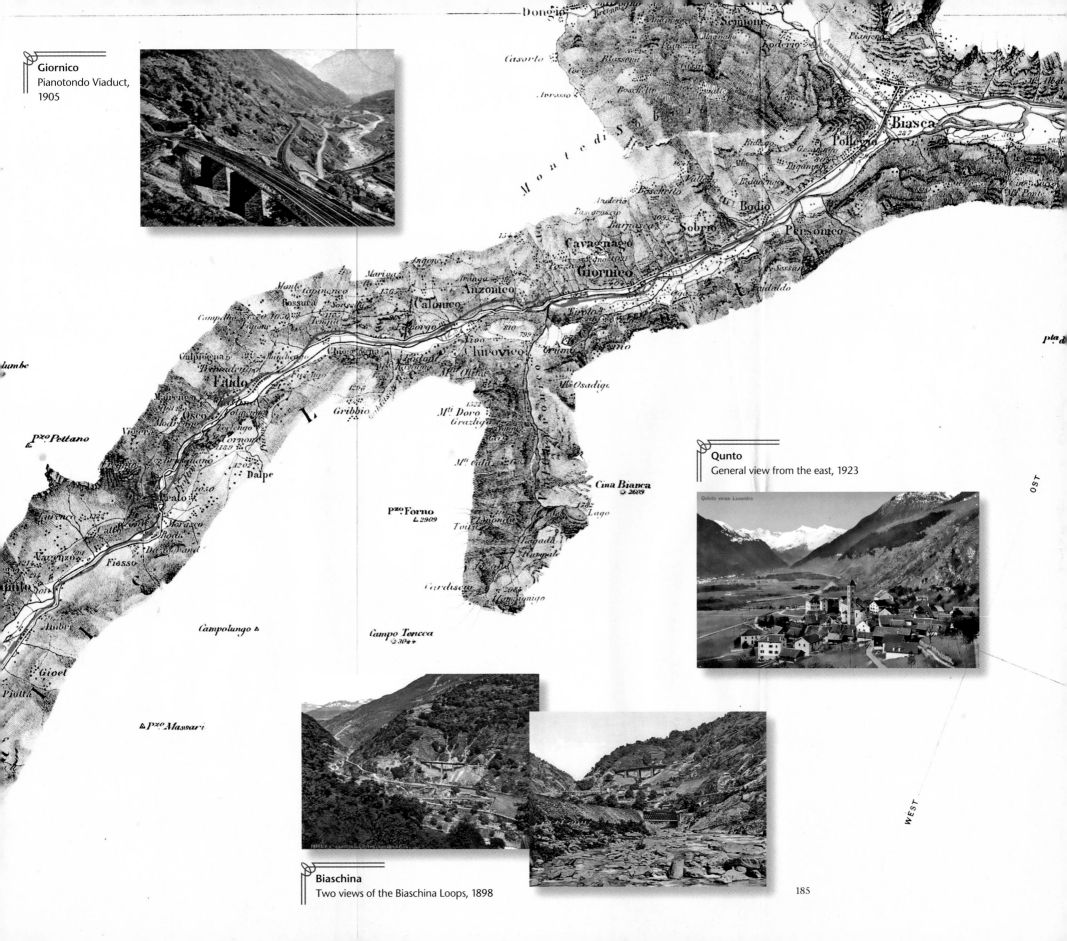

Giornico
Pianotondo Viaduct,
1905

Qunto
General view from the east, 1923

Biaschina
Two views of the Biaschina Loops, 1898

Piotta
Two views from the mid-1930s

1674 Piotta, 1012 m.s.m.

Faido
General view, 1914

5 Faido - Veduta generale

Rodi
View from the south, 1924

S. Gottardo   Piora

186

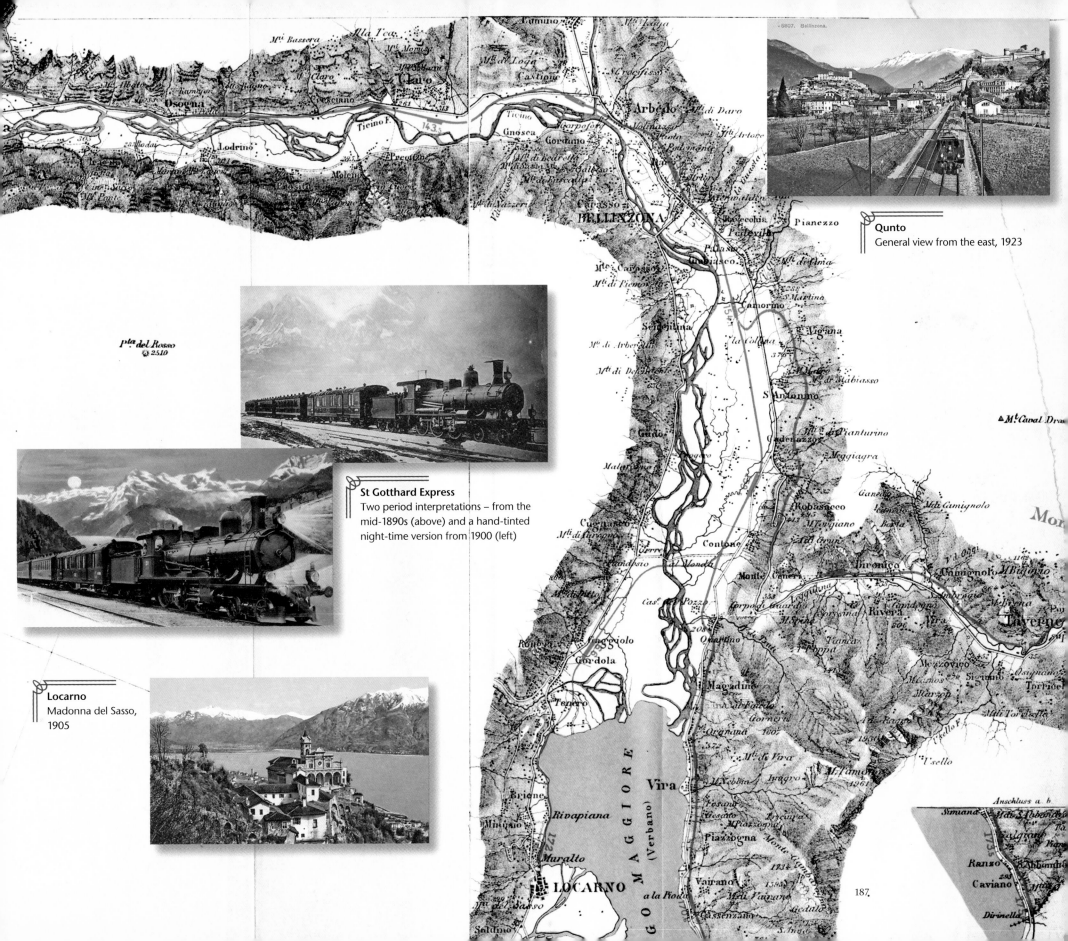

Bellinzona

Qunto
General view from the east, 1923

St Gotthard Express
Two period interpretations – from the
mid-1890s (above) and a hand-tinted
night-time version from 1900 (left)

Locarno
Madonna del Sasso,
1905

187.

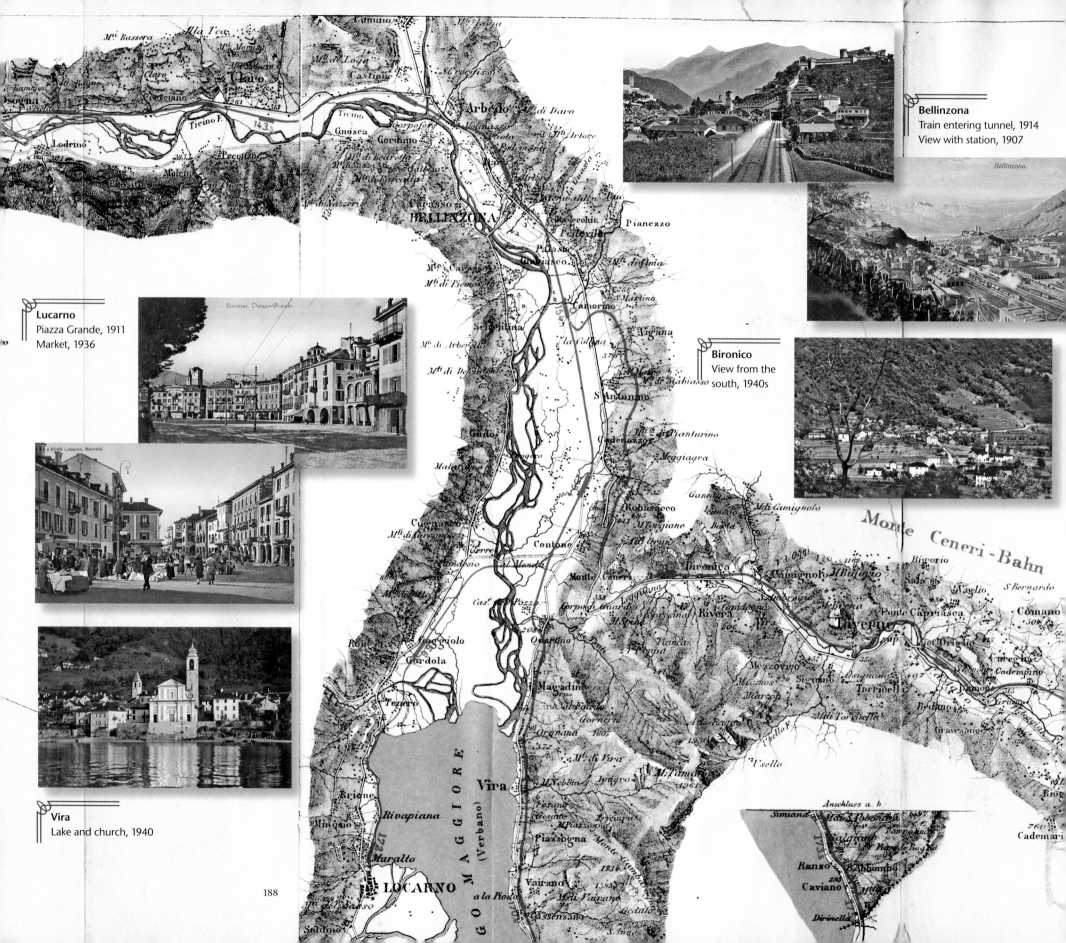

Bellinzona
Train entering tunnel, 1914
View with station, 1907

Lucarno
Piazza Grande, 1911
Market, 1936

Bironico
View from the south, 1940s

Vira
Lake and church, 1940

188

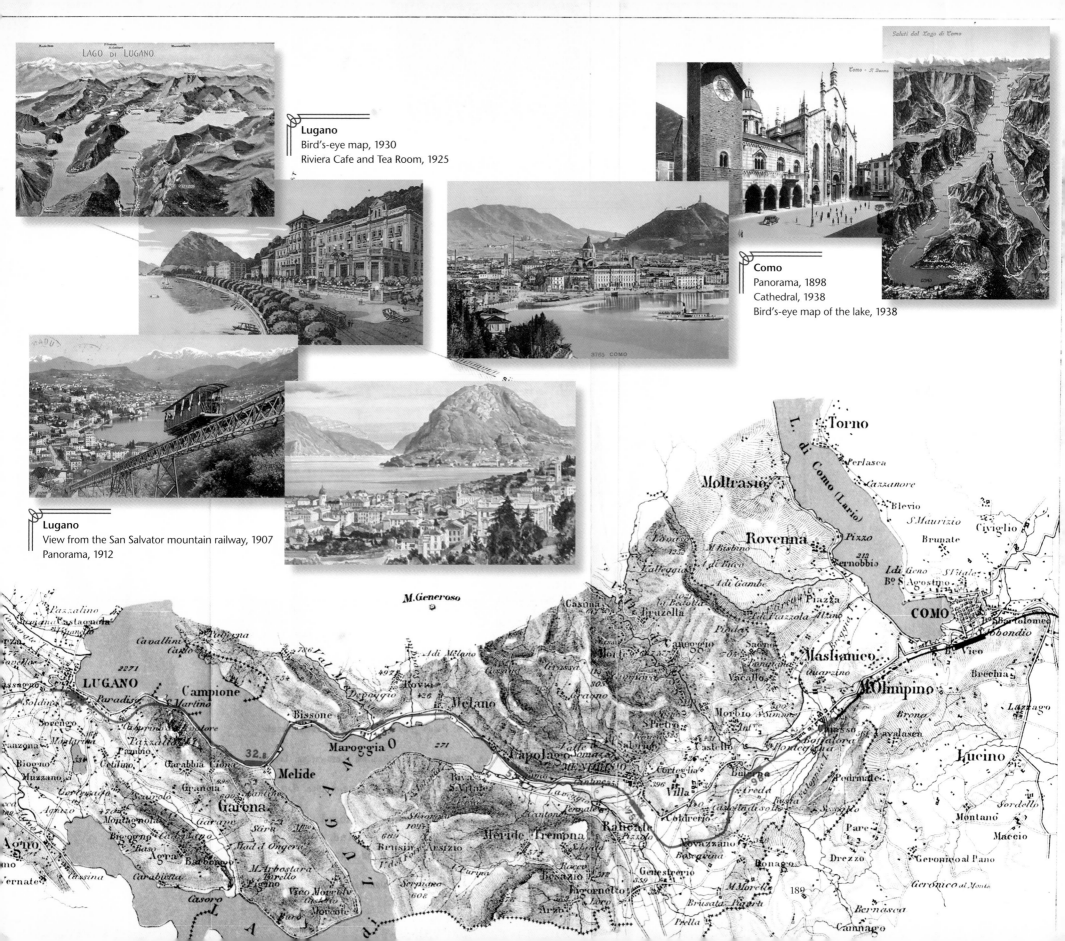

Lugano
Bird's-eye map, 1930
Riviera Cafe and Tea Room, 1925

Como
Panorama, 1898
Cathedral, 1938
Bird's-eye map of the lake, 1938

Lugano
View from the San Salvator mountain railway, 1907
Panorama, 1912

THE SIMPLON ROUTE

Switzerland's Second Trans-Alpine Route

The Simplon Tunnel opened one of the last main traditional trans-Alpine routes, the first having been the Mont Cenis Tunnel route linking France and Italy, which had opened thirty-five years earlier. In conjunction with other lines, notably the Lötschberg route, the Simplon Tunnel offers the shortest route between northern Europe and Italy. Highlighting the speed and directness of the route, the famed *Simplon Orient Express*, introduced after the First World War, used the new tunnel as opposed to the more traditional *Orient Express* route via Vienna.

Tunnel operations were electrified from the beginning, initially wired using the Italian three-phase system, and later re-electrified with the Swiss single-phase standard. Simplon traffic grew rapidly after the First World War, and a parallel second bore, slightly longer than the first, was opened in 1922. The twin northern portals are located southeast of Brig near the village of Termen. Their impressive stone facing inscribed with the dates of construction offers a sight which might well have come straight out of Tolkien's fantasy fiction.

The Italian portal of the Simplon Tunnel at Domodossola, *c*.1910 (above).

A 1906 postcard showing an SBB Simplon-Express at Iselle station on the Italian side. In the left background is an SBB electric locomotive used to pull the train through the Simplon Tunnel (right).

A north–south railway via the Simplon Pass was envisioned in the 1850s, but it took half a century more to be realised. Key portions of the route were built well in advance of the great Simplon Tunnel, with track reaching Brig, near the site of the north portal, in July 1878 and considerable consolidation of the Jura–Simplon network being completed ahead of tunnel construction. By the time the SBB assumed operation of the Jura–Simplon network, construction of the tunnel was well under way, its completion being among SBB's early priorities. The initial bore was completed in February 1905, and at 19.7 km it was for many years the world's longest railway tunnel.

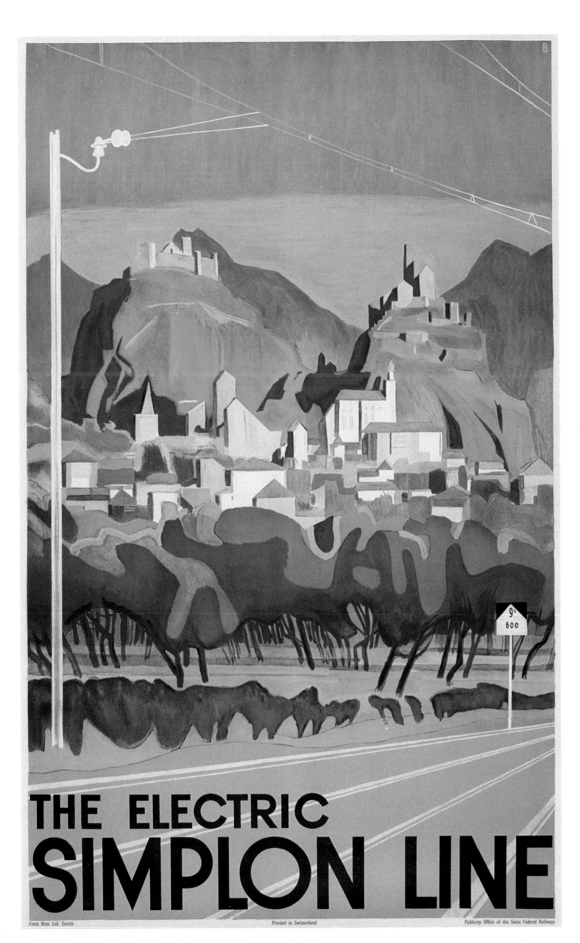

THE ELECTRIC SIMPLON LINE

Fretz Bros Ltd. Zurich   Printed in Switzerland   Publicity Office of the Swiss Federal Railways

The Electric Simplon Line poster, artist unknown, 1955 (far left).

Timber supports were used temporarily to strengthen the Simplon Tunnel as it was driven (left).

The tunnel portal, 1908 (below).

Churchman's cigarette card showing tunnel construction (bottom).

Le Tunnel du Simplon à Iselle.

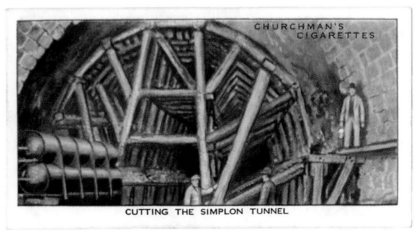

CHURCHMAN'S CIGARETTES

CUTTING THE SIMPLON TUNNEL

THE LÖTSCHBERG ROUTE

The Last Classic Alpine Rail Crossing

Official opening celebration of the Lötschberg Tunnel on 14 May 1911; the first electric locomotive passed through the tunnel on 3 June (above).

Life undergound for tunnellers working on the Lötschberg (right).

A 13 2–10–2 (1E1) 2,500hp electric locomotive stands in Goppenstein station at the south end of the Lötschberg Tunnel, 1927 (opposite, top left).

Poster for the Lötschberg route, Eric Hermès, 1949 (opposite).

Poster of Blausee bei Kandersteg on the Lötschbergbahn, by E. Hodel, date unknown (opposite inset).

Opened in 1913, the Lötschberg Route was one of the last primary standard gauge Swiss main line links completed in the classic era of European railway travel. Although effectively integrated with the Swiss Federal Railway (SBB) network, this route was operated by the Compagnie du Chemin der Fer des Alpes Bernoises Berne–Loetschberg–Simplon, better known by its initials BLS.

The route runs on a north-west–south-east diagonal across western Switzerland, connecting Berne with Brig via the Lötschberg Tunnel under the Bernese Alps. It provides a direct route for express trains running from Holland, Belgium, and north-eastern France, via the Simplon Tunnel, to Italy and beyond. It obviated the need for a circuitous detour south-south-west for trains heading over the Alps via the Simplon Route by offering a natural extension of the Simplon Line. While through carriages are handled, BLS operated its own equipment. Historically its locomotives were rugged electric types painted a utilitarian uniform brown, which contrasted with the serene and stunning scenery of the line.

Although this route had been projected in the mid-nineteenth century, it was only in 1899 that Berne Canton started work on the project, partially with the assistance of French financing.

Like many Swiss main lines, the BLS route offers important international connections. At Berne, BLS trains operate via SBB, crossing the world's largest four-track viaduct spanning the Aar River Gorge. Originally constructed of steel, the bridge was later supplanted by a reinforced concrete span. Rolling south-eastward, the snow-crested peaks of the Bernese Alps

192

are visible to travellers from the moment the train leaves Berne. At Thun, on the shores of the lake of the same name, BLS trains leave SBB rails for their own. Lake Thun, considered among the most picturesque of all Alpine lakes, is famous for its clear blue water which reflects the sky and the surrounding snow-topped peaks. As the line approaches the Kander Valley, passengers may get glimpses of some of Switzerland's more famous peaks, including the Blümlisalp.

Spiez, at an elevation of 616 m, is a classic Swiss village with a handsome station located near a key junction where a line diverges, running to Zweisimmen via Erlenback, to connect with the Montreaux–Oberland–Bernois Railway. Further south at Mülenen, the BLS connects with the Nissen funicular line. After many miles of relatively gentle running through Alpine valleys, at Frutigen the BLS begins its steep ascent of the Kander Valley, where the ruling grade reaches 2.7 per cent. Since the valley floor rises more steeply than is possible for the grade to keep pace with, at Mitholz the railway grade employs spirals to loop back on itself. Passing below the romantic ruins of Felsenburg Castle, it zigzags above the Kander, offering stunning views of the mountains beyond.

At Kandersteg, 1,178 m above sea level, the railway faces the formidable wall of the Bernese Alps, escaping by virtue of the 14.6 km Lötschberg Tunnel, emerging again at Goppenstein. Having crossed into the Mediterranean watershed, the line descends into the Rhone Valley where, from high on a shelf, views of SBB's Simplon Line running hundreds of feet below come into view. Gradually the two lines come together and finally join at Brig, not far from the portal of the Simplon Tunnel.

THE RHAETIAN RAILWAY AND GLACIER EXPRESS

Switzerland's Narrow Gauge Marvels

· ALBULA - BAHN ·

BERNINA-BAHN

Direkte Verbindung vom Engadin nach Italien. 2256 ü.M.

Narrow gauge railways allow for tighter curves, lighter equipment and steeper grades than standard gauge operation. This enables cheaper construction, and permits railways to reach places where standard gauge lines would be prohibitively expensive. South-eastern Switzerland was well suited to the benefits of narrow gauge, and among the most interesting Alpine railways is a spectacular narrow gauge network that straddles the Alpine watersheds of the Rhine, Rhone and Danube rivers. Historically the different elements of the network have been operated by different companies, each characterised by different styles of construction and operations. Working together, these lines hosted Europe's slowest, highest, and scenically most impressive 'express' trains, notably the *Glacier Express* from St Moritz to Zermatt.

The Rhaetian Railway (Rhätische Bahn or RhB) network features exceptional engineering, exemplified by the Albula Pass crossing between Chur and St Moritz. Unquestionably one of the most impressive railways in the world, highlights include the much-photographed Landwasser Viaduct, a sharply-curved semicircular stone arch bridge which emerges dramatically from the side of a cliff before crossing a deep precipice and plunging into a tunnel on the far side.

For the passenger, the RhB's circuitous ascent of the Albula Gorge between Bergün and Preda offers a dizzying thrill. The railway line winds up and over itself repeatedly to gain altitude on a steady gradient within the confines of a narrow mountainous pass, all without the aid of a rack. Opened in 1904 and originally operated with steam locomotives, the line ascends 417 m on a serpentine route which takes 12.5 km by rail to travel just 6 km as the crow flies. To achieve this requires remarkable spiral tunnels and towering stone viaducts which make three complete loops — an envy of model railway builders everywhere. At Preda the railway plunges into the 6 km long Albula Tunnel, cresting at over 1,800 m. The difficulties of using steam locomotives made the RhB an early candidate for electrification, and its entire route was under wire by 1922. Among its iconic locomotives are the famed jack-shaft-powered 'baby crocodiles', so-called because of their olive-brown paint, long nose sections, and small driving wheels.

Among the lines connecting with the RhB is the Bernina Line, consolidated with the RhB in 1943, which crosses the Bernina Pass and descends through the Poschiavo Valley, providing a link between the Alpine resorts around St Moritz with Tirano in Italy. Built between 1908 and 1910, the Bernina Line was electrified from the beginning, and is among the most steeply-graded adhesion railways (relying only on the friction between the locomotive's driving wheels and the rail to drive the train) in the world, with maximum gradients of 7.1 per cent.

To the west the RhB linked with the Furka–Oberalp Bahn at Disentis. This steeply-graded railway is named for the two high Alpine passes it crosses. Completed in 1926, it was one of the last through railways built in Switzerland, and has several long rack sections. On the Furka Pass it skirted an avalanche run using a seasonally removable bridge, lifted before the heavy snows arrived and restored in the spring. At Brig the Furka–Oberalp Bahn connects with another narrow gauge line which continues via Visp to Zermatt, the terminal for the short but exceptionally steep Gornergrat Bahn rack line, which ascends a 20 per cent ruling grade to an elevation of 3,120 m.

RhB Ge 4/4 III with a Regio Express train from St. Moritz to Chur on the famous Landwasser Viaduct. Note the two first 'panoramic' coaches (above).

Poster for the Albula-Bahn, Anton Reckziegel, 1903, showing a steam locomotive crossing the Bergbach (opposite, top).

Poster for the Bernina-Bahn, artist unknown, c.1916 (opposite, bottom).

Poster for the Rhaetische Bahn, *Graubünden-Schweiz*, Walter Koch, 1909 (right).

Poster for the Davosersee (Davos Lake), F. Hugo d'Alesi, 1900 (far right).

THE JUNGFRAUBAHN

The Highest Railway in Europe

Adolf Guyer-Zeller, visionary railway builder responsible for the creation of the Jungfraubahn (above).

Jungfraujoch, the highest railway station in Europe and top end of the line at 3,454 metres (right).

The Jungfraubahn beginning its ascent from Klein Scheidegg station (opposite, top).

A collection of images from the Jungfraubahn's early days, 1895–1912 (opposite, bottom).

The Jungfraubahn (Jungfrau Railway) claims the title as Europe's highest railway, and is among Europe's steepest. When visionary builder Herr Guyer-Zeller conceived the line in the late nineteenth century, many people dismissed his idea as an impossible fantasy, yet through his clever engineering and persuasive abilities he secured necessary permission and financing to make his vision a reality.

Construction began in July 1896 at Klein Scheidegg, the 2,061 m high terminus of the Wengernalpbahn (Wengernalp Railway), and proceeded upwards toward the railway's namesake Alpine peak. Unlike Swiss main lines designed to carry a variety of through and local traffic, from the beginning the Jungfrau was only intended as a tourist line, with the sole objective of carrying passengers to high altitudes to enjoy Alpine panoramas previously only available to the most dedicated mountaineers.

The railway was built in stages, and as each portion opened tens of thousands of passengers flocked to the line. Sadly Guyer-Zeller succumbed to a heart attack in 1899, before the most difficult part of the line was started. Yet, despite especially difficult engineering and occasional financial problems, construction was pushed relentlessly forward. The line was cut into the mountain, ascending above the snowline into harsh glacial territory. Despite the exceptional remoteness of the route, combined with difficult stone, terrible winter conditions and threats of avalanche, the engineering teams worked on the line year round. The top of the line, Jungfraujoch at 3,454 m, was reached in August 1912. The peak of Jungfrau towers over the summit station, rising to an altitude of 4,158 m above sea level.

The entire line is only 9.3 km long, ascending at grades of up to 25 per cent, and more than 6 km of the line are inside the mountain, including some of the intermediate stations as well as the Jungfraujoch terminus. Such a climb is well beyond the capabilities of an ordinary adhesion railway, so when it was built most of the line was equipped with the Strab rack system, employing a central cog-rail engaged by a toothed driving wheel to allow trains to claw their way up the mountainside. Steep gradients, tunnels, and exceptionally tight curvature lent themselves to narrow gauge construction, and the line was built as a meter-gauge route, electrically powered by three-phase overhead.

Passengers travelling on the Jungfraubahn reached the line via connections from Interlaken, with a choice of routes via either Lauterbrunnen or Grindelwald. A change of trains was required at Klein Scheidegg. Typically three-car trains carry passengers on the ascent, which begins sharply as soon as the train leaves the bottom station. Since much of the line was hidden in the inky black of tunnels, engineers carved massive windows in the rock to give passengers glimpses of the surrounding Alpine scenery. Eismeer ('Sea of Ice') Station, located within the confines of the mountain supported by massive stone columns, offered windows of the sprawling Fiescher Glacier, and even more magnificent vistas open up immediately above the railway's subterranean Jungfraujoch terminal.

6°30'   7°   Longitude East of Greenwich   7°30'   8°

North Latitude

Drawn for the heliogravure process at

N° 35. ATLAS DER SCHWEIZ Bibliothek des Geograph. Lexikons, Neuenburg.

Eröffnung der Bahnen:
1847 – 1855
1856 – 1860
1861 – 1870
1871 – 1880
1881 – 1890
1891 – 1900
1901 – 1908
Ausländische Bahnen
Projekt. Bahnen

1:500000

HISTORISCHE ENTWICKLUNG DER EISENBAHNEN

POLAND

In 1795 Poland was partitioned, its territory divided between Prussia and the Austrian and Russian Empires. During the nineteenth and early twentieth centuries these nations built railways across Polish territory to serve the needs of their respective empires. Yet Poland maintained a strong awareness of its national identity, and this was reflected in international travel guides of the period. *Bradshaw's Guide* for 1893 listed timetables for 'Russia in Europe, including Poland', further noting that the Russian Empire 'incompassed 60 governments', including Poland's.

When the Republic of Poland was established in 1918, its national railway network, Polakie Koleje Panstwowe (Polish State Railways or PKP) was formed from components of the previous Austrian, German and Russian systems. While this resulted in a single Polish network, it brought with it a host of operation challenges. Not only had Polish infrastructure been ravaged by the war, but its component networks were not designed for uniform working. One of the hardest challenges was the difference in track gauge between former Russian lines that used a 5 foot (1.52 m) gauge, and lines elsewhere in Poland which had been built to the standard continental gauge of 4 feet $8^{1}/_{2}$ inches (1.44 m). PKP also faced difficulties in amalgamating a phenomenally wide variety of locomotives and rolling stock.

During the interwar period Poland developed new routes designed to benefit the unified Polish state. Noteworthy was the north–south coal corridor running from the mines of Silesia to the newly-developed Baltic port of Gdynia, completed with French financing in 1933. Other main lines, such as the Kutno–Lodz link, improved the network further.

During the Second World War, Poland's railways were again ravaged by armed conflict, and as a result of Soviet invasion many routes were again re-gauged to the Russian standard; some reverted to standard once more in the postwar period. After the war, Poland's borders were redefined, with both frontiers shifted considerably westward. The Soviet Union reclaimed much territory in eastern Poland, assigning it to its Belarussian and Ukrainian provinces, while the border with Germany was moved to lines established by the Oder and Neisse Rivers. Railways in former German territory retained their Germanic characteristics, including the continued operation of German-built steam locomotives, some surviving until the early 2000s.

Warsaw Rembertów station, 1866 (top).

Tarnów station in southern Poland, 1910 (above).

Poznan station, 1863 (bottom left).

Construction of the Terespol Station in Warsaw, 1866 (below right).

Trzebinia station crew, 1905 (opposite).

BERLIN–WARSAW

A Key West-East Connection

Poznan station around 1910 (opposite).

Poznan station in the 1920s (below top).

Locomotive taking on water at Kutno, 1923 (below).

Kutno station around 1910 (below right).

Among the principal Polish railway corridors were the lines connecting the Polish and German capitals. These were first developed in the mid-nineteenth century, when Warsaw was an Imperial Russian city. In this period the German–Russian frontier was located between Slupca and Strzalkowo, west of Konin; during the interwar period the Polish–German frontier on this route was located west of the important junction at Zbaszyn. The end of hostilities in 1945 resulted in the shifting of the German–Polish frontier westward to the River Oder, near the German city of Frankfurt-am-Oder. Polish State Railways operated internal Warsaw–Zbaszyn express trains as well as international services between Warsaw and Berlin.

Among the most famous and important places on the Berlin–Warsaw route is Poznan, a city which over the centuries has been variously administered by Polish and Prussian authorities. In the tenth century it served as Poland's capital, while some histories describe it as the oldest large town in Poland. The 1933 Thomas Cook timetable lists westward trains arriving at 'Poznan' while departing from 'Posen', a judicious means of reflecting the differences in Polish and German spellings. In the railway era Poznan became an important junction and hub serving many routes, as well as the location of a major locomotive works.

East of Poznan there were two routes to Warsaw. The older and shorter of these ran via Konin, Kutno and Lowicz, measuring 377 km versus the 391 km route via the industrial city of Lodz. Poland's name is derived from Latin 'Polonia', which translated means 'nation of the plain'. True to this descrip-tion, both Warsaw routes crossed open flat country. While this made for easy railway engineering and

simple operations, the landscape from the carriage window is uninspiring. Today trains clip along at high speed on this route, though historically Polish trains were notoriously slow, even on level straight track, a tradition maintained on many secondary lines. There were, however, exceptions; in 1933 the premier *Nord Express* departed Berlin at 6.20 p.m., with a scheduled arrival in Warsaw at 6.18 a.m. the following morning, having covered 558 km.

Kutno, on the northern Poznan–Warsaw route, is a major junction 134 km west of Warsaw where five routes intersect. Closer to Warsaw is Lowicz, another junction, where the direct route from Warsaw to Lodz diverges. The town was famous for its historic horse fairs. Near Warsaw the line passes near Zelazowa-Wola, birthplace of the pianist and composer Frédéric Chopin; nearby are the picturesque ruins of a medieval castle.

WARSAW—MOSCOW

A Railway Between Two Worlds

When much of Poland was part of the Russian Empire, the Warsaw–Moscow journey was effectively a domestic one, yet that made it anything but swift. In 1893 a through train to Moscow departed from Warsaw at four in the afternoon, and took 6 hours 40 minutes to plod the first 214 km to Brest-Litovsk, an historic fortified town on the River Bug which developed as a regional railway hub. The train finally reached Moscow at 11.35 on the second morning, having travelled 1,022 km east from Brest-Litovsk. It was among the longest slow journeys in Europe. A further complication for foreign travellers resulted from the fact that at that time Russia's calendar was twelve days behind Western Europe, so despite the glacial pace of the trains travellers would find that they had arrived in Moscow before they left London!

When Poland was re-established after the First World War, lines inherited from the Czarist Russian network were in exceptionally poor condition. As Russian forces had retreated from advancing German armies they laid waste to railway infrastructure. Stations, signal boxes and railway employee housing were among the casualties. *Railway Wonders* estimated that four out of every five bridges were destroyed, while the general condition of tracks and rights of way suffered from years of neglect, if not outright destruction. Despite these setbacks, Polish State Railways set about rebuilding railways from the ruins of the old system. This

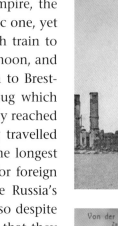

Destruction of railway infrastructure by the retreating Russian army; Gdansk Station in Warsaw, and the station at Lötzen (present-day Gizycko) in northeast Poland (right).

Terespol Station, Warsaw, 1920s (below).

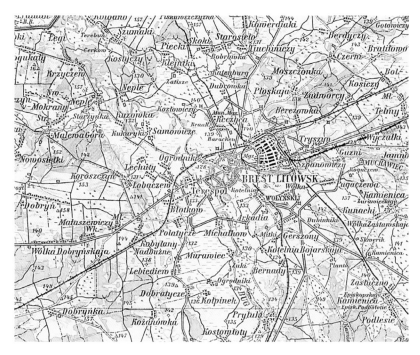

required substantial re-gauging of lines, since the Russian network had been constructed to five-foot gauge.

Poland's eastern frontier during the interwar period was substantially further east than after the Second World War, and many railway lines crossed the Polish–Soviet frontier. Most important of these to international travellers was the primary Warsaw–Moscow route, which ran for 1,305 km in a north-easterly direction via Lukow and Terespol, crossing the frontier east of Stolpce, near the Belarusian capital of Minsk. Stolpce, on the River Niemen, was notable for having a large prewar Jewish population.

During the Second World War invading Russian forces rapidly re-gauged key Polish routes back to the Russian standard, many of which were again re-gauged to western standards after 1945. By that time Poland's frontiers had been again redrawn, with the new border with the Soviet Union located between Terespol and Brest-Litovsk.

The difference of track gauge has long limited railway traffic between Poland and Russia and its gauge-similar satellites. Through passenger trains between Warsaw and points east typically used Russian-gauge carriages, which are generally much larger than those used in Western Europe. Re-gauging activities at the border were typically coincident with the time-consuming petty bureaucratic activities of Soviet Russian customs officials. While running speeds across western Poland were slow, lines in the east were even slower. For the Western European passenger, the relatively bland scenery of the rolling Polish plain could be relieved by the thrill of heading further and further east to lands unexplored and decidedly foreign.

Terespol Railway locomotive No. 1, *Friedrich Lembert*, 1866 (above left).

Brest-Litovsk around 1910, map and station building (above).

Jewish women being used by the German army as forced labour on the railway at Stolpce, 1943 (left).

WARSAW–VIENNA AND SOUTHERN POLAND

Into the Heart of the Carpathian Mountains

Kraków main station and Vistula Bridge around 1912 (below).

Small stations in the Carpathians in the 1920s: Rabka-Zdrój and Nowy Sacz (right).

The Kraków–Tarnów line at Jordanowie (opposite).

The busy station and goods yard at Zebrzydowice, 1910 (insets opposite).

Warsaw's Vienna Station served as a gateway to the west, with through services to Berlin, Paris, Prague and Rome, as well as Vienna and many other intermediate destinations. Running in a south-westerly direction from the Polish capital, this standard gauge route allowed for through connections at Kraków via Austria's Kaiser Ferdinand Nordbahn. Prior to the First World War Kraków was within the Habsburg monarchy's Austrian Empire, but after the redrawing of political frontiers in 1918 it became part of Poland, with the railway crossing the new Polish–Czech frontier near the station at Zebrzydowice, where to accommodate customs facilities a sizeable goods yard was developed.

Kraków also served an east–west route connecting the German city of Breslau (later Poland's Wroclaw) with Katowice via Kraków, then continuing eastward via Tarnów, and Przemysl to Lemberg, later Polish Lwów, which after the Second World War was absorbed by Soviet Ukraine and today is known as L'viv. Historically Lemberg had served as the Austrian capital of Galicia, and was a major railway gateway to the east. Architecturally the city shares a similarity with the Bohemian and Moravian capitals of Prague and Olomouc, also key cities in the Habsburg Empire. Despite the many changes in national frontiers, Lemberg remained an important railway junction.

South of Kraków, Polish State Railways lines reach into the Carpathians, a marked contrast with the flatland running experienced elsewhere in Poland. Its routes connected many popular resorts; notable is the scenic dead-end branch running to Zakopane high in the mountains near the Slovakian frontier. Southwards from a junction at Tarnów, a minor trunk line winds its way over the mountains, serving winter resorts and health spas near Nowy Sacz and Krynica, at the same time providing an outlet for Polish coal to industrial centres in eastern Slovakia and Hungary. Among the scenic highlights is the broad horseshoe curve near Grybów, where the line loops around to gain elevation, affording passengers a view back along the line they just travelled. South of Nowy Sacz the line traverses the forested Dunajec River valley, which serves in part as the border between modern-day Poland and Slovakia.

Kraków. Dworzec kolejowy. Krakau. Bahnhof.

Widok z wieży zamkowej w Krakowie. — Ansicht vom Königl. Schloss in Krakau. Vue prise de la tour du château à Cracovie.

RABKA ZDRÓJ

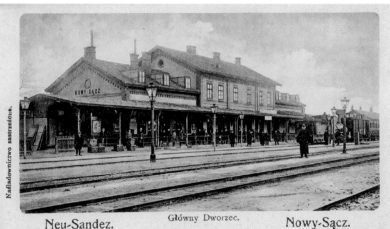

Neu-Sandez.   Główny Dworzec.   Nowy-Sącz.

WARSAW'S MAIN STATIONS

Railway Portals of the Polish Capital

Poland's capital and largest metropolis is located near the centre of the nation, and also close to the geographical centre of Europe. This strategic location makes it a key transport gateway between east and west, and facilitated Warsaw's emergence as an international railway crossroads.

By the end of the nineteenth century Warsaw was ringed by railway terminals – Vienna Station, south of the centre, served trains toward Berlin and Vienna; in the north-west the Vistula Station (later Dworzec Gdánski) was the terminus for trains for Danzig (Gdánsk in Polish). To the east of the Vistula River, in the suburb of Praga, was St Petersburg Station for trains to that northern Russian city, and nearby was Terespol Station for trains toward Brest-Litovsk (Brest-Litewski) and Moscow.

Gdansk (Kowelski) Station, 1908 (right).

St Petersburg Station, 1921 (below).

Traffic changes as a result of Polish independence following the First World War saw the redrawing of the Warsaw railway map. A new electrified junction railway was built to facilitate connections between the major international lines; this included a central cross-city line and a new Vistula River bridge.

Postwar plans also included the construction of a unified centralised terminal, although unlike the new cross-city railway it took a half century to be realised. In the meantime a new main station (Warsawa Glówna) was built near the site of Vienna Station in the 1920s and 1930s, and was largely rebuilt following its destruction in the Second World War.

The site of Terespol Station was redeveloped in the 1920s as Wschodnia Osobowa (East Passenger Station), together with a new station to the west of the city called Warszawa Zachodnia (Warsaw West).

In the mid-1970s Warsaw Central (Warszawa Centralna) was finally constructed in a massive concrete style characteristic of Soviet-era architecture. Its four underground platforms make for a gloomy welcome to Warsaw.

Warsaw Vienna station in 1905 (main picture).

Warsaw's railway terminals in 1905, from *Dr Koch's Eisenbahn und Verkehrs-Atlas Europa* (left).

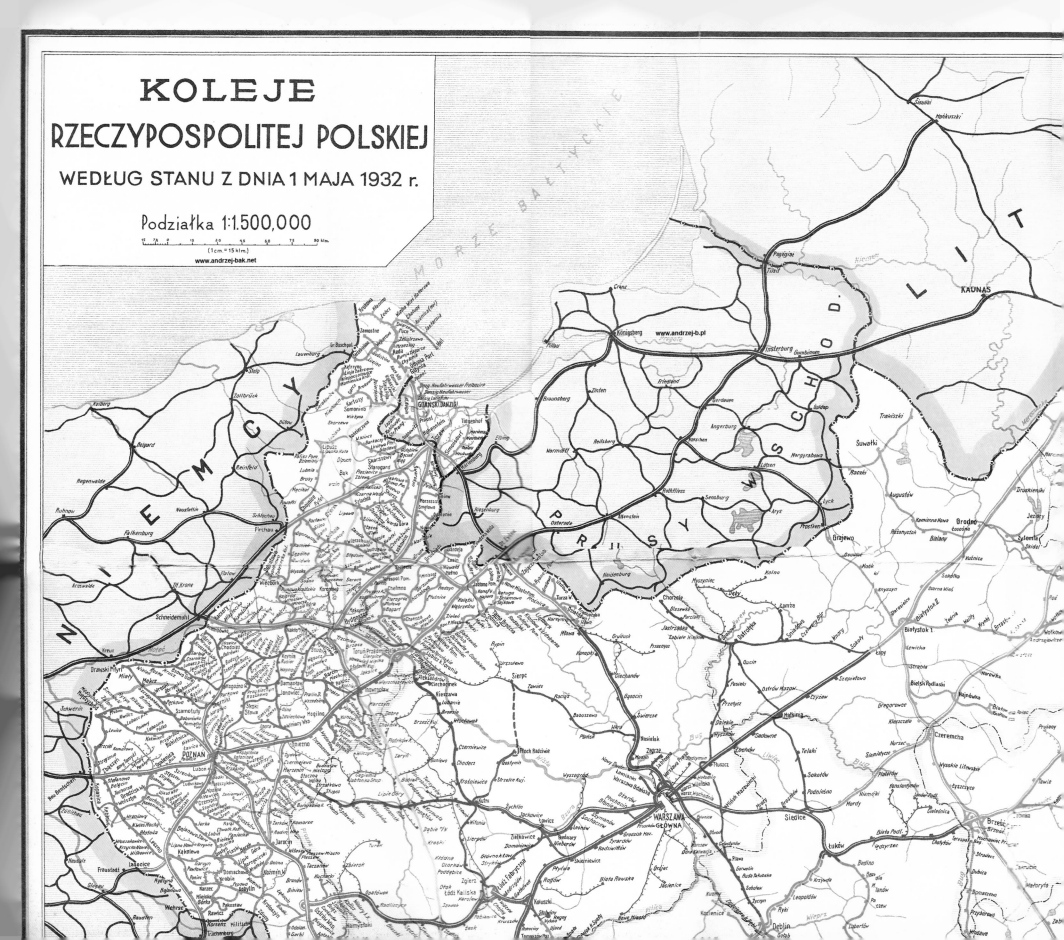

KOLEJE
RZECZYPOSPOLITEJ POLSKIEJ

WEDŁUG STANU Z DNIA 1 MAJA 1932 r.

Podziałka 1:1.500,000

15 7,5 0   15   30   45   60   75   90 klm.

(1 cm. = 15 klm.)

www.andrzej-bak.net

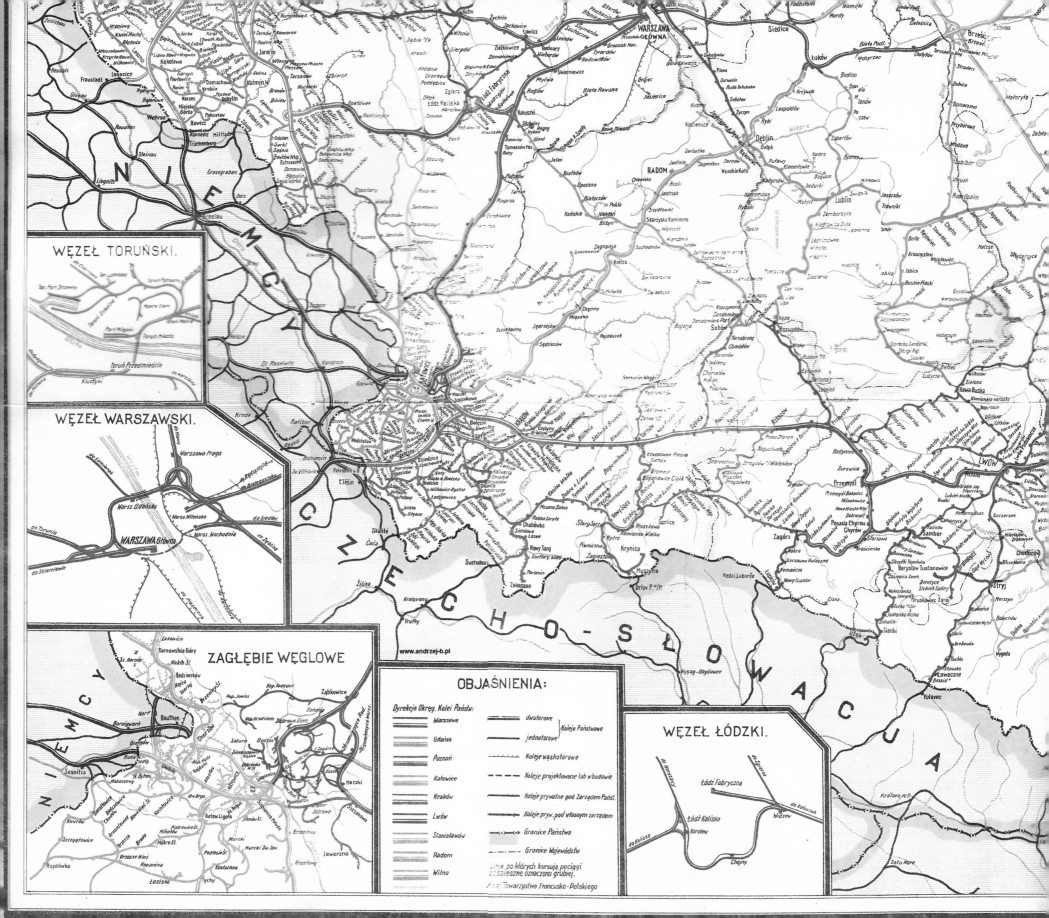

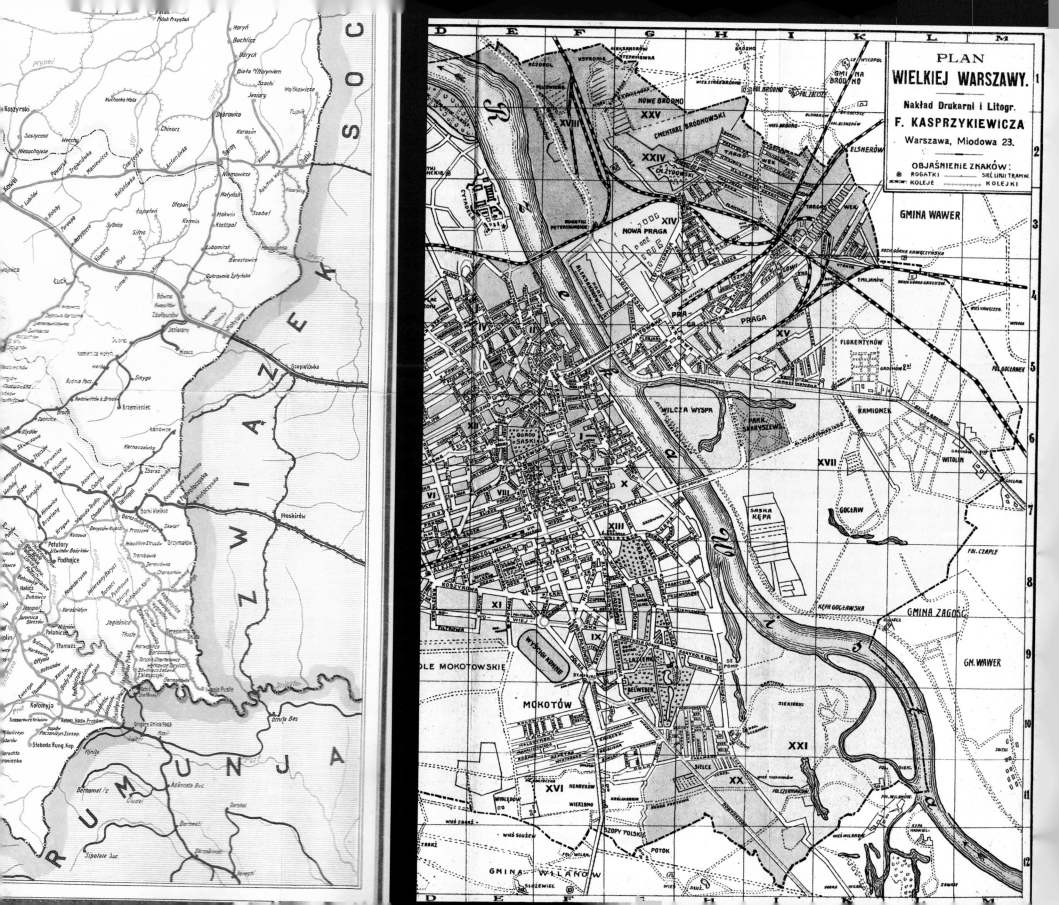

RUSSIA

Russia is a vast country, and although railway transport would later prove the best way of traversing the country's great distances and harsh terrain, the development of a rail network took longer to establish than in most parts of Europe.

Before Nicholas I came to the Russian throne, very little consideration had been given to railways. A few mines and factories in the Ural Mountains used tramways, but they used horses or men to pull the carts over short distances. Several proposals were made to build railways, but none were accepted until the Austrian engineer Franz Anton von Gerstner pushed through his proposal to build the St Petersburg–Tsarskoe Selo Railway. Work began in March 1836, and in November the Tsar and his family were among the lucky passengers to be pulled on an exciting voyage up and down the five kilometres of completed track headed out of St Petersburg towards the imperial suburb of Tsarskoe Selo. On 30 October Gerstner himself drove the line's brand new engine the whole 26 km to Tsarskoe Selo, with a huge audience of ministers and officials.

Work on other lines began soon after this triumph. The 647 km Moscow–St Petersburg line, allegedly designed by Nicholas I by drawing a line on a map between the two cities using a straight-edge and a pencil, was completed in 1851 – the journey took 22 hours. Between 1866 and 1899 the Russian railway network increased from 5,000 km to 53,200 km.

Until the early 1880s all Russian railways were operated as private companies, but as they grew in number and complexity many private railways found themselves in financial difficulty. The Tsarist government, who had in many cases already provided guarantees and securities to many of them, now took some of them over, resulting in a mixed system of private and government railways.

In several cases the government was able to turn around money-losing railways and make them profitable, while the remaining private companies now had a strong incentive to operate more efficiently in order to avoid nationalisation. The result, according to historian A. Boublikoff, was that 'Russian railways gradually become perhaps the most economically operated railroads of the world'. Profits were often high, and by the turn of the century Russian railways were generating over 100 million gold rubles a year for the government.

After the Russian Revolution of 1917, all railways in Russia were transferred into Soviet ownership. During the next forty years the Soviets put massive effort into the Russian railway system, introducing almost universal electrification, building new lines, double-tracking, installing automatic couplers, brakes and signalling, and even founding Railway Universities. In many respects, including freight traffic, electrification, profitability and railway education, Russian railways were for many years some of the best engineered and efficiently operated in the world.

A remote station in the Urals, 1912 (above).

The Irtysh River bridge near Omsk, 1897 (opposite).

Perm station, mid-1920s (below).

217

MOSCOW—ST PETERSBURG

Tsar Nicholas's Pioneering Line

Russia joined the railway age rather later than the main European nations, but Tsar Nicholas I, who ruled with an iron fist, soon set about building a line that was more ambitious in scope than the efforts of its rivals. The Moscow–St Petersburg line was not only the longest outside America at the time, it was also built to a very high standard, demonstrated by the fact that most of the route has been retained to this day.

In many respects the difficulties and issues facing the construction of what became known as the Nikolayev Railway (later renamed the October Railway following the October 1917 revolution) were to be repeated, on a grander scale, half a century later when the issue of whether to build the Trans-Siberian was debated. Just as with the Trans-Siberian, it was an epic project in terms of railway construction whose main purpose was to consolidate the power of the Tsar. Despite his lofty position, Nicholas I took an intense supervisory role in every detail of the construction of this key railway.

The scale of this project, in a country that was still largely agricultural and barely industrialised, was daunting. The Tsar had the advantage of being able to use serfs who were paid little or nothing to work on the line. The best estimate suggests that there were fifty thousand serfs employed by the railway at its peak, and perhaps 10 per cent of those died mostly from the periodic epidemics of typhoid and dysentery which spread through an ill-treated and hungry workforce.

There were numerous obstacles for the project to overcome. As well as slave labour, the project required skilled engineers who were in short supply, which meant most had to come from abroad. George Whistler, a former American army officer who had worked on several US railroads, was effectively the chief engineer, but the Tsar was intent on presenting the project as a Russian achievement, and therefore appointed two of his countrymen engineers to be responsible respectively for the north and south sections. There was such a small supply of home-grown engineers in a country with very few universities and technology colleges that in 1843 the entire graduating class of the Imperial School of Engineering was drafted to the railway.

The topography was not easy. Much of the terrain was undulating and intersected by rivers and gorges, as well as deep swamps and dense forests. With the route designed largely as a straight line, extensive cuttings and embankments were required. It was, too, a project on an unprecedented scale. Apart from churches and castles, nothing that required such large numbers of workers and sophisticated techniques had previously been accomplished in Russia.

Nicholas's reputation as an authoritarian figure might be wholly justified, but the oft-told tale about the slightly odd route taken by the railway has largely been debunked. He is said to have ordered the route between the two cities to follow a straight line which he drew using a ruler, and it is indeed straight apart from three rather inexplicable kinks. These are said to have been where his fingers projected over the edge of the ruler, but were more likely to have been determined by the difficulties of the terrain through which the line passed. A similar tale arose later over a much longer curve, the Verebinsky bypass, added to the line to avoid a gradient; since this deviation was built in 1877, more than two years after Nicholas's death, this too must enter the realm of myth.

The government had enormous difficulties in finding the money to finance the scheme. Raising taxes on an already overburdened agrarian population was not only difficult, but risked fomenting revolts. Nicholas's constant emphasis on military rather than civil spending led to repeated delays during construction as money ran out. The speed of construction was also not helped by the Tsar's insistence on overseeing minor decisions.

As a result the line took nine years to complete, twice the expected time. It also cost double the original budget. Yet it proved to be a triumph as it was used heavily by both passengers and, not surprisingly given the state of the roads, freight. Even though the 400-mile rail journey took about 20 hours, the volume of traffic far exceeded expectations. In 1852, the first full year of operation, the railway averaged nearly 2,000 passengers per day and carried large quantities of freight, mostly flour, grain and livestock.

The truth or fiction about another feature of the line, its gauge, is more difficult to disentangle. While the Tsarskoe Selo line was 6 foot, and the Warsaw–Vienna railway used the standard European gauge of 4 feet 8½ inches, the Moscow–St Petersburg line, and subsequently nearly all of Russia's rail network, used 5 foot. The standard explanation is that Nicholas, obsessed with military considerations, ordered the adoption of this wider gauge for defensive purposes, knowing that the requirement to change gauge at the Russian frontier would hamper any potential invader. The truth is almost certainly more prosaic, that it was the American engineer George Whistler who suggested the wider gauge.

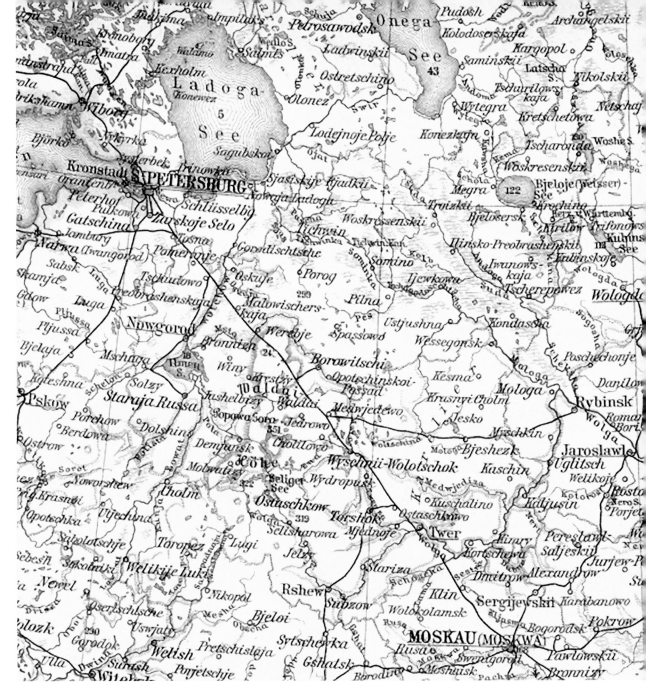

A 1906 German atlas map of the Moscow-St Petersburg route (above).

Typical stations on the route – Udelnaya and Pushkino (left).

Tsarskoe Selo station; the depot and roundhouse at Tver; the St Petersburg terminus (opposite).

THE TRANS-SIBERIAN RAILWAY

The Longest Railway Line in the World

While many railways can lay claim to be the world's most astonishing construction feat, there is one that towers above the others for the sheer scale of the enterprise – the Trans-Siberian Railway, which stretches nearly 5,750 miles from Moscow to Vladivostok on the Pacific coast. It is not only the world's longest railway by far, but was also built in the most hostile environment on the planet, and through largely deserted country with consequent difficulties in finding both labour and materials.

The decision to build the railway was also quite remarkable. In the mid-1880s when the idea was being discussed, Russia was impoverished, with a very small affluent aristocracy and a huge peasantry, only recently liberated from serfdom. Despite concerns that the country could not afford such a massive enterprise, Tsar Alexander III, one of the last absolute monarchs, insisted it should be built, and the go-ahead was given in 1890.

There were compelling reasons, both military and economic, for the construction of the line. In terms of economics, Siberia had been a distant and mysterious land, mostly populated by tribes, but was seen as having great potential for agriculture and minerals. The Russian government hoped that building a railway would open the way for settlers in the same way that had happened in the USA, but because of the harsh conditions and Russia's sparse population, the line did not prove to be the catalyst for economic development as it had been in America.

The Russian Empire was only loosely held together, and for the first time the railway offered a relatively fast and reliable form of travel over the long stretches of little-populated land

Императоръ Александръ III,
Царь-Миротворецъ.

Августѣйшій Основатель Великаго Сибирскаго пути.

The two men who made the Trans-Siberian Railway a reality – Tsar Nicholas III and Sergei Witte (above).

A special church carriage for the Trans-Siberian Railway, built to commemorate the birth of Grand Duchess Olga Nikolaevna; it was consecrated on 14 November 1895 (bottom left and opposite).

The bridge across the Ob River (left).

of Siberia. Russia wanted to establish a trade route with the East and, more important, protect its eastern flank. The fact that Canada had recently completed its own first transcontinental was seen as a threat, since troops would now be able to come from Europe, notably from Britain to whom Russia had recently lost the Crimean War, far faster than previously. Fears that China, weak at the time, would emerge to become a regional power also spurred the building of the line. In fact, Russia took advantage of China's weakness to locate the original route through Manchuria, a decision that would help trigger the Russo-Japanese War, although later a route to the north, entirely within Russian boundaries, was completed in 1916.

The construction of the railway faced many obstacles including marshes and mountains, severe weather and Lake Baikal, the largest lake in Asia. Moreover, there was the sheer nightmare of Russian bureaucracy to be overcome, as well as rife corruption. Another problem was the sparse population, which meant that it was difficult to recruit labourers locally. The railway was built eastward from Chelyabinsk and westward from Vladivostok, and was by far the biggest railway

Photographs from a 1904 commemoration album to celebrate the building of the Trans-Siberian Railway: (opposite) building the Yenisei Bridge; a double-headed train near Tomsk; the station and goods yard at Kyzyl; (top right) Krasnoyarsk station; (bottom right) the Tom River bridge near Yaya, east of Tomsk.

project ever undertaken, at its peak employing more than 89,000 men. Work conditions were poor, and almost all work was done by hand using simple and primitive instruments. It is estimated that the cost of the project was at least 855 million rubles (around £85m in today's money), a staggering sum for such a poor country with a small tax base.

As with most major projects, a visionary promoter and champion was needed. Sergei Witte fulfilled this role perfectly. A former railway clerk who had, unusually, climbed up the social scale to be a government minister, he took charge of the project and worked closely with successive Tsars to see it through.

The railway was not just a single track running through the steppes, but was from the outset seen as part of a wider transport network that would help to connect Siberia with the rest of the Russian Empire. The railway also connected 25,000 miles of navigable waterways to create a transport system that could be used in the summer months when the rivers were ice-free. These same rivers were vital in transporting supplies during the construction of the line.

Amazingly, it took barely a decade to build this lengthy railway in the most inhospitable conditions ever faced by railway builders. When work started in 1891 it progressed relatively smoothly in western Siberia, but on the central section around Lake Baikal – which eventually was the last section to be completed – conditions were often a nightmare. In the foothills of the Saian mountains the ground only melts for three months per year, and then it becomes a swamp. This meant the navvies often had to labour in up to two feet of water. In the mountainous sections, especially where the railway ran around the southern end of Lake Baikal, much difficult engineering and tunnelling work was needed.

Corruption and inefficiency were a major problem. Materials were often not supplied to the right standard or location, and contractors did not carry out the work they were

supposed to. The labour force was augmented by prisoners who had been sent into exile being used to work on the line. Promised two years remission for every year worked on the line, they proved to be enthusiastic and willing workers.

In order to complete the line in such a relatively short time, many short cuts were taken and the original line was built to a very low standard. Rails were lightweight, bridges rudimentary, and sleepers were often carved out of unseasoned wood which soon perished.

In the early days the line was a ramshackle affair with frequent derailments and breakdowns, and it took up to a month to travel its length. The route was soon being improved, however, and services were speeded up. Foreigners, especially diplomats, began to use the railway instead of sea travel as a quicker way to reach China and the Far East.

Militarily, however, the line was a disaster. Its construction triggered the 1904–5 war with the Japanese, resulting in a terrible defeat for the Russians. The line played a key role in the Russian Civil War, too, as the East was the last redoubt of the Whites, the opponents of Communism. Famously, as portrayed in the film *Dr Zhivago*, Trotsky ran the war from an armoured carriage on the Trans-Siberian.

Today the Trans-Siberian is an all-electrified modern line, and a vital part of Russia's infrastructure, carrying vast quantities of freight as well as passengers.

Photographs taken during the building of the Trans-Baikal section of the Trans-Siberian Railway between 1895 and 1904.

A 1906 map showing the route as built, and possible inland variants between Irkutsk and the head of Lake Baikal (opposite); the present-day route is close to the westernmost of these variants.

The opening of the summit tunnel on the Trans-Baikal Railway in 1904 (left).

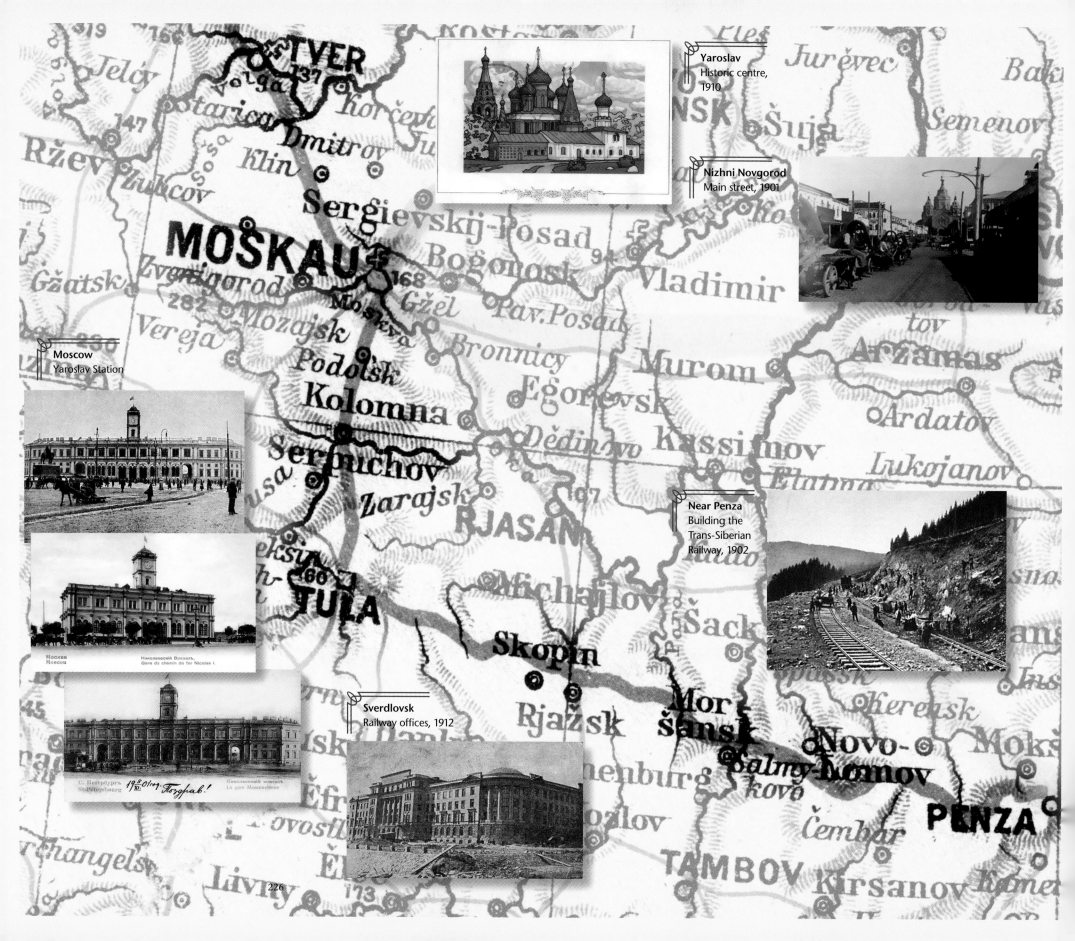

Yaroslav
Historic centre, 1910

Nizhni Novgorod
Main street, 1901

Moscow
Yaroslav Station

Near Penza
Building the Trans-Siberian Railway, 1902

Sverdlovsk
Railway offices, 1912

Vologda-Viatka
Babaevo Station, 1906

Perm
Two views of the bridge over the Kama River, c.1898

Nizhni Novgorod
Railway yards, 1910

Yaroslavl
Quay Bridge on the old north railway, 1907

Samara,
Southern Station, 1905

227

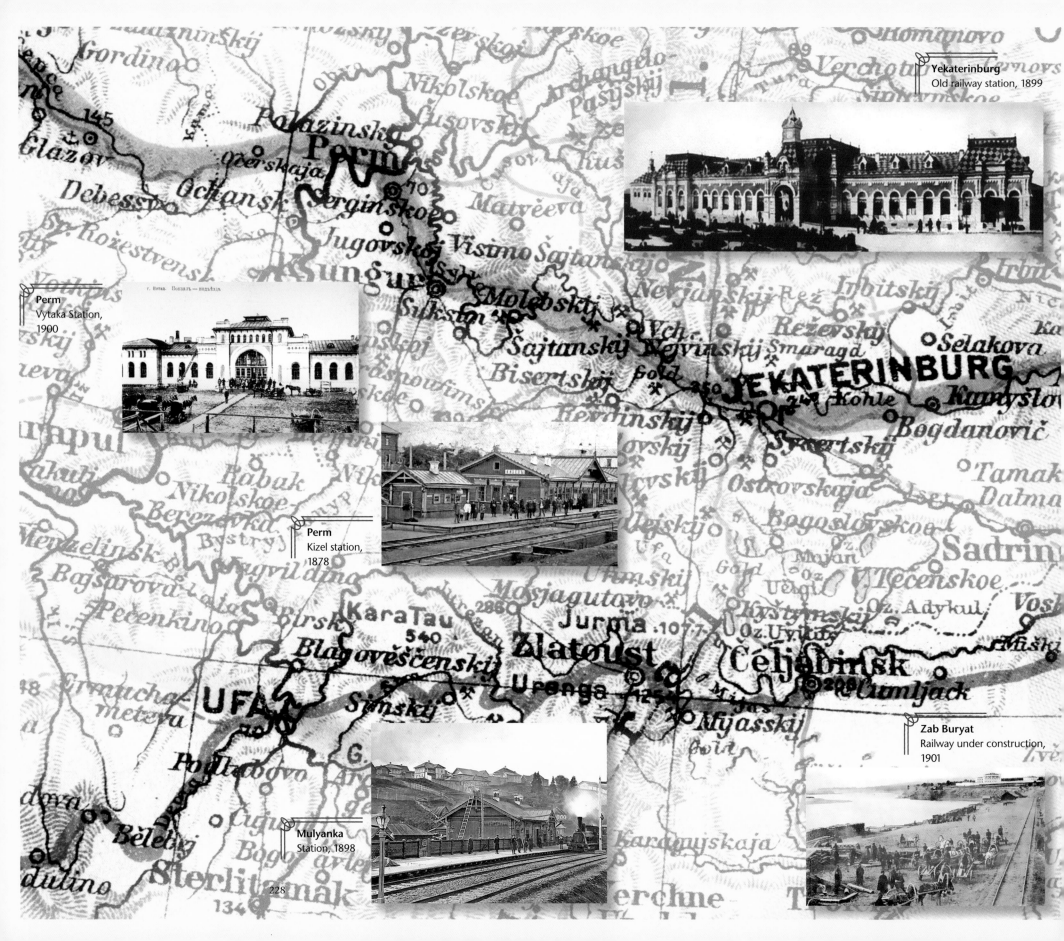

Yekaterinburg
Old railway station, 1899

Perm
Vytaka Station, 1900

Perm
Kizel station, 1878

Zab Buryat
Railway under construction, 1901

Mulyanka
Station, 1898

228

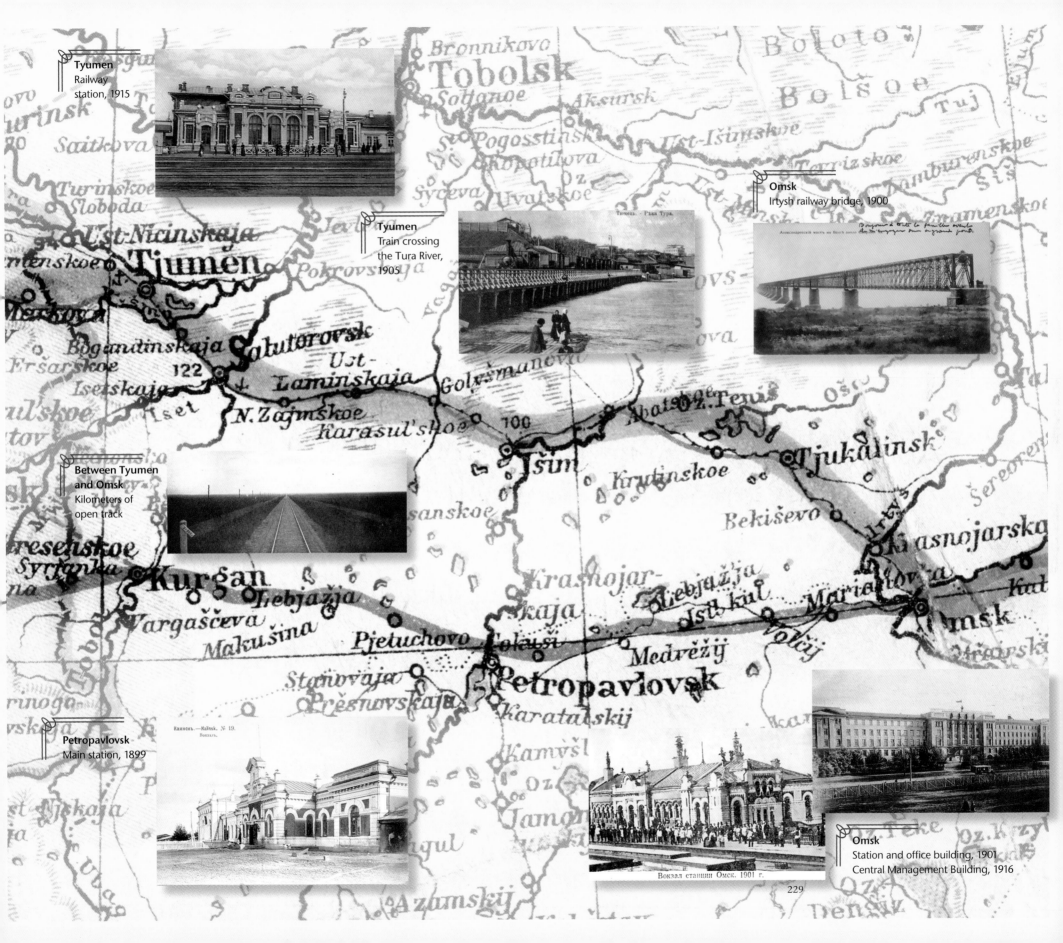

Tyumen
Railway station, 1915

Tyumen
Train crossing the Tura River, 1905

Omsk
Irtysh railway bridge, 1900

Between Tyumen and Omsk
Kilometers of open track

Petropavlovsk
Main station, 1899

Omsk
Station and office building, 1901
Central Management Building, 1916

229

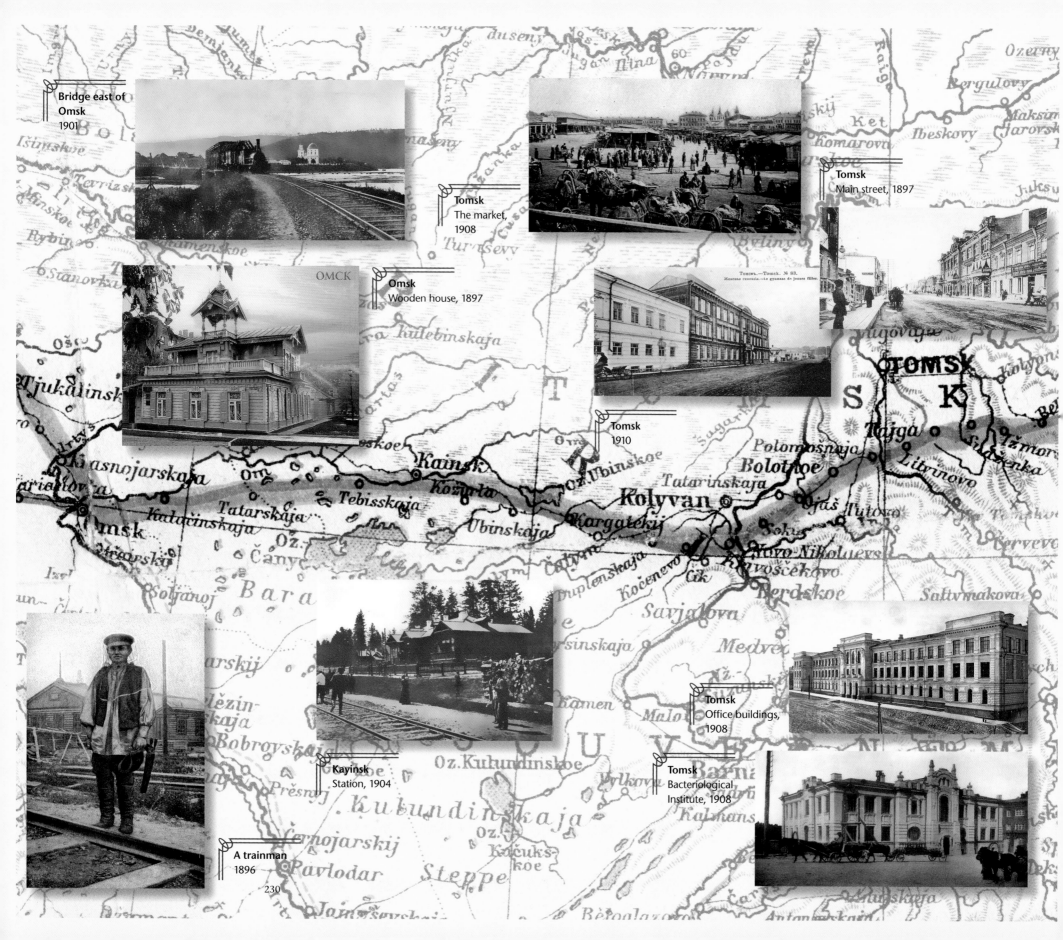

Bridge east of Omsk
1901

Tomsk
The market, 1908

Tomsk
Main street, 1897

OMCK

Omsk
Wooden house, 1897

Томск.—Tomsk. № 83.
Женская гимназія.—Le gymnase de jeunes filles.

Tomsk
1910

Tomsk
Office buildings, 1908

Kayinsk
Station, 1904

Tomsk
Bacteriological Institute, 1908

A trainman
1896

230

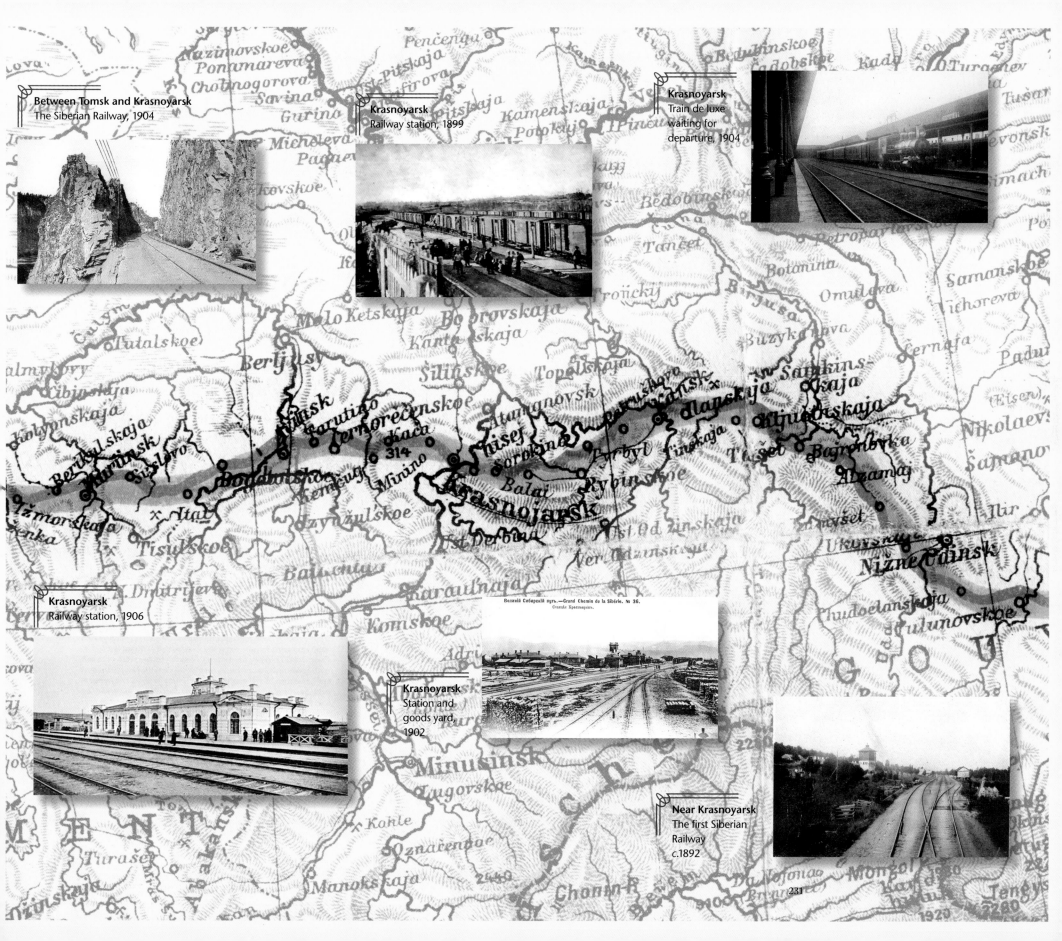

Between Tomsk and Krasnoyarsk
The Siberian Railway, 1904

Krasnoyarsk
Railway station, 1899

Krasnoyarsk
Train de luxe
waiting for
departure, 1904

Krasnoyarsk
Railway station, 1906

Великій Сибирскій путь.—Grand Chemin de la Sibérie. № 36.
Станція Красноярскъ.

Krasnoyarsk
Station and
goods yard,
1902

Near Krasnoyarsk
The first Siberian
Railway
c.1892

231

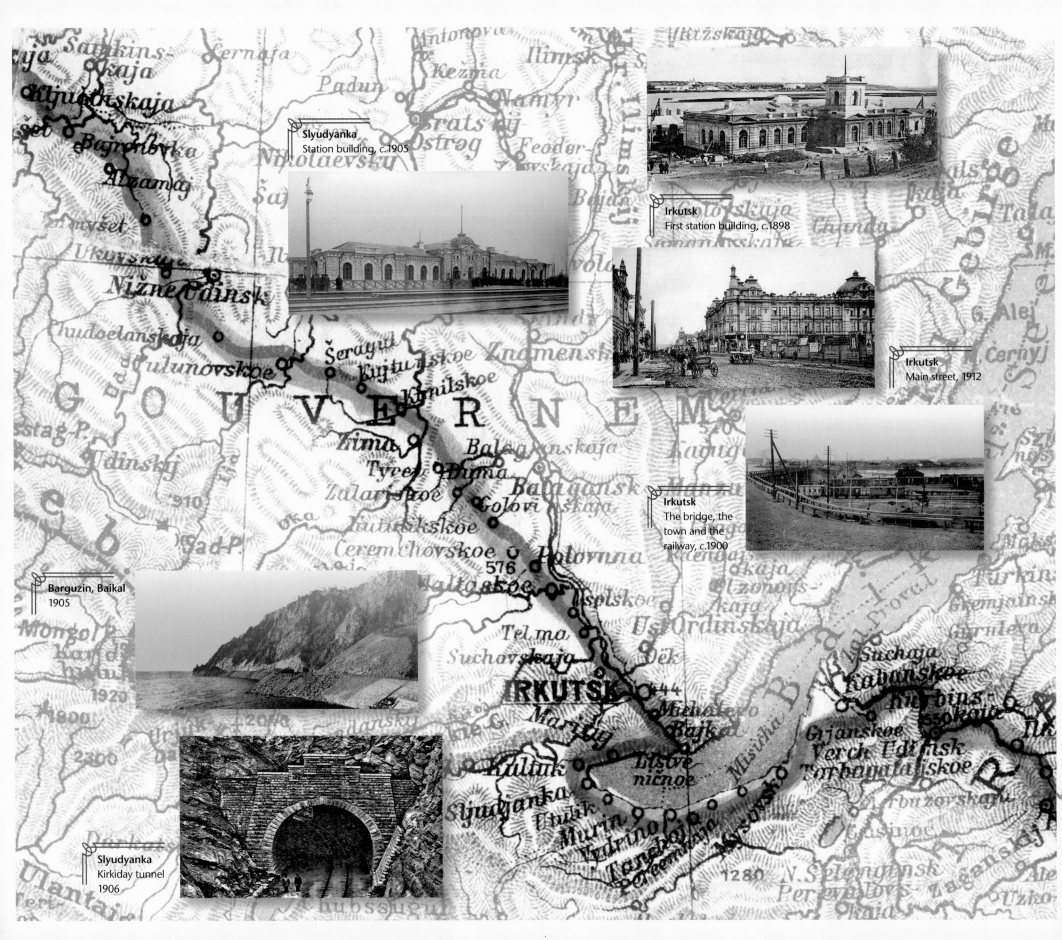

Slyudyanka
Station building, *c.*1905

Irkutsk
First station building, *c.*1898

Irkutsk
Main street, 1912

Irkutsk
The bridge, the town and the railway, *c.*1900

Barguzin, Baikal
1905

Slyudyanka
Kirkiday tunnel
1906

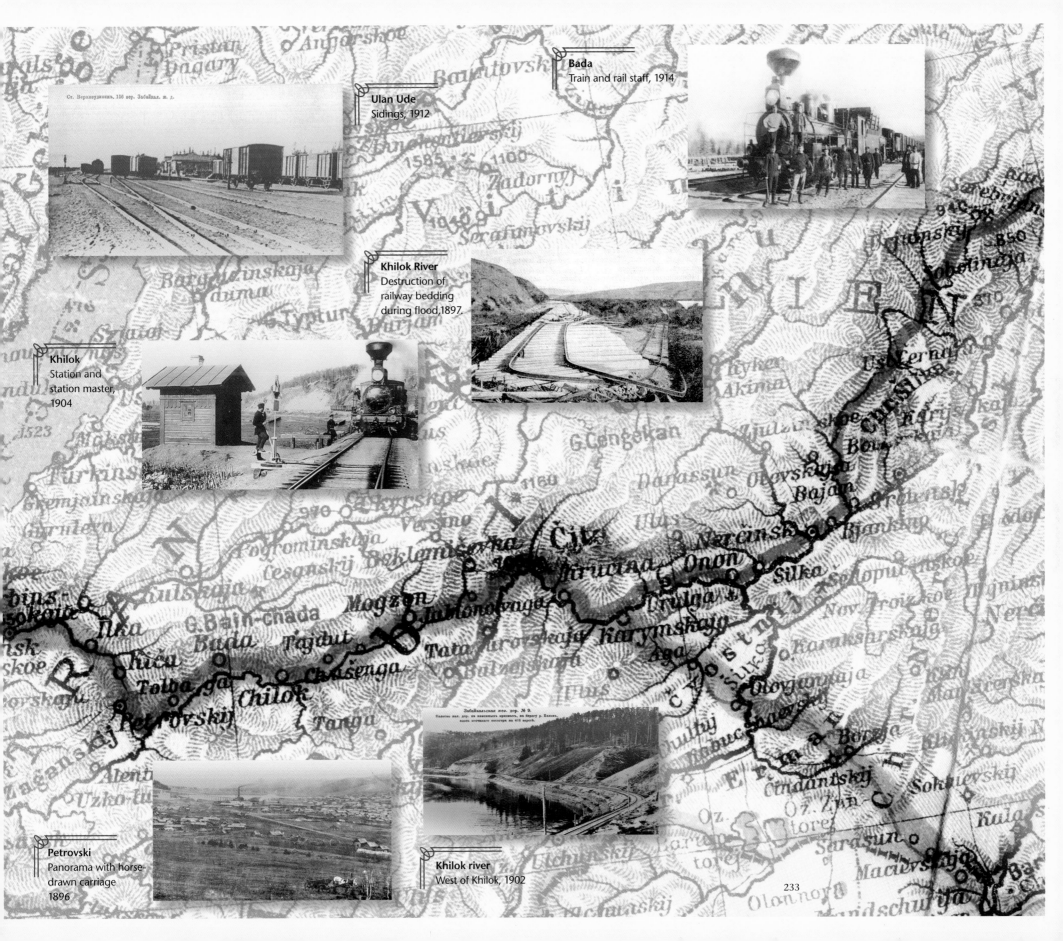

Ulan Ude
Sidings, 1912

Bada
Train and rail staff, 1914

Khilok River
Destruction of railway bedding during flood, 1897.

Khilok
Station and station master, 1904

Petrovski
Panorama with horse-drawn carriage 1896

Khilok river
West of Khilok, 1902

233

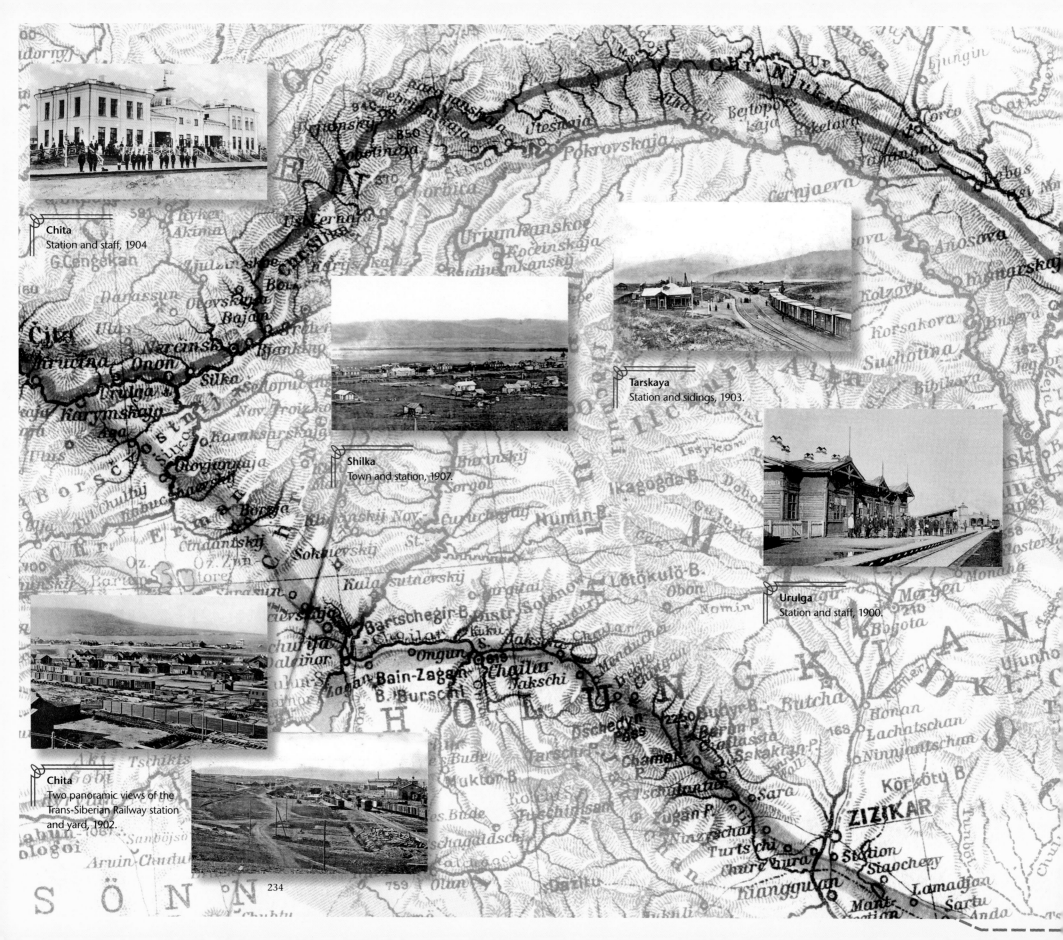

Chita
Station and staff, 1904

Tarskaya
Station and sidings, 1903.

Shilka
Town and station, 1907.

Urulga
Station and staff, 1900.

Chita
Two panoramic views of the
Trans-Siberian Railway station
and yard, 1902.

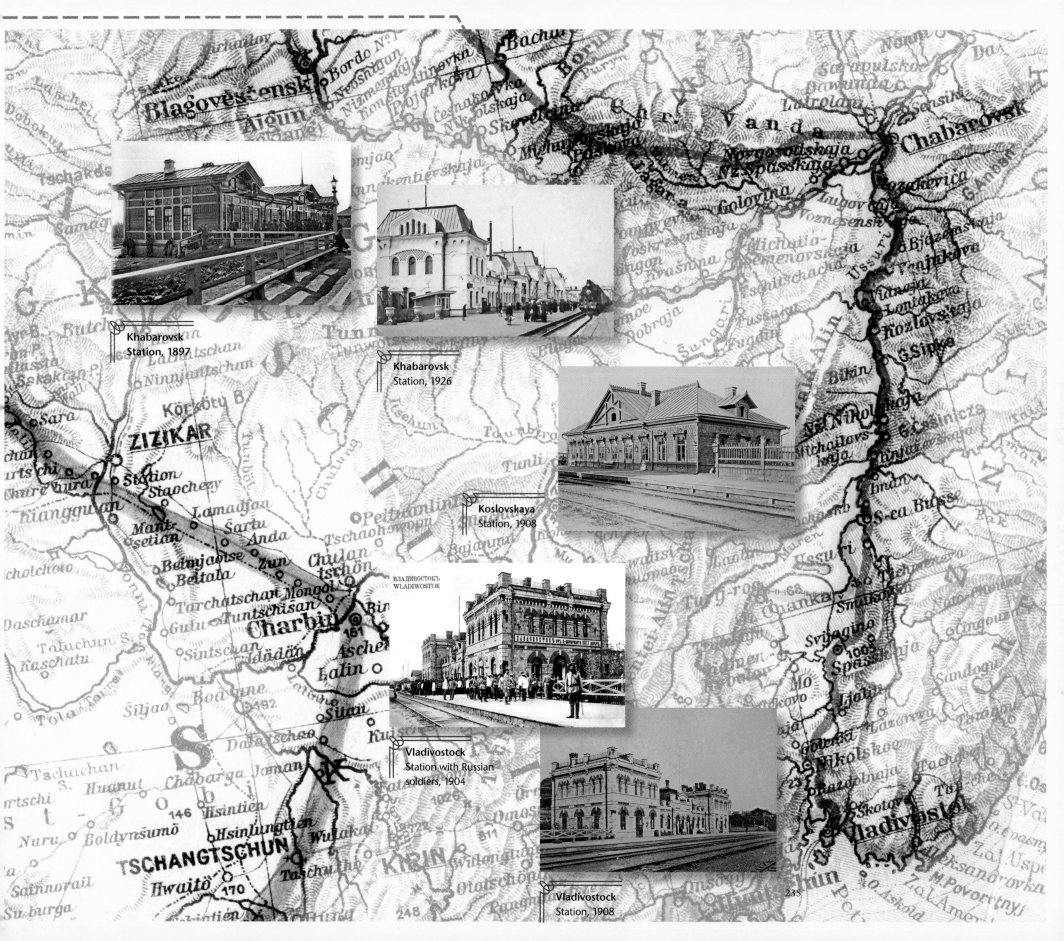

Khabarovsk
Station, 1897

Khabarovsk
Station, 1926

Koslovskaya
Station, 1908

Vladivostock
Station with Russian
soldiers, 1904

Vladivostock
Station, 1908

235

Norge — Bromma St. Bergensbanen

SCANDINAVIA

Railway building in Scandinavia technically started in 1844, when a railway was opened between Altona and Kiel in the Duchy of Holstein, at that time in union with Denmark as King Christian VIII was both King of Denmark and Duke of Holstein. When, as a result of the Second War of Schleswig, Holstein was ceded to the German Confederation in 1864, it became a German railway even though it had been built under the Danish monarchy. The true history of rail transport in Denmark began in 1847 with the opening of an easily-built railway across flat terrain between Copenhagen and Roskilde.

Norway and Sweden came late to railway building, the first Norwegian railway, the Hovedbanen between Oslo and Eidsvoll, opening in 1854, and the first Swedish steam-driven railways being the Nora–Ervalla railway in Närke, opened in 1856, and the Arboga–Köping railway in 1857.

In the period between the 1860s and the 1880s Norway saw a boom of smaller railways being built, including isolated railways in central and western Norway. The predominant gauge at the time was 3 feet 6 inches (1.07 m), but some lines were built in standard gauge 4 feet 8½ inch (1.44 m). The height of the era came in 1877 when Rørosbanen connected central Norway with the capital. In 1883 the entire main railway network was taken over by Norges Statsbaner (NSB), though a number of industrial railways and branch lines continued to be operated by private companies.

The second Norwegian railway construction boom started in the 1910s, and included the Bergensbane through the mountains from Finse to Bergen, connecting eastern and western Norway. Large-scale projects continued to be built through the 1920s, including the Dovrebanen northwards to Trondheim. This period also saw the first electrified railways, and a steady conversion from narrow gauge to standard gauge.

Sweden hesitated on the question of railway building for several years, mostly because of the costs involved. In 1845 the Swedish count Adolf Eugene von Rosen received permission to build railways in Sweden, and started building a railway between the town of Köping and Hult, a small port in Lake Vänern. The Köping–Hult railway was intended to be the first part of a railway between Gothenburg and Stockholm, but von Rosen ran out of funds before the project could be developed beyond its original short route.

Following a parliamentary decision in 1854, naval engineer Nils Ericson was asked to plan Sweden's first main lines. He proposed that the line between Gothenburg and Stockholm should run south of Lake Mälaren to avoid competition with shipping, and that the line between Malmö and Stockholm should run via Nässjö and Falköping, where it would meet up with the Gothenburg–Stockholm line.

In Finland, the first railway line between Helsinki and Hämeenlinna was opened on 31 January 1862. As Finland was then the Grand Duchy of Finland, a territory of Imperial Russia, railways were built to the broad Russian track gauge of 5 feet (1.52 m). An extension from Riihimäki to the new Finland Station in St Petersburg was opened in 1870, though the Finnish and Russian rail systems remained unconnected until 1912, and Russian trains could not anyway have used the Finnish rail network because of its narrower loading gauge. Before the First World War the Finnish loading gauge was widened to match the Russian load gauge, with hundreds of station platforms or tracks moved further away from each other.

A timetable from Sweden's first railway, the Köping–Hult Jernväg (above).

Two postcards from about 1910 of stations on Norway's Bergensbanen between Kristiania/Oslo and Bergen – Bromma and Geilo (opposite and left).

Gjeilo, Bergensbanen

THE BERGEN LINE

'Not a Thing To Be Forgotten'

The cover, map and cross-section of the Bergensbanen, from the celebration booklet printed to mark the opening of the line in 1909.

Bergen is a colourful historic port on Norway's rocky west coast. In 1910 its population of 76,870 people made it Norway's second largest town after Oslo, then known as Kristiania. The town itself is situated south of the harbour on a peninsula reaching out beyond a splendid bay, with the railway station a short distance from the historic centre. Ringed by mountains, the town faced difficult overland transport to inland regions, and the railway east to Oslo required complex engineering to traverse the spectacular but demanding Scandinavian landscape, such that the 1910 *Bradshaw's Guide* described the route as offering 'some of the finest and most varied of scenery, a panorama of rivers and fjords, mountains and ravines, and glaciers.'

Howard Preistman, who described the route's construction in a 1902 issue of *Railway Magazine*, eulogised about the journey. Explaining that the 108 km line from Bergen to Voss had opened in 1883 as a narrow gauge route, he wrote that the experience was 'not a thing to be forgotten, for the train is incessantly running through cuttings and tunnels as it winds it tortuous way beside the deep water of three fjords. Any observant passenger can see that everywhere it is not in the tunnels which comprise fully one tenth of the route, the greater part of the line has been blasted out the face of solid granite cliffs.'

The extension of the Bergen Line from Voss to Kristiana was approved in 1894, but the severe nature of the remote territory and the construction challenges faced meant that the line was not fully opened until 1909. Beyond Voss the railway climbed eastward into the rugged uplands, requiring considerable tunnelling, tunnels which eventually numbered 184 and measured 39 km in total. Of special note is the famed 5.3 km Gravahals Tunnel, built on a rise with a summit two thirds of the way through.

Myrdal, a lonely outpost on the windswept high mountain plateau east of Voss where the line crosses the Flåm valley, became an important railway junction in the 1930s. The Flåmsbana, a 20 km branch line between Myrdal and the village of Flåm, connects the Oslo–Bergen main line with boat services on the Sognefjord. The line's elevation difference is 863 m, with ten stations and twenty tunnels. The maximum gradient is 5.5 per cent, making it the steepest standard gauge railway in Europe. Because of its steep gradient and dramatic setting, the Flåm Line is now almost exclusively a tourist service.

East of Myrdal the Bergen Line crests at more than 1,280 m above sea level, then descends to Finse, the highest station on the line at 1,222 m. The 484 km line climbs well above the snowline, which means that it requires regular maintenance, especially when heavy snow buries the line. Near the summit snow fences and sheds protect the line from drifts, and from its early years massive rotary snow ploughs were used to clear the line, driven forward by two or three heavy engines.

From its opening the Bergen Line was promoted as a northerly link between Great Britain and Russia. In the 1910s weekly steamships left Newcastle-on-Tyne for a 28-hour North Sea crossing to Bergen, where passengers would continue their journey overland by rail.

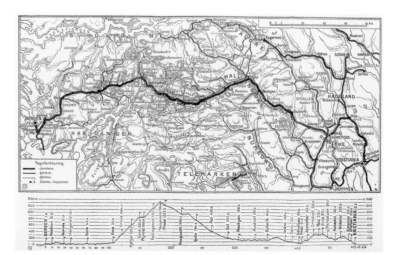

November 1909: the official opening ceremony at Voss; clearing the line of snow; Myrdal station (above).

The Reinunga Tunnel near Myrdal, 1909 (left).

239

STOCKHOLM–NARVIK

Lines to the Edge of the World

Among Europe's northernmost railways is the Malmbanan or Lapland Railway, a remote iron ore railway built across the top of Sweden, entirely north of the Arctic Circle, to a purpose-built port on the scenically sublime Ofoten Fjord at Narvik, Norway. The last 46 km of the route, known as the Ofotbanen, runs through Norway. While the Lapland Railway does not link with the rest of the Norwegian network, at Boden near the south end of the route it connects with the Swedish network, thus forming a through link between Stockholm and Narvik. Technically speaking the Lapland Railway's southern terminus is near Luleå, at Svartön Harbour on the Gulf of Bothnia, where large docks were built to facilitate the transshipment of iron ore to sea-going ore carriers.

In the latter part of the nineteenth century the discovery of large deposits of iron ore in this remote region encouraged railway construction. The Luleå–Gällivare line opened in 1888, the route was extended to mines near Kiruna in 1899, and the final portion across the Norwegian frontier was completed in 1903. In its first decades steam locomotives worked the line, but the volume of heavy ore trains made it an early candidate for overhead electrification, which was completed between 1915 and the mid-1920s.

Although ore remained the driving force for operations on the Lapland Railway, it also offered tourists access to this exceptionally remote and wildly scenic region. In summer this is the land of the midnight sun; in winter a spectacular desolation of snow and ice. North of the Arctic Circle the summer sun dips low on the northern horizon but never sets, making for a prolonged surreal twilight. In winter darkness prevails for months.

Before the railway was built this region was largely unsettled, inhabited only by nomadic Lapps and their herds of reindeer. The thin thread of steel was the only lifeline connecting the remote mining settlements at Gällivare and Kiruna with the rest of humanity. A trip over the line was an adventure to the edge of the world. The run north from Stockholm was typically scheduled overnight, the route running through evergreen forest, rocky glaciated plains and desolate moors.

The line crosses the Arctic Circle shortly before reaching Gällivare, but this demarcation on the globe could easily go unnoticed by travellers as there was nothing but forest at this stage of the journey. North of Kiruna the landscape takes on an otherworldly appearance; for many miles the train runs above the long narrow arctic lake of Torneträsk, which shimmers in the midnight sun, reflecting peculiar swirls of clouds in the Arctic sky.

From an engineering perspective the Norwegian end of the line is the most impressive, clinging to a shelf above the Ofoten Fjord, in less than thirty miles passing through 23 tunnels on its sharp descent toward the harbour at Narvik.

The Nordal Bridge on the Ofoton section of the Malmsbanan, shown here in 1988 before the line was upgraded (below).

A passenger train approaches Narvik on the upgraded line, December 2010 (below right).

An iron ore train skirts the shores of Torneträsk (main picture).

Two photographs from 1906 show an empty ore train about to leave Narvik, and the station at Riksgränsen on the Swedish–Norwegian border (insets).

HELSINKI STATION

The Finnish Capital's Iconic Terminal

Helsinki's main railway station ranks among the world's great railway terminal buildings. Although completed toward the end of Europe's great station building era, architecturally Helsinki Station has more in common with Finland's civic structures than traditional European terminals.

Instead of the neo-classical or neo-Gothic styles typical of most European terminals, Helsinki station exhibits Art Nouveau motifs. Built between 1911 and 1914, at a time of rising nationalism when Finland was under the yoke of the Russian Tsar, Helsinki station embodied the essence of Finnish symbolism. The renowned Finnish architect Eliel Saarinen drew upon ideals of the Vienna Secession movement, blending elements of the Arts and Crafts with traditional Finnish rural architectural themes to deliver a bold reactionary style that contrasted sharply with the Russified architecture of earlier decades. Today the station is used by some twenty thousand passengers daily, making it Finland's most-visited building.

Finland's railway network was a product of Tsarist Russian domination, and shared the Russian broad gauge track rather than the standard European gauge, together with other elements of Russian railway practice. This allowed for larger locomotives and carriages than those used by most continental railways. After Finnish independence, Russia remained Finland's primary railway connection, with through passenger services connecting Helsinki with St Petersburg and Moscow.

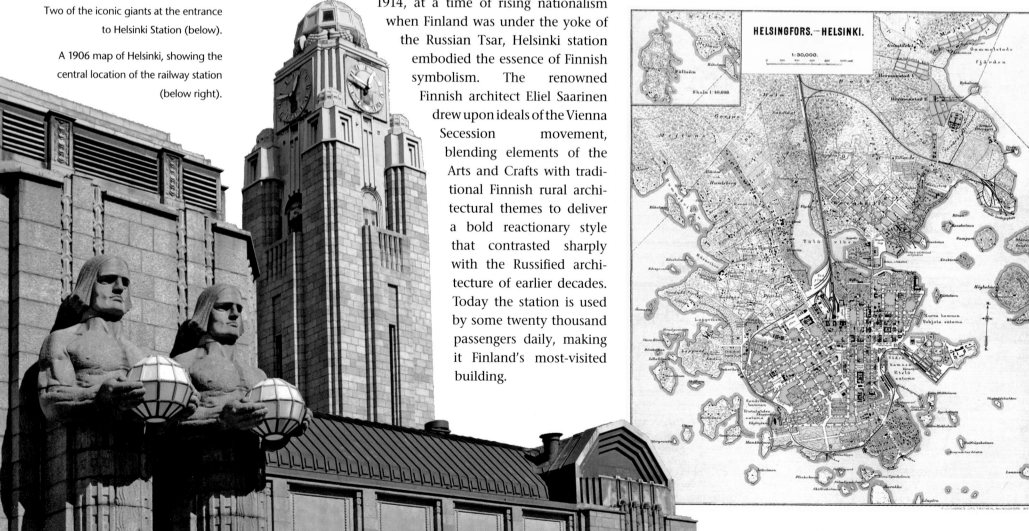

Two of the iconic giants at the entrance to Helsinki Station (below).

A 1906 map of Helsinki, showing the central location of the railway station (below right).

HELSINGFORS.—HELSINKI.

1:30,000.

An aerial view of Helsinki Station, taken in 1934.

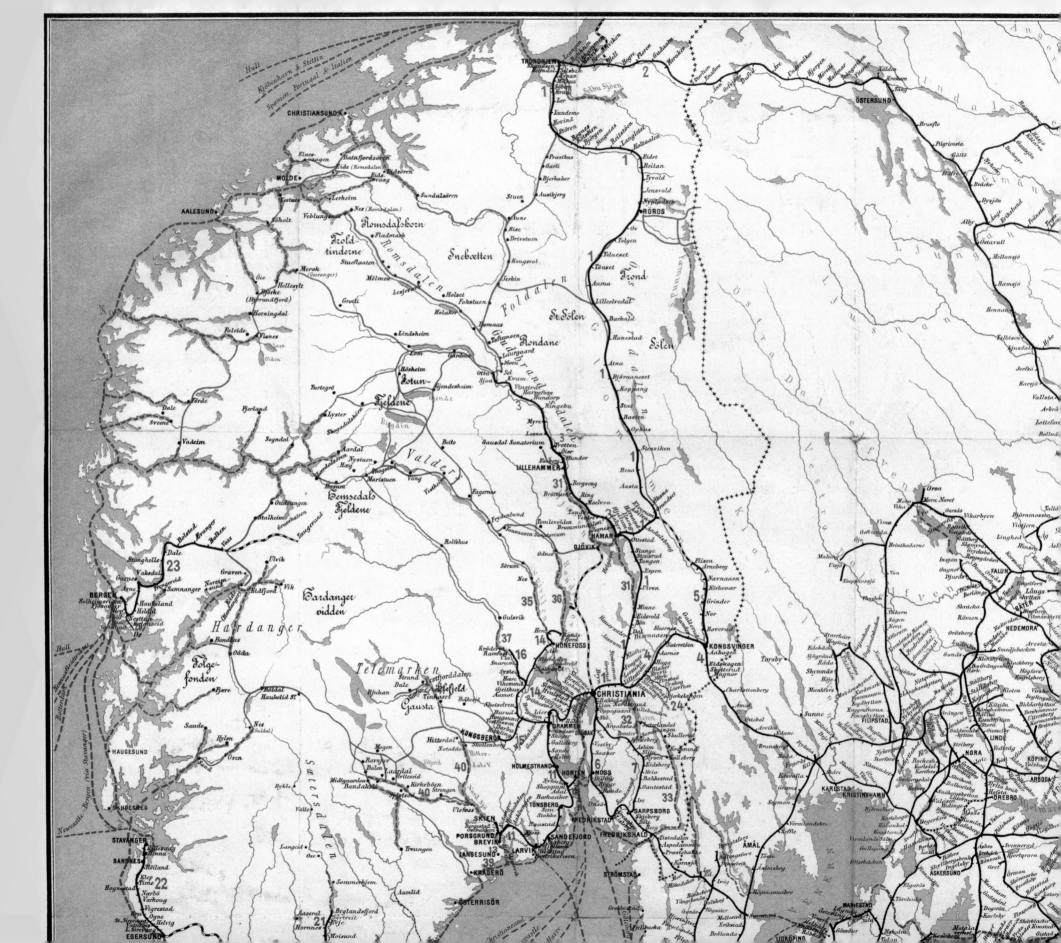

The Bergensbanen under construction near Finse, summer 1906.

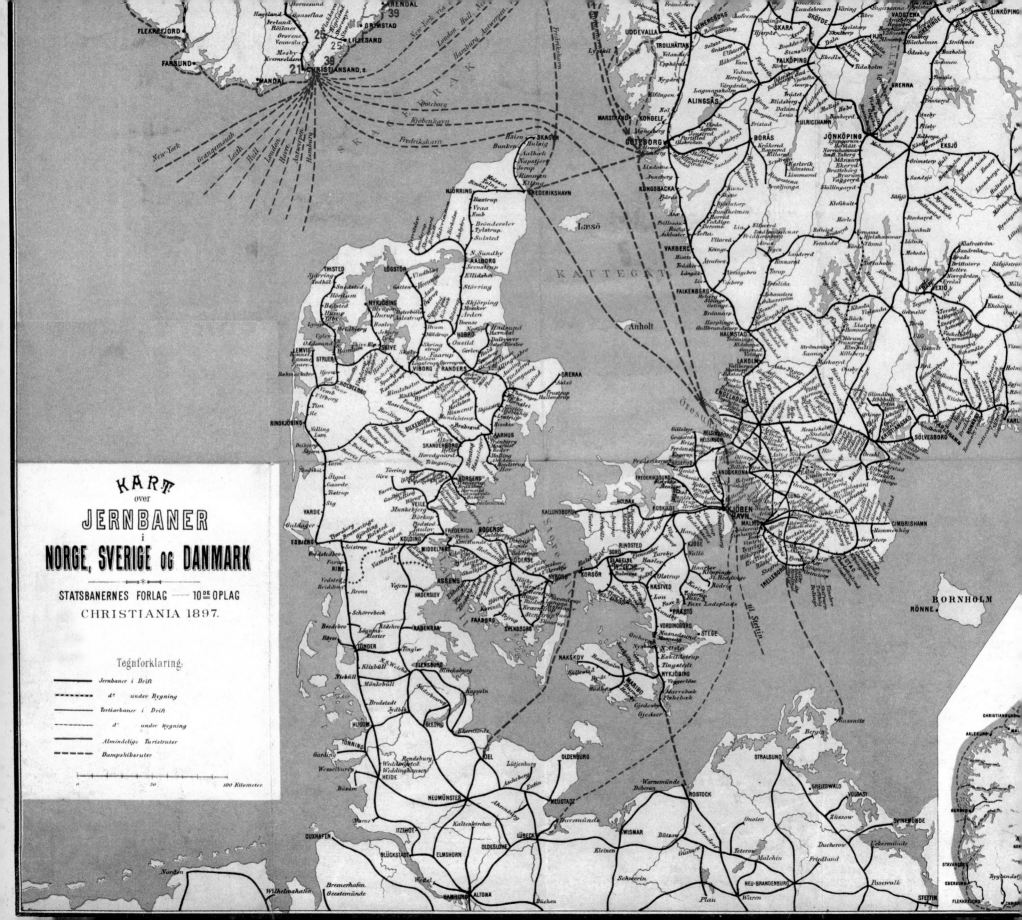

KART
over
JERNBANER
i
NORGE, SVERIGE og DANMARK

STATSBANERNES FORLAG — 10DE OPLAG

CHRISTIANIA 1897.

Tegnforklaring:

Jernbaner i Drift
dᵒ under Bygning
Tertiærbaner i Drift
dᵒ under Bygning
Almindelige Turistruter
Dampskibsruter

50   100 Kilometer

A Norwegian express train near Hönefoss, early 1920s.

THE CLASSIC EUROPEAN LOCOMOTIVES

No railway subject has a greater volume of literature than locomotives, their development, refinement and application. In 1829 Robert Stephenson's *Rocket* was demonstrated and won at Liverpool and Manchester Railway's celebrated Rainhill locomotive trials. This crucial design set the essential pattern for main line locomotives around the world. It combined three principal elements of reciprocating steam locomotive design – a multi-tubular (fire tube) boiler, forced exhaust draft, and direct coupling between pistons and drive wheels.

Initially British builders led the way, producing many influential locomotives. By the 1850s, railways across Europe began refining the locomotive in myriad variations by developing machines peculiar to the necessities and limitations of their respective systems. Over the years there was a consistent push to produce faster and more powerful machines, balancing the desire for increased efficiency with the cost of maintenance, and keeping machinery within the allowances of existing infrastructure.

In the nineteenth century steam ruled supreme, but early in the twentieth century new forms of motive power took hold. Electrification involved high initial cost, but offered great power and efficiency. Urban and underground networks,

Stirling No. 1 at the National Railway Museum in York, England (below).

followed by Alpine railways and other mountain lines, were early to take advantage of electricity. Following the First World War, and more so after the Second World War, continental railways moved toward the widespread electrification of main lines. Internal combustion power also gained interest, first applied successfully for self-propelled railcars, and later in the twentieth century refined for heavy locomotive work. Although prolific in Britain and dominant in small nations like Ireland, diesel traction did not gain the dominance in Europe that it found in America.

Classic Steam

Britain's early railway development, combined with its numerous private lines and an unusually inventive spirit, produced a great variety of refined designs. Handicaps can often result in creative solutions – Britain's constrained loading gauge, limiting the size of engines which could be used, contributed to inventive approaches toward improving performance. The late-Victorian and Edwardian periods represented a golden age of steam, and among the great designs were Francis Webb's compounds built for the London and North-Western, among them three-cylinder Teutonic Class express engines first built in 1889, and the four-cylinder 0–8–0 heavy goods engines of the early twentieth century. Patrick Stirling perfected express engines using a single set of enormous driving wheels; Great Northern Railway's famed Stirling Singles were exemplified by the 4–2–2 type of 1894, and had driving wheels more than eight feet tall. Other railways took a more conservative approach, developing the 4–4–0 for passenger work, and later progressing to the 4–6–0. Great Western Railway's G.J. Churchward refined the 4–6–0 before the First World War, and the railway continued to perfect it until the end of steam. After the First World War, British locomotive designers perfected the 4–6–2 Pacific; most famous were Sir Nigel

Gresley's machines built for the London and North-Eastern Railway. His A3 class reached its zenith in engine 4472, *Flying Scotsman,* perhaps the most famous steam locomotive of the twentieth century, while his streamlined A4 Pacific of 1935 is best remembered by engine 4468 *Mallard*, which set the world steam locomotive record of 126 mph in 1938.

Continental development tended to progress along national lines. German railways were characterised by straightforward standardised designs, mass-produced for simplicity, efficiency, and easy repair and maintenance. Among the memorable engines was the Prussian P8 4–6–0, a large class which entered service in 1906, built as an express locomotive. The German Second World War era 2–10–0 Kriegslok ('war locomotive') was well suited to heavy goods work, and exceptionally capable; German passenger trains of this era depended largely on fast O-class 4–6–2 Pacifics.

French railways will be remembered for their supreme development of compound locomotives, the most famous being Nord's engines designed by Alfred DeGlehn, and later P-O/SNCF types refined by André Chapelon.

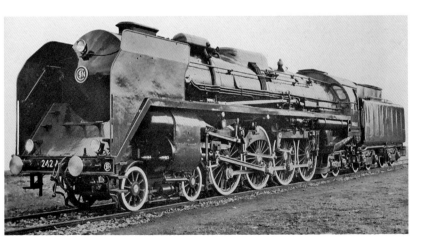

Austrian steam locomotives of the mid-nineteenth century had a decidedly individual appearance, resulting from the elaborate spark arrestors on their chimneys. In Iberia, where locomotives were unhindered by restrictive gauge and operated over long distances, many reached North American proportions; it was one of the few places in Europe where the 4–8–4 triumphed.

British GWR 4–4–2 express locomotive No. 103 of a De Glehn compound design (top left).

Prussian P8 No. 2455 (top right).

Kriegslok No. 52 4867 (above).

Chapelon SNCF Class 242 A1 used the 4–8–4 wheel arrangement (left).

EUROPEAN RAILWAY CARRIAGE DESIGN

A FIRST-CLASS TRAIN ON THE LIVERPOOL AND MANCHESTER RAILWAY 1833

A SECOND-CLASS TRAIN ON THE LIVERPOOL AND MANCHESTER RAILWAY, 1833.

First and second class carriages were introduced from the very beginning of rail travel, as shown here in contemporary illustrations of the Stockton and Darlington Railway (above).

Early European railway passenger carriages evolved directly from stage-coach practices. The earliest carriages were little more than stage-coach bodies on railway wheels, but the design soon progressed into a series of stage-coach compartments placed on a common rigid frame, with a continuous roof overhead, built in both four-wheel and six-wheel variations; six wheels allowed for a longer frame and a more comfortable ride. Compartments spanned the width of the carriage, with seats facing one another and doors along the sides without interior connections between compartments or carriages. Belgian railways adopted corridor-style carriages in the late-1830s, but this now common style remained unusual for many years.

Three classes of carriage were standard. First class, by far the most expensive, was aimed at the gentry and wealthy travellers, and involved more spacious accommodation with fewer people assigned to each compartment, along with cushioned seats and pleasing décor. In the formative years, first class

was relatively austere compared with accommodation in later years; compartments were unheated, and lacked lavatories and running water, and at best were lit with a dim oil lamp.

Second class accommodation varied considerably; on British lines it was not substantially different from first, and in Germany it was deemed excellent. In other countries it was decidedly inferior. In the early years British third class offered minimal accommodation; half-height partitions separated seating areas and passengers were packed in, leaving them only a small amount of personal space on crowded trains. On many lines third class carriages were originally accommodated only by low priority all-stops trains, such as Britain's mandated 'Parliamentary runs'.

In the 1870s new styles of passenger carriages came into vogue. The saloon offered an open format, akin to a parlour, with movable chairs and end doors permitting movement between carriages. Sleeping cars appeared in several formats on British railways and on the Continent – Russian railways had adopted sleeping cars in the 1860s, but had had little influence on other European railways. The earliest sleeping cars used the standard rigid wheelbase common to passenger carriages since the dawn of the age. C.H. Ellis attributes the first application of sleepers to the North British Railway in 1873. These were an adaptation of the saloon style, each featuring two compartments connected by a central corridor, with both lavatory and luggage facilities. Décor was dominated by lush red velvet. Julian Morel, the author of *Pullman*, notes that in the same year Britain's Midland Railway took a more radical approach, working with the American Pullman Company and buying American-style corridor sleepers riding pairs of bogies. The cars were built in America to the constraints of the smaller British loading gauge, and assembled in Midland's Derby Works. These were decidedly American in appearance, complete with end platforms and clerestory-style roofs. In the early years the cars were operated under contract by the Pullman Company, much in the same way Pullmans were handled on American lines. A similar arrangement was negotiated in Italy, where cars were assembled near Turin.

Pullman's influence in Europe was wide-reaching. Early continental sleepers used four-wheel carriages, but bogie sleepers had been adopted by the late 1870s. Impressed by Pullman sleepers on an American trip in 1868, Georges Nagelmackers, founder of Wagons-Lits (the International Sleeping Car Company), was the leading force in implementing high-class overnight services in Europe. By the First World War, Wagons-Lits dominated the international sleeping car business across the continent. Despite this, the 'Pullman' name never became synonymous with this business in Europe as it had in North America. Instead, by the early twentieth century, European Pullman carriages tended to infer a better class of day travel. C.H. Ellis noted that in Britain, the third class Pullman service introduced on the London, Brighton and South Coast in 1915 offered greater comfort than first class carriages of ordinary design.

The restaurant carriage evolved in parallel with sleepers, and by the early twentieth century many trains de-luxe carried them. Until the 1920s passenger carriages were constructed from wood. Improvement came with the introduction of steel frames, and then all-steel cars. Beginning in the 1930s, some railways experimented with light-weight designs employing aluminum and other modern materials.

'The most luxurious train in the world' – London, Brighton and South Coast Railway pullman express 'The Southern Belle', hauled by 4–4–2 'Atlantic' class superheated locomotive No. 426, 1923 (top).

The dining car of the *Orient Express* in 1928 (above left).

A London, Brighton and South Coast Railway parlour saloon, 1910 (above right).

RAILWAY MUSEUMS AND SIGHTS TO SEE

Great Britain, the country which launched the railway movement, became more than 120 years later the pioneer of the modern preserved railway. In 1951 the Welsh narrow gauge slate-hauling Talyllyn Railway made the first steps toward becoming an historic railway, setting important precedents. Today Great Britain is blessed with dozens of first class preserved railways, and North Wales is famous for its quaint narrow gauge lines. Among them is Festiniog Railway, which runs from the mountainous slate-quarrying town at Blaenau Ffestiniog to Porthmadog, linking there with the reconstructed Welsh Highland Railway, which offers a 65 km narrow gauge journey to Caernarfon across stunning Snowdonian mountain scenery. The Festiniog Railway operates double-ended Fairley-type steam locomotives, typical of those used on the line since the 1870s.

Adams 4–4–2T No. 488 hauls a train at Sheffield Park station on the Bluebell Line (below).

An exact reproduction of Germany's first steam engine, *Adler*, runs at Koblenz; it is housed at the DB Museum in Nürnberg (right).

Among the finest of British preserved railways is the Bluebell Line, south-east of London, which runs some fine Edwardian carriages, and operates a recreated *Golden Arrow Pullman* with period equipment. The Severn Valley Railway in Shropshire and the North Yorkshire Moors Railway both operate long sections of reconstructed secondary main line using period equipment, with immaculately-maintained stations and signalboxes. The National Railway Museum at York displays one of the finest and most complete collections of railway equipment anywhere in the world. Nor are period operations relegated to preserved lines; in addition to main line steam excursions, steam traction is regularly scheduled on some main line services such as the summer season Fort William–Mallaig run on Scotland's West Highland Railway.

Germany is very proud of its railway history, and has many museums and preserved lines. The DB Museum at Nürnberg dates back to 1899, and is the oldest in Germany, housing a wide range of historic equipment and artefacts. In Munich, the Deutsche Museum's Transport Museum, located at Thresienhöhe, has fine exhibits of period trams, U-bahn cars, locomotives, sleeping and dining cars, and vintage German signalling. The former East Germany operated several narrow gauge networks with steam right up to its reintegration with the West, and several of these continue the tradition of steam operation. Most spectacular is the Harzer Schmalspurbahnen's network of lines, including the corkscrew-like ascent of Brocken Mountain. In addition to frequent main line period excursions, Germany is also famous for its Plandampfs, where steam locomotives and period equipment regularly work standard schedules in place of modern trains.

Poland kept the spirit of steam alive longer than in the West. The steam roundhouse at Wolzstyn never succumbed to diesel, and is the last fully active such facility in Europe. It supplies engines for both daily passenger services and excursions, also offering courses for steam-train drivers. The roundhouses at Jaworzyna and Chabowka are active railway museums, and maintain serviceable locomotives for main line excursions. Several narrow gauge lines have likewise preserved steam power.

In the Netherlands, Het Spoorwegmuseum (Railway Museum) at Utrecht has excellent displays of period Dutch railway equipment, including examples of Wagons-Lits international carriages. It is one of more than a dozen Dutch railway heritage sights open to the public.

Switzerland and Austria have excellent railway museums and heritage lines. Several railways maintain historic railway stock for both excursions and daily operation. It is not uncommon, for example, to find period locomotives and cars working Rhaetische Bahn routes. A portion of the original Furka Pass line has been rebuilt as a seasonal steam-powered excursion line. The Swiss Transportation Museum in Lucerne displays a collection of steam and electric locomotives.

In addition to the wide variety of first and second class passenger trains operated daily by European railways, several tour companies, such as that using the historic name Orient Express, offer scheduled luxury railway excursions to popular destinations, with equipment elegantly decorated in the spirit of classic railway travel.

Nineteenth-century Pullman coaches on display at Het Spoorwegsmuseum in Utrecht (above).

The roundhouse at Wolzstyn in Poland (left).

The modern-day Simplon–Venice–Orient Express (below).

BIBLIOGRAPHY

Books

Allen, Cecil J. *Modern Railways – Their Engineering, Equipment and Operation*. London: Faber and Faber Limited, 1959.

— *Switzerland's Amazing Railways*. London: Thomas Nelson & Sons Ltd, 1953, 1965.

Baedeker, Karl. *Paris and Environs with Routes from London to Paris*. Leipzig: Karl Baedeker, 1891.

— *Northern Italy*. Leipzig: Karl Baedeker, 1899.

— *Switzerland*. Leipzig: Karl Baedeker, 1901.

— *The Rhine*. Leipzig: Karl Baedeker, 1926.

Behrend, George. *Grand European Expresses – The Story of the Wagons-Lits*. London: George Allen & Unwin Ltd, 1962.

— *Railway Holiday in France*. Newton Abbot: David & Charles, 1964.

— *Railway Holiday in Switzerland*. Newton Abbot: David & Charles, 1965.

— *History of Trains de Luxe – From the Orient Express to the HST*. Glossop, Derbyshire: The Transport Publishing Company, 1977.

Beller, Steven. *A Concise History of Austria*. Cambridge: University Press, 2006.

Biddle, Gordon. *Great Railway Stations of Britain*. Newton Abbot: David & Charles, 1986.

Binney, Marcus and David Pearce. *Railway Architecture*. London: Bloomsbury Books, 1985.

Boag, George, L. *The Railways of Spain*. London: *The Railway Gazette*, 1923.

Bolton, W.H. *The Pageant of Transport Through the Ages*. London: Sampson Low, Marston & Co Ltd, 1930.

Carter, E.F. *Famous Trains of the World*. London: Frederick Muller Ltd, 1959.

Dethier, Jean. *All Stations: A Journey Through 150 Years of Railway History*. London: Thames and Hudson, 1981.

Dover, A.T. *Electric Traction – A Treatise on the Application of Electric Power to Tramways and Railways*. London: Sir Isaac Pitman & Sons Ltd, 1925.

Douglas, Kimon A. *The Railroads and the State*. New York: Columbia University Press, 1945.

Ellis, C. Hamilton. *Famous Locomotives of the World*. London: Frederick Muller Ltd, 1957.

— *The Pictorial Encyclopedia of Railways*. London: Hamlyn, 1968.

— *The Trains We Loved*. London: George Allen & Unwin Ltd, 1947 (reprinted by Pan Books Ltd, 1971).

Evans, Martin. *Pacific Steam: The British Pacific Locomotive*. Hemel Hempstead, Herts: Percival Marshall, 1961.

Fayle, H. *Narrow Gauge Railways of Ireland*. Wakefield, UK: EP Publishing Ltd, 1970 (originally published by Greenlake Publishers, London in 1946).

Gana, Giles Della. *A History of the Swiss Federal Railways*. Essex, UK: Heath Publishing Services, 1995.

Hall, Cyril. *Wonders of Transport*. London: Blackie & Son Limited, 1900.

Harter, Jim. *World Railways of the Nineteenth Century – A Pictorial History in Victorian Engravings*. Baltimore: The John Hopkins University Press, 2005.

Kalla-Bishop, P.M. *Italian Railways*. Newton Abbot: David & Charles, 1971.

Kann, Robert A. *A History of the Hapsburg Empire 1525–1918*. Berkeley and Los Angeles: University of California Press, 1974.

Lake, Charles S. *The World's Locomotives*. London: Percival Marshall & Co, 1905.

Lartilleux, H. *Géographie des Chemins de fer d'Europe. Suisse–Italie*. Paris: Library Chaix, 1951.

McPherson, Logan Grant. *Transportation in Europe*. New York: Holt and Company, 1910.

Meeks, Carroll L.V. *The Railroad Station: An Architectural History*. New Haven, CT: Yale University Press, 1956.

Monkswell, Lord. *French Railways*. London: John Murray, 1911.

Morel, Julian. *Pullman*. Newton Abbot: David & Charles, 1983.

Mullay, A.J. *Streamlined Steam, Britain's 1930s Luxury Expresses*. Newton Abbot: David & Charles, 1994.

Murray, Kevin. *The Great Northern Railway (Ireland) Past, Present and Future*. Dublin: Great Northern Railway, 1944.

Pearson, J.P. *Railways and Scenery. Series 1, Vols. 1 to 4*. London: Cassell & Co Ltd, 1932.

Pratt, Edwin A. *Railways and Nationalization*. London: P.S. King & Son, 1908.

Protheroe, Ernest. *The Railways of the World*. London: Routledge & Sons Ltd, 1914.

Robinson, F.F. *Through the Garden of Ireland – an Illustrated Tourist Guide*. Dublin: The Dublin & South Eastern Railway, 1914.

Roth, Leland M. *Understanding Architecture, Its Elements, History and Meaning*. Colorado: Westview Press, 1993.

Rowe, D. Trevor. *Railway Holiday in Portugal*. Newton Abbot: David & Charles, 1966.

Rowe, D. Trevor. *Spain & Portugal*. London: Ian Allen, 1970.

Rowe, Vivian. *French Railways of To-Day*. London: George G. Harrap & Co. Ltd, 1958.

Shepherd, Ernest W. *The Dublin & South Eastern Railway*. Newton Abbot: David & Charles, 1974.

Shepherd, Ernie. *The Midland Great Western Railway of Ireland*. Leicester: Midland Publishing Limited, 1994.

Solomon, Brian. *Railroad Stations*. Phillipines: Metrobooks, 1998.

—— *Bullet Trains*. Osceola: Motorbooks International, 2001.

—— *Railway Masterpieces: Celebrating the World's Greatest Trains, Stations and Feats of Engineering*. Iola: Krause Publishing Company, 2002.

—— *The World's Most Spectacular Railway Journeys*. Oxford: John Beaufoy Publishing Limited, 2011.

Spooner, C.E. *Narrow Gauge Railways*. London: E. & F.N. Spon, London, 1879.

Steinman, David B. and Sara Ruth Watson. *Bridges and their Builders*. New York: Dover Publications, 1957.

Stretton, Clement E. *The Development of the Locomotive: A Popular History 1803–1896*. London: Bracken Books, 1896.

Veenendal, Augustus J. *Railways in the Netherlands: A Brief History, 1834–1994*. California: Stanford University Press, 1998.

Winchester, Clarence. *Railway Wonders of the World, Volumes 1 and 2*. London: Amalgamated Press, 1935.

Winkworth, D.W. *Railway Holiday in Portugal*. Newton Abbot: David & Charles, 1968.

Wolmar, Christian, *Fire and Steam: A New History of the Railways in Britain*, Atlantic Books, 2007.

—— *Blood, Iron and Gold: How the Railways Transformed the World*, Atlantic Books, 2009.

Periodicals

ABC Guide for Travellers. Ireland.

Baldwin Locomotives. Philadelphia, PA.

Bradshaw's Continental Railway Guide. England (various years 1881–1939). *Bullet Trains*.

Electric Railway Journal. McGraw-Hill Company, USA.

Jane's World Railways. London, UK.

Journal of the Irish Railway Records Society. Dublin, Ireland.

Railroad History, formerly *Railway and Locomotive Historical Society Bulletin*. Boston, MA.

The Railway Magazine. London, UK.

Thomas Cook, European Timetable. Peterborough, UK.

Today's Railways. Sheffield, UK.

The maps reproduced in the regional map sections of this book

GREAT BRITAIN
Stanford's London Atlas of Universal Geography, London, 1894, Map 11.

IRELAND
Map from *The Second Report of the Vice-Regal Commission on Irish Railways*, 1910.

BENELUX
Maps from Baedeker's *Belgium and Holland*, 1905.

FRANCE
Chemins de Fer et Lignes Télégraphiques de la France, Gobert/Beaurain, Paris, 1885.

ITALY
Le Ferrovie Italiane, Ulrico Hoepli, Milano, 1890.

THE BALKANS AND GREECE
Dr W. Koch's Eisenbahn und Verkehrs-Atlas Europa, Leipzig, 1905, Maps 56 and 57.

IBERIA
Letts's Popular Atlas, 1881, Map 17.

CENTRAL EUROPE
Post und Eisenbahn-Karte von Mittel-Europa, Carl Flemming, Glogau, 1895.
Reise-Karte des Oesterreichischen Kaiserstaates, Vincenz Schulser, Vienna, 1862.

SWITZERLAND
Stanford's London Atlas of Universal Geography, London, 1894, Map 25.

POLAND
Koleje Rzeczpospolitej Polskiej, Warsaw, 1932; *Plan Wielkiej Warsawy*, Warsaw, 1910.

RUSSIA
Carl Flemmings Generalkarten No. 33, *Russland*, 1914.

SCANDINAVIA
Kart over Jernbaner i Norge, Sverige og Danmark, Statsbanerner Forlag, Christiania, 1897.

INDEX